If you are born a human in this time, you are born a warrior.

A warrior who doesn't know or live his or her identity, becomes depressed, fatigued and even suicidal.

Take up your sword. Do it on purpose,

SPIRIT

WARRIOR

Written with love for all my human brothers and sisters, by

CARAF AVNAYT

I dedicate this writing to the memory of my mother Annamarie Eley and Ed's mother, Constance. Everything I am today, is because of these two women, who in lifetime after lifetime, and through eternity have poured their soul into me; trusted me to uphold their love of truth, their love of beauty and their incredible refusal to partake in evil, no matter what.

They are both gone on ahead to other dimensions, but whenever I am weak and doubt myself, I find this fire in my blood that won't die. I find this glowing power of God in my spine that refuses to call good, evil and evil, good. I find a resolve in my flesh to speak the truth and the truth only.

I recognize it as my mothers, my Divine Mother.

YOUR MOST POTENT WEAPON IS YOUR NATURE.

FIND YOUR SPIRITUAL WARFARE STRENGTHS AND WEAKNESSES USING YOUR ASTROLOGICAL BIRTH CHART.

THIS WRITING IS NOT BASED ON TRADITIONAL WESTERN OR EASTERN ASTROLOGY BUT IS THE WITNESS IN THE SPIRITUAL VISION, OF ME, CARAF AVNAYT, IN THE YEAR 2024, OF HOW HUMAN AND DEMON FIELDS OF PARTICULAR PLACEMENTS ARE MANIFESTING IN THIS TIME AND REALM.

Cara Is Spirit
@Carahasangels

You already won; when you were born you.

5:41 AM · Nov 23, 2023 · **897** Views

The Warrior

There's a difference between a warrior, and someone who wields a sword.

Anyone can wield a sword. But it the warrior who believes he has the right to exist, to live, just the way he is in that moment; therefore, he fights for that right.

The thugs have demeaned humanity, making us feel we are not worthy to live as we are.

They have surrounded us and swamped us with soulless fake humans and told us that that ugliness, degeneration and honor-less existence is also human.

They have made us feel that our bodies have to be a certain way or we don't qualify to live.

The warrior knows this one thing, and he or she knows this from her feet placed on this earth.

If I am here, it is to conquer.

That I am here, means the river of Life has brought me here to win.

That I am here, means I am equipped inside me, with all that I need, to win.

Introduction

Dear Ed,

For a long time now, I've wanted to share what I know about energy warfare. I've had the privilege to have been taught a lot by my Granddad John Waltham and directly by God, to manage the harsh experiences I've survived as a ritual torture subject, and someone constantly under ritual assault of several types for energy harvesting.

The topic is so huge, Ed, that I was and even now am so daunted. Even after deciding to write this, Ed, I'm sort of shaking and shivering inside.

You know, my darling, even to dare to write this while sitting here in the very eye of the devil, so to speak, takes a lot of courage. I had to get a blood red carnelian to keep me going, and a moonstone to keep me from shutting my feelings down, because for me, Ed, this is emotional. I'm wearing all the things I wear to remind me of Granddad, my mothers, and I have your name on my wrist.

And I'm still shaking a bit, Ed.

You know why, because the world is never going to be the same again, Ed, as I type these words I'm typing. These my words to you, Ed, are from my deepest heart, my deepest truth. I have fought a war to be here this moment, Ed, to write these things to you, and I will fight a war to finish and get this out.

But it won't matter, Ed, because I already won when I was born me. And every human soul whose path this writing comes into, Ed, already has won by being born them.

You might say, Ed, that this war I'm fighting to get this out, is one of celebration, more than anything else.

Let me tell you, Ed, how exactly I got up the courage to actually start writing this.

See Ed, when I was born, my mother was killed and my dad was arm-twisted and tricked into letting a relative couple who had lost a baby look after me. This is how I came to be trafficked. The foster family was one of those entirely fake setups the ritual torture and human trafficking industry maintains specifically for these situations.

Anyhow, so I was given the birth and baptism certificate, and name and everything, of the baby I replaced. My whole life till I was 28, even though I knew I was not of the foster family, I was in a sort of haze or double mind. In that stupor, I thought I was actually born on the day the birth certificate said I was, and so on.

My whole life, Ed, the astrology thing always came out pure nonsense. Nothing ever matched me really. I therefore had very little respect for anything to do with astrology.

Just a few weeks ago, though, Ed, on some instinct, I decided to put in my real date of birth and time and such on an internet website and check out my birth chart. This time, I gave it a leisurely look over and I was so surprised, Ed; Gobsmacked, really. There, Ed, I could see my nature mapped, my strengths and my weaknesses. And Ed, to my absolute shock and some horror, I found that many of my questions about myself that never were answered before, were answered now. I actually got life guidance from my birth chart, Ed.

But the wheels of time had only just turned in that direction, Ed.

One evening, our son Gabriel, playing around, broke not one but three glass things in the kitchen. I don't know how it is for others, but for me, whenever there's a huge change of consciousness coming, breakable things in the house seem to fly off shelves, slip out of our hands and shatter.

Over two days, Ed, 3 plates and 2 jars and one mug broke, those which had survived years with us. I braced myself because I knew the change of consciousness coming was going to be huge. Our energy field frequency had changed drastically and we were now going in a new direction.

Then one night, just as I was going to lie down to sleep, I got this feeling, Ed, like you were telling me to check out your birth chart too. I was kind of surprised. In all these years it never occurred to me to check out your birth chart because I don't know your time of birth. I'd assumed one needed that.

But because I felt like you'd asked me to, I thought I'd check and see what I could get for just a birth date. And then Ed, all of a sudden, I realized that if I found out where the moon was overhead, the day of your birth, I might be able to get close to your birthdate.

Now Ed, I have to say here. My ancestors have worked with a form of astrology since time immemorial. It is inherited in the mother's line and my Granddad John Waltham learned it from his wife and taught it to me. It's pretty simple. The planets are seen as living energy fields and their influence seen plainly in the energy field. For example, expansion of the field is Jupiter, contraction is Saturn, cell generation is the Sun, cell purification is the Moon and so on.

I have seen energy fields all my life, so I grew up with this. Only I never connected my inherited knowledge with the astrology of others. In my mind I never even thought of it for some reason.

Yet Ed, when I was sitting right here, a few weeks ago, I knew that if I found out where the moon was the day you were born, and if the moon had changed signs (changes every 2 days or so), during that day, I'd know more or less, which time of day you were born, because I can see in your photos which zodiac your Moon was in.

I was right. On your birthday, in those 24 hours, the moon had indeed been where I knew it had been from your photo, and had changed signs too. I now had information that you weren't born before 5.15am.

But that was still a long time, and the various "houses" change every 2 ½ hours so I needed to get more specific.

One more time I decided to look at your photo to see your rising sign. I was a little confused then, but I managed to work it out, and found your rising sign.

Now I was a little dismissive, Ed, at this point, because it seemed like I was just playing about and as I wrote to you that day, "I don't want to falsely accuse of things by reading the wrong birth chart."

But since I'd come that far, Ed, I thought, "Let me put in the timing I now have by my instinct, and see what comes." So, I filled the form and clicked, "Calculate".

The page then loaded, Ed, with your birth chart, and me, Ed, I did not know where I was. Was I sitting or standing, flying or stationary. For there in front of me, Ed, I felt the glory of God manifest. My soul could feel the stars and the heavenly bodies overhead as they were the time of your birth.

And Ed, I never thought a birth chart could be sexy. But yours SO is.

And I knew that I'd got it right, because there was no chance, I'd have had that vision of your energy field if it wasn't right.

At that moment, also, Ed, I realized that all the astrology I'd read online was insufficient. Call me whatever, Ed, I felt that the reading of a chart ought to be worship of God, who has manifested as that person. I had never come across that sort of astrology before, Ed.

And how could I? In our times complete bio-bots are passed off as human and they have birth certificates and sun signs and everything. It means crap to those who have no soul. The soulless never were born and for them astrology is a mind game. A suggestion. There is a base primal pull of the heavenly bodies on the flesh, the flesh they have stolen from humanity, and it invariably pulls them to their death. But it is all so fatalistic and ultimately meaningless, really.

But here, oh my God, Ed, I was looking at the heavens the day that my very own manifestation of God took birth in this realm. This was not a thought in my mind at all. I confess I was actually thinking of so many other things at the time. But it is what I experienced, Ed. I felt like you were standing right in front of me, you just as my soul remembers from time before, and from eternal times I have seen you in my meditation. But now, like never before, I felt your reality as a man in this realm.

In that moment, Ed, my inherited field of learning – the energy field workings fused together with what I was seeing in front of me, the website generated birth chart; and just like that, Ed, I was able to read and understand things so clearly.

Days and nights your birth chart revealed itself to me, like all living things do when you love them. I will never be the same again. That person I was, before that moment I saw your birth chart.

Because as I began to process my experience, I realized how perfect we humans are, right at birth.

We are born, completely equipped to deal with everything coming at us in this realm. The heavenly bodies which are also what we are made of, quite literally and physically, dance in this perfect dance where they match up above in the skies, exactly what we are in our souls.

This is what I learned, Ed, reading your chart and then mine, with new eyes:

Your most potent weapon, is your nature.

Why you need to know what YOUR weapons are

A person can wield a weapon that is someone else's forte for decades, Ed, and get nowhere with it really, because the weapon does not match their own energy flow.

But the day you find the weapon that your own energy works with, you become a lethal force.

The thug world puts us all into school and gives us a tiny range of options to choose from in how we express our energy. But there are infinite ways of self-expression and weapons of warfare.

In the heavens above at the time of our birth are rather defined clues to which weapons our energy will vibe with and be able to wield with the most fluency and flourish.

So that's why I'm writing this. For each human to know their own nature of warriorhood, and their own weapons.

Furthermore, Ed, in our times, if we wish to have the things in our life that we consider precious – our soulmate, our beloved children and family, land, pets, plants and so on; we must know how to protect them; and we cannot do that till we have come into our own as a warrior. That is how the times are.

Life will wait for us to take up our sword and be the warrior we are born to be, before bringing us our soulmate and all our precious destiny, so that we are able to sustain the blessings in our lives.

History and literature, are full of humans begging demons to show mercy to humanity and the earth; and the demons refusing.

History then shows the human taking up the sword to bring justice back.

Because God has destined it, that we do not live as beggars, but as those who can take our freedom, defend it and keep it.

Because we are not made weak, though we might be gentle.

And we are not losers, though we do not wish to hurt anyone.

We are born winners, because we are born of God, the original program that generated this entire universe. We ARE the code.

The Energy Fields of the Planets, Zodiacs & Houses

Before I get to the energy warfare bit, Ed, I've got to give you a quick idea of how I see these in the human energy field, Ed. I don't hold these mentally in my mind. My readings and seeing of the energy field is pure observation in the minute. But in my mothers' line this is how these are seen.

The Planets

The planets are called "Thrones" in my ancestral knowledge. There are twelve thrones in a circle. On each of these sit the twelve emanations of God. Each soul is born, by the rays of these twelve thrones meeting in the center of the circle. We are therefore made of them.

Of the twelve, traditional astrology made reference to seven most often. I am listing them in the traditional order, according to which the days of the week are named in every ethnicity. The English name of the day, the Sanskrit derived Hindi name, and the planet.

Sunday – Ravi-vaar (The day of the Sun) - Sun

Monday - Soma-vaar (The day of the Moon) - Moon

Tuesday - Mangal-vaar (The day of Mars) - Mars

Wednesday - Budh-vaar (The day of Mercury) - Mercury

Thursday - Guru-vaar (The day of Jupiter) Jupiter

Friday – Shukra-vaar (The day of Venus) - Venus

-vaar (The day of the Saturn) Saturn

These seven planets were seen by my mothers as the forces ruling the external or conscious brain manifestation of one's life energy flow.

Like the sperm has a head and a tail, so these 7 rule the head of the sperm. The tail or the subconscious is ruled by the other five.

The rulers of the subconscious brain can be seen as aspects of the conscious brain, or reflections of them in a way.

Two famous ones in Indian astrology are Rahu and Ketu, the north and south nodes of the elliptical energy field of the moon's magnetically made energy field over us.

Imagine you're running around a small field. After you've run around a few times, you don't have to remember to turn at the corner. Your body knows it has to turn there. You've made a magnetic field by running around in the same path so many times.

The Moon has done that since so long, so we have a potent energy field, the thickest one compared to the other heavenly bodies' fields, because it contains what is called Soma in Sanskrit – or "elixir" and is also the name of the moon. It is the energy that a woman's orgasm liquid has, and the very same that is in the Pineal gland directing our lives in so many ways. It rules the water in our bodies, and through it the blood and the lymph.

Our realm's immediate mother is the moon, for without her would be no water and without water there would be no earth, or air or anything.

Her path over us, is therefore the closest, thickest layer of energy atmosphere over our realm. The very elixir of life – the bliss of the mother, which then as amniotic fluid holds the baby formed, is the energy of the moon field.

All the other heavenly bodies are seen by us through this layer. All their rays must pass through this layer.

So the North node and the South Node of the path of the moon overhead at the time of our birth, called Rahu and Ketu in Indian astrology, are these powerful vortex points where energy bends.

Just as the moon went to one of these points and then turned and came back, so energy flows to these points, and then turns to return.

It's like the tides on the seashore. The waves come rushing at the shore, but there at the shore, they turn and go back.

Energy flows in our brain and in our systems just like that. Conscious to subconscious, back to conscious, and then back to subconscious.

This is how our very life energy flow is directed, a dance between our conscious decisions and our subconscious influences, ever going from one to the other. More about this later.

What in modern astrology are named the planets Uranus, Neptune and Pluto are long used to describe the other 3 thrones that rule the subconscious. These were removed from common astrology in eons past and only recently re-introduced. They were re-introduced without their true benevolence and power explained, because information about how our subconscious works is still restricted from the common sphere.

My path in describing these, Ed, is not going to by a logical path, but by how my spirit leads, weaving in and out of my consciousness, taking me here and there, so you'll have to be flexible to do this dance with me.

SATURN

Dear Ed,

Today's 8/8/2024 so I'm going to get straight into that mysterious force called Saturn.

When I was a baby, Ed, and I was placed in another family not my own, I was given the name and birth certificate of a child born the year before me, on the 8th of June. For the next 28 years of my life at least, I thought that was my birthday, and when people asked me for my birthday, that's what I said.

In India, Ed, people recoil at the number 8. It's a bad number. That's what they'll say outright. It's Saturn's number. I didn't respect astrology or numerology because of that sort of crap. "Oh, you will have a bad life. Oh you will have a lot of difficulty. This is the lifetime in which you will pay for your karmas of the past lives." That's the kind of thing people used to say to me.

Because I was Christian, and Christians for the most part consider astrology a science of the devil, I had something to fall back on to help me ignore the prophets of doom.

But it was something that kept troubling me inside over the years. God knew I was pure hearted. Why would God punish me – or any innocent human – by making us be born on a bad day? Does the Bible not say that God looked at all they had created and see that "It is good?" (Genesis 1:31 in the Bible)

I couldn't believe God was sadistic, Ed. I know God personally, Ed. God has been my father and mother, brother and sister, and it was through God that I found you too, Ed. There is not one sadistic bone in God. He would never want me to suffer in the least. Was he not the one holding me through my childhood when I cried that I did not have clean shoes, or that my nose looked blobby; and all those little things that make a child and girl cry? I felt the love and compassion of God then, as I do today.

So I knew, Ed, that something was just off with all those "warnings" about how 8 was a bad number and Saturn was a planet that brings pain and suffering.

Move to 2006, Ed. I was 25, and living in the Himalaya mountains of north India. I had chosen my own path in life, by then, leaving behind the dogmas in my own mind, and the fake family of abusers that had held me back. I had seen you in my meditation one day, God showing up as a man, and my whole life now was about you.

I read an ancient book called the "Shiva Purana". It talks about how in primeval times, the manifestation of God as a primal man called Shiva, lived. He was very in love with his wife, but her father disrespected Shiva at a function and she got enraged and burned herself. That can happen, Ed. I have anger like that so I understand. Anyway, Shiva was distraught for many hundreds of years after that.

Meanwhile his wife took birth as a daughter of the mountains, named Parvati. From her young age she knew she was in love with Shiva and born only to love him. So as soon as she was of age, instead of gallivanting about like the others, she took to meditation to call him to her.

Now Ed, I thought to myself, "Why that is exactly what I should do! I'm in exactly the same situation, aren't I? That is what I'm already doing!"

Thence started in my life, deep and intense meditations to invoke you, from the spiritual side to come to me. To be honest, one reason I wanted to spiritually invoke you, was to release my anger at why you hadn't already arrived in my life. I had already been waiting for three years for you then. Age 23 -25, Ed, every day is like an eternity if you're waiting for the man you love. So I was quite angry.

And I had tons and tons of unreleased trauma from my life up until then, so I was quite heavy and troubled.

My meditation was simple. God would lead me to a book, or an old temple or such, or I would overhear someone in the café talking about some aspect of God and if it stirred my heart I would go home and set my mind on you as that and invoke you.

Because I have experienced God as EVERYTHING and that everything showed up in your form, your face, your features, I know that in you is everything.

And Ed, I was attracted to your dark side. Because if there's one thing that's been my thing since I was little, it was that God is my sweetheart and there's nothing of God I would fear. My whole life, Ed, was full of fears and tensions. Terrible dangers, such tense situations. But God was my zone.

And your dark side, Ed, I felt that in it my soul would find the recluse from the evil world that I sought, in it I would find you without any of the extra shenanigans one puts up with in the world, like pleasantries and all that. I was fed up of it all. I wanted the core of you and the depth of you and I wanted to immerse myself leaving nothing above ground.

It was in various such meditations and ecstatic experiences when I found the depth and bliss I sought, that a shop owner of crystals and such told me that dreaded thing again. "You're born under Saturn. That's hard."

I went home and looked at you in the Spirit and said, "You're Saturn too, aren't you?" (All the planets are simple aspects of God force or Life force.) "So, I'm going to invoke you, and you come right on and kill me if you must. I'm ready."

I really was quite ready. So, I got a "Shani Mantra" or mantra of vibrations of Saturn off the internet and got straight to it. I don't remember how many thousands of times and how many days I did that for now. It's all quite immaterial. As Granddad used to say, "The many repetitions of anything are just so you get it right just once. When you get it right once, you've opened the lock."

I must've opened the lock many times. I always know when I've opened the lock, because I feel your presence then, and my whole being fills up with joy and bliss.

But I would continue to practice of the mantra (not saying it loudly but saying it inside) for the number of days I had decided at the start. This is a good discipline in anything. So I think, it was 88 days or something like that.

Ed, I feel the aspect of you/God that's Saturn smiling at me with that special smile that someone has in memory of times together, as I type this. That evening was a rainy one in the mountains. Stormy as hell. If ever a weather described you as Saturn, it is the storm. My door to the balcony was open and the cumulative sound of rain over the mountains for hours and hours came in like the sound of ocean. At the same time, there was the rock of the mighty mountains not just beneath but by my side as one side of the flat I was living in, had the mountain rock as the wall.

It was about 8 in the night – not planned by me, but so it was. And I was hungry, there was nothing to cook in the house, so I called and ordered pizza.

Domino's Pizza there had a thirty minute guarantee or you got it free. On those mountain roads too, they made it in 23 or 24 minutes.

I go to the door when the pizza arrives, with my wallet, and discover to my horror, that I have no cash to pay for the pizza. I'd completely forgotten about it. This was back when you either paid with your credit card online or paid in cash when the pizza arrived.

I told the delivery guy that I had no cash, but that I would go to the ATM – about a mile from there – and get it. I was steeling my body already for the lashing of my life in the rain on the mountain highway in the dark. I had no transport of my own and if I had, I wouldn't have gone driving in that rain. But I was going to do it to pay for the pizza.

To my surprise, the pizza delivery guy says, "No way. The pizza is free today." I couldn't believe my ears. Pizza was pretty expensive in this town and certainly not something anyone would give away for free. I thought maybe he meant I could pay them the next day or something like that. "No, no," he insisted, "It's free today."

"Does your Dad own the pizza place?" I asked him in shock. He laughed and was about to go, when I said I was definitely going to pay for the pizza the next time I ordered. The bill was on the pizza box, so I got a pen and asked him to write his name on it, so the next time I ordered, I could show that bill to whichever delivery guy came and pay it. He said it wasn't necessary at all, but if I absolutely wanted to, he'd write his name on the bill. He wrote it.

It was, "Shani", or Saturn.

"That's your actual name?" I asked in shock. He laughed, "Yes, that's my actual name."

He left and I never saw that dude again. It was a small town in the mountains and – this is kind of embarrassing, Ed – but there was only one Pizza joint there and I knew all the four delivery guys by sight. I pretty much lived on pizza in those days. It was the only food you could order on the phone in that place, so it wasn't even a choice really. But I never saw Shani again.

The great God aspect Saturn gave me such a sweet gesture of acknowledgment, Ed, at the end of the time I invoked him/you.

That night, as I was falling asleep, I felt messages about Saturn arising in my soul.

Understandings and realizations of the nature of God force called Saturn.

These became the bedrock of my life and the covering over my head. My God and my eternal love in one, inside of which I need never be afraid or scared of anything.

If I hurt, I would heal. If I died, I would live again. If I failed, I would come right back and succeed.

The Grace of God is Saturn, Ed; holding each living being to their destiny of joy, bliss and love – unfailingly and unflinchingly through time.

When I was in my late teens, I'd complained to my Granddad one day. "Every time I enter someone's life, everything of their life falls apart. Then there I am comforting them, helping them. I move away, and everything becomes alright in their life again. Do I bring people bad luck?"

"No," my Granddad said, "You arrive to hold them together when it's time for them to go through a bad patch. You leave when they're able to walk on their own."

I now know, Ed, that that is the role that people born with Saturn dominant in their birth-charts play. They are healer angels who learn to grow unafraid of and even enjoy the dark side of life. They have the natural ability to see the obstacle as the path and therefore they achieve things that others could consider near superhuman. Their life will have some challenging times, but the grace of God on them, will far, far, exceed it all, bringing them out of it like the champions they are. Like you Ed, and Gabriel (our son).

People with Saturn dominant in their birth-charts are:

Those born with Saturn in their 1st house, or 8th house; or Saturn in the constellation of Capricorn, or a collection of 3 or more planets in the 8th house; or those born on the 8th, 17th and 26th of the month.

But whether or not a person is born with Saturn dominant in their charts, a time in life will come for all humans, when Saturn force is strong and then they might be attracted to this writing and go Saturnian for a while, as a necessary part for their achievement of their destiny in this life.

In every human's body and life, Saturn is both a start and a finish, because it is that God force that prepares a person for battle, and is the God force that receives them back from the battlefield each time, wounded and in need of repair, more training, and another deployment; or victorious and ready for the reward.

That is why in our journey to be a warrior, we start with Saturn.

Energetic Effect of the God-Force called Saturn & The Basic Energy Function of Each Planet or Throne

A lot of people worldwide, are attracted to Swords, Sabers, Guns and weapons in general, Ed. The majority of them are attracted to those because of the sense of power they imagine it would give them, to hold something in their hands that could destroy another. They imagine that when they hold that weapon in their hands, others will be naturally terrified of them, maybe not trouble them anymore and so on.

Fear rules the thug world realm, Ed. And weapons inspire fear because of the damage they might do.

However, Ed, in the energetic realms, or the realms of REALITY, the sword is about mastery, being expert in something and it is only that which gives you actual power, because then you're not just slashing everything aimlessly, but you're using your power to reach your goal.

Saturn is that God-Force, Ed, that is **our learning to use a weapon**, the sword, the knife; that which we can use to protect, defend, and most importantly do justice.

Having a weapon is something anyone can do, Ed. Millions of people are in jail all over the world for possessing weapons. What use was it to them?

Knowing how and when to use the sword to advantage, that's Saturn.

In pure energy terms, let me tell you how the planet aspects of God, work. I'll be repeating it lots, so you'll end up knowing these easy soon enough.

But it's like this.

The Sun is the when energy flows out from the center.

This is the basic first function of life energy.

The Moon is when energy flows back in to the center from the circumference. Without this nothing would exist as energy would simply move eternally outwards.

The Moon therefore causes the creation of all "forms" or beings of Life.

Mars is the vitality or basic life force with which energy flows – whether outwards or inwards. The speed, you could call it.

Mercury is the sparking or friction between life energy flowing in opposite directions, giving rise to new cells or formations, causing all growth from primal energy into vibration, life, form, everything really. It is the spark of intelligence or where consciousness goes from being "everything" to "I am THIS," and then back to "everything". Replace "everything" with "nothing" if you swing that way.

Buddha for example is named literally after Mercury as "Budh" is Mercury in Sanskrit.

Jupiter is expansion of life force in all its manifestations. It expands all the force mentioned before this. It's the compound interest of life force. The Sun and Moon make a zygote. Mars makes it have the heat to keep alive; Mercury makes the first friction happen inside and awakens the intelligence to create a new cell just like the first one.

Jupiter is the force that makes all this happen over and over and over, so the baby's body grows. As that growth happens new intelligence is gathered and given to the first four forces to use as they make new cells.

Here's where Saturn comes in. If Saturn doesn't come in here, we're going to have a big ball of cells ever growing, but never becoming anything that will actually be effective in the consciousness of the universe.

But Jupiter is never without Saturn. It's like this.

If you're building a house, and you're digging the foundation; Jupiter gives you the force to move forward and cover the area of the house, but Saturn gives you the force to dig downward.

To build a house, you need a certain depth of foundation. If you want to build a one story house, the foundation needn't be so deep. But if you want to build a skyrise, you need a much deeper foundation, and then columns that go down into the earth that will support the building.

So as every cell of us is made, while Jupiter is giving us the ability to expand like that, Saturn is doing the opposite of expansion, which is deepening.

This makes every cell of the universe able to exist. Until now it's all energy flowing. But now, it's energy forming as matter or STABLE vibration, because Jupiter and Saturn are creating this field where the energy is both flowing out, and flowing down, so the energy is **anchored** in time while flowing out at the same time.

This force field is the only environment in which anything can exist.

Let me give you more examples of this.

If Jupiter gives you the blessings of travel, Saturn gives you the blessing of being rooted or settling somewhere.

If Jupiter teaches you a new language or art; Saturn gives you mastery or the ability to actually use what you're learning.

If Jupiter gives you a lot of wealth, Saturn gives you the intelligence of investment so that that wealth makes sense to you. Saturn is often misunderstood as causing the loss of wealth, expenditure and so on, but actually Saturn is bringing balance to the energy field so it can continue existing true to its spiritual nature.

For example; if a man wants to find love in his life, and he earns a lot of money; Saturn will cause him to have expenditure that will curtail his spending power so that he stays in a place where he will find love, rather than go to a place – fantastic though it might be on paper – where he won't find love.

If he wants to find love, and he has to move to another place to find love, and he's earning less money, Saturn will increase his expertise or depth in something, so he earns more or makes connection with those forces that enable that move. It could even come through a tragedy that makes him pack up suddenly and move even on a very low budget. OR Saturn can make him experience depression, disconnection and such until he moves. You never know how.

Saturn anchors our energy flow to our life purpose and destiny and that is why it is synonymous with fate and destiny.

This anchoring of our energy flow to our life purpose is also called Justice; because when we are anchored right, we set off vibrations in the universe that make everything shift and move to do justice to us.

And that is why I call Saturn the Sword of God. Because through the Saturn force, God removes that which we don't need in our lives, that which takes us away from our path, that which dilutes our strength and power making us lose it in places instead of investing it right.

Saturn is therefore the rule of healing and correction, rejuvenation (which can only happen when we re-align to our life purpose), death and rebirth (which are the same thing and can happen without us leaving the body) and achievement of realization or fulfillment of life purpose, finding satisfaction.

Now, in the arrangement of the days of the week, Ed, you'll find Venus stuck in-between Jupiter (Thursday) and Saturn (Saturday), as Friday. The ancients found the force of Venus coming right in-between these two mammoths, as the force that determines the aesthetics of HOW Jupiter or Expansion works with Alignment or Depth finding, Saturn.

If we want to build a house, Jupiter will give us the ability to make it be as spacious and lavish as we want it to be; Saturn will make it strong, with a good foundation and sturdy walls; but Venus, is what will make it a home.

Venus will make us feel it's beautiful. Without Venus it will be walls and doors and windows and floors and ceilings and appliances.

The God-Force of Venus is much misunderstood, because in the thug civilization, Ed, the God-Force of Venus is drastically, drastically limited right now.

Have you seen the buildings of old, Ed? The temples and churches? The profusion of color, and sheer art? Those can never be made in these times, now, Ed, because the God-Force of Venus, is withdrawn from the thug civilization. They can only make boxes now and boxes stacked on boxes. The God-force of Venus, is withdrawn.

Venus is the ability of energy flow in each cell of us that makes us tune our vibration to something or the other.

Every natural living being is constantly tuning their life energy outflow to what they love, and that is what we experience as BEAUTY.

Pigeons will fly back to the place of their birth across distances. Birds will go back to their nests. Other birds will fly long distance to a place they've never been to, because their whole family is going and they got to be with those they love.

People in prison put pictures on the walls, of those they love. Animals spend all day looking after their young, or winning the mate of their dreams.

All of nature is tuning itself and pointing itself to what they love.

But the thugs have created a fake human civilization where we are taught to tune ourselves to things other than what we love. We are taught to aim our life energy at things that are concepts, ideas, things we're told we NEED, rather than what we want.

This perverts our Venus energy function.

A man, a woman, can forget what they even love as they work for decades doing what someone else wants them to do, to buy what they're told they need to buy, and live a life they're told they need to live; when what they want is in a whole other direction.

A population like this is bereft of art, music, beauty, joy, and all those things that make life worth living. That's the hell of this thug world, Ed. This is what is depressing children and teenagers. What's the point of an existence like this?

When Venus energy goes weak or withdraws in a person's life, Ed, it means they're no longer tuning towards love, or sexual fulfillment. Their Jupiter will stop expanding; their Saturn will start pulling them to death to start somewhere else; their Mercury will stop creating sparks, their mind will go zombified; their Mars will dull so they find it hard to even move; their Moon will dim making the water in the body to start coagulating and going stale and stinking, flesh will decay; the Sun will dim so they no longer feel like doing anything... No motivation, no excitement, no life force.

I've been there, Ed. At death's door. Many times. I've observed this process many times and I've also been blessed to have reversed this by exercising Venus in me, tuning to what I love; exercising my Saturn by upholding my life purpose in all I do; exercising my Jupiter by overcoming fear to expand my life and go towards what I love; exercising my Mercury by honoring those times I felt the spark of life and letting my energy flow into that; exercising my Mars by simply believing that if God has kept me here it means I'm provided the strength to do what I have to; exercising my Moon by surrendering to the pull that draws my awareness inside, into the things of my soul; exercising my Sun, by honoring my life energy flow in all my living. You know what it is. Each person knows what they really want to do in life. That's our life purpose and fueling it is our life force.

This has brought me back from the dead, Ed. That's why I can write all this so confidently. I'm not trying to be poetic. This is hard core reality, Ed. This is healing that works. This makes cancer go away. This makes hair-fall stop and new hair grow. This makes wrinkles go away. This makes an infertile couple conceive and give birth and have a family.

This is the real deal, Ed.

Now these are just 7 of the 12 thrones, Ed, that make each soul.

The other four are the Rahu-Ketu or North Node-South Node Axis of the Moon Field, Uranus, Neptune, Pluto .

Uranus, Neptune and Pluto are new discoveries as "planets", Ed, but the energy concept of them has been around since forever.

In my family's system these last five ruled the deep consciousness or the area of the consciousness in the brain stem; the deep sleep area.

The herbs that go this deep are the poisonous ones, like Datura, Sauromatum Venosum, Oleander and the death causing mushrooms and these are used as medicine for problems with these areas.

These thrones literally are our deep subconscious. Here is a short description of each.

Uranus was considered in our system "the splitting of the nail". In the old times, when a person became fed up of something in life, like if he had inner rage building up, and he had no way to let it out, his or her fingernails would appear to split. I have never seen an example so you'll have to imagine it. Granddad said it used to be like a tree branch splitting because its insides were termite eaten.

Uranus was called "The Splitter" or the "The Rennet" because that is the God Force that splits a person's consciousness to evict quite rudely what is no longer wanted.

Granddad said that this planet literally only appeared in the skies in recent centuries, just as the need for splitting arose.

It literally signifies the splitting of world consciousness; where what is real will continue on one path and the unreal will go into oblivion. It used to be considered an invisible force before.

It is the spiritual force in the consciousness of humanity that ends one eon and begins another, and it has the same effect in the birth chart of a person. But more about that later.

Neptune was known as Neptune, the ruler of the deep. Neptune was the energy force that brought out from deep consciousness, into conscious awareness, that which was on the sea bed so to speak; things the soul had allowed to sink beneath the waves of time.

The trident of Neptune is also the trident of Shiva and it symbolizes the arising of the primal nature of the person.

As the Lord of the Sea or deep consciousness, Neptune in a birth chart shows where the person's deep consciousness energy flows the most into manifestation. More about this later.

Pluto was seen as the "Ball of the Heel". To put this into perspective; the famous avatar, Krishna, orchestrated his own death by sleeping in the undergrowth of a forest with only the ball of his heel visible. A hunter mistaking it for something else shot an arrow into it, killing

Krishna, and ending the Dwapara Yug or third cycle of time and starting the Kali Yug or final cycle of time.

The ball of the heel is the place where we connect to earth energy, and on it depends the entire core energy structure of the body. It is where we stamp down our foot insisting on something and refusing to budge; and when we decide to change, we turn on our heel and walk away.

On an energetic level, our place in space, in time, depends on the energy point here.

This has very direct impact in our lives, because if we aren't connected through our heels to the earth field, our body flops, the bones go out of joint, everything swims this way and that. The brain itself atrophies.

Pluto is that energy force that keeps us in a point in space in consciousness. Depending on where in the birth chart Pluto is, we will be the most impactful or instead, destructive. A required destructive. It is where our power to say, "Yes, Live," or, "No, Die" manifests.

This is the God-Force that makes us make changes in our lives; drastic and unexpected, that change everything for everyone.

The Energy Patterns of the Zodiacs, and the Houses

Ed, there is a lot of information about this online, but my way of seeing this is different, for the following reasons:

1) Both Western and Eastern Astrology have reached us by going through the process of being interpreted for the soulless or fake humans over the centuries. How the zodiacs and houses impact the soulless is quite different from their effect on natural humans. My Granddad taught me to always see those differences, because that's the critical difference that makes the human able to actually use the information.

2) Granddad never told me this was "astrology". For us, the zodiacs and the houses are not places up in the sky, so much as zones in the human consciousness. I only realized very recently that you can apply the same thing both ways, because in reality the sky above represents our consciousness.

   But because of this, we see the planets, zodiacs and houses, as spiritual zones first, and their effects as conscious entities, rather than the contemporary astrology which sees these powers as something like machines that produce the same output if you put in the right raw materials.

   It's the difference between a human drawing your portrait, and an AI bot generating your portrait after being given some information about you. The former is worth everything no matter how imperfect; the latter is worth nothing however perfect.

   Soul is everything.

3) The aim of the astrology of my family was the adoration or worship of a person. Every birth chart was seen as the description of a form of God or Goddess. These were often inscribed on gold or silver plate and carried or kept in a beautiful place at home, very much like a deity. My Granddad's

wife wore a small silver plate inscribed with his birth chart around her waist. He said that before that, they had had starting trouble in their marriage, but that sort of started things off, and next thing, they had three daughters.

The birth chart was like a spiritual identity and life purpose reminder, more than anything else.

But since those times, Ed, Granddad found he could use the same methods of understanding the planets, zodiacs, and houses, to solve various problems and understand hidden things of the deep consciousness.

He didn't teach me these things directly but they were in the way we spoke about energy fields and life energy flow, and that is how I acquired my unique understanding of these.

So for me, it's all about basic life energy flow. That's my view point of all of this. I'm not an astronomer or traditional astrologer, I'm a viewer of energy fields and energy flow. So that's where I'm coming from.

I got to say, Ed, I have seen the planets in the night sky with a telescope and they are beautiful.

But let's get to the meaning of the zodiacs, or star systems in the sky above our earth, and their corresponding places in our consciousness.

ARIES

The area of consciousness ruled by Aries, Ed, is that part of our consciousness where we start new things.

Pretty simple, huh?

TAURUS

The area of consciousness where we nurture ourselves for the journey of our lives.

GEMINI

The area of consciousness where we count or check how much energy we have at our disposal for our life journey.

CANCER

The area of consciousness in which we make little bundles of sustenance from our store for our journey.

This is something like me making tea bags, Ed. I'll have maybe four or five herbs and spices and I'll want to make say twenty tea bags (for my travel or a gift to someone). So I make twenty pieces of cheesecloth and I put a little of each herb and spice in each piece of cloth and then tie it up with string.

The energetic function of dividing energy resources up like that happens in the zone of Cancer.

LEO

The zone of consciousness in which all resources are collected up and we look up at the journey ahead.

VIRGO

The zone of consciousness in which we dip our feet and touch the water. The first taste of the wine, the first testing of the bridge strength, the first testing of the medium or vehicle we wish to use on our journey.

LIBRA

The zone of consciousness in which we coordinate our left with our right. The pulling together of opposite energies.

SCORPIO

The zone of consciousness in which we point our sword, our vision, our telescope, our wand, at the particular point on the horizon we want to reach.

SAGITTARIUS

The zone of consciousness in which we gather up all our resources for the journey.

CAPRICORN

The zone of consciousness in which we find we are already moving, and we have just to adjust our speed, fine tuning things as energy carries us on.

AQUARIUS

The zone of consciousness in which we shift gears, or paradigms, or change lanes.

PISCES

The zone of consciousness in which we are flying, or moving in a zen state.

The twelve houses of a birth chart, Ed, are the progressions of a person in expressing their energy, starting with self-realization or self-awareness in the 1st house and leading up to transcending one's limitations and becoming infinite, in the 12th house.

FIRST HOUSE

In this zone of consciousness, we develop in our minds the image of who we are as a person, and that, along with various unconscious and subconscious mind influences forms our body, appearance and outlook in general.

SECOND HOUSE

In this zone of consciousness, we develop strengths and weaknesses, assets, and things we fall back on in hard times. Something like money in the bank or gold buried in the backyard.

Most of our childhood, we collect up information about our environment, all kinds of trivia, because we believe this will come in handy sometime. Some people continue the learning, some people hoard stuff. It all comes under this house.

It's like in the Bible, on knowing that seven years of famine were going to come, Joseph and the Egyptians stored up grain in huge warehouses in advance.

This is also the house of stored sexual energy or Jing, the kind we access when all our moving or working energy is finished in some kind of accident or trauma.

This is the house of "second wind"; that which takes over when we are depleted of our first layer of energy.

THIRD HOUSE

This is the zone of consciousness in which we develop energy thriftiness, and management. Every living being learns when young, what to expend, how much energy on. What's important, what's not that important; how to energy hustle; that's all in this house.

How to deceive, how to be nimble, how to escape; that's all here.

Mind games, trickery – humans have to learn these to survive in the thug world.

FOURTH HOUSE

This is the zone of consciousness in which we telecast or throw our energy field out beyond our bodies into an energy field that includes those we trust, places we feel safe in or call "home". It is our trust zone and the start of our establishment in the lifetime.

FIFTH HOUSE

This is the zone of interaction between our home energy field and others. In this world, it is very rare that we actually truly fully interact with someone as our naked soul. 95% of the time at least, our interaction is through layers of personality, history, commonly accepted culture and so on. Our personality game with the rest of the world happens in this zone.

SIXTH HOUSE

This is the zone where we focus our energy on one or a few aims in life, and focus on them. We define our ideals, our beliefs and with them our limits, our boundaries and how far we're willing to go, or not, towards certain goals.

You can see, Ed, how all the previous houses weigh in here. How for example, our idea of who we are as a person defines how much we believe we can aspire for in life, and therefore where we perceive our limitations are.

So this is where we begin to take care of ourselves health-wise and energetically, because we have an estimation of where we're lacking, and where we're over-expending ourselves.

The body begins to protest habits and foods that don't suit us, the protest showing up as illnesses, allergies and the like.

This house pretty much determines if we will conserve our energy to finish the cycle.

SEVENTH HOUSE

This is the zone where our energy reaches out for energy combustion through joining up with others who have similar energies. In traditional astrology, Ed, this house has ruled marriage, marriage not in the love-sexual creation sense, but marriage as a form of domestic partnership. A lot of the fake humans throughout history, have never experienced marriage as anything beyond a domestic partnership where sexual needs are met, or not.

In reality, this zone is where our energy prepares the ground, the environment for the reception of real sexual energy from our soulmate and the children or the fruit of that union.

We all have an environment, whether we live with our tribe like primal humans or in a flat on our own in a place where we know no one personally. It's an energy environment made up of who we allow into our lives as friends, influences, and spouses.

The spouse is someone who influences this environment more than anyone else, because we SHARE the environment with a spouse and this is that zone in which we create that shared environment.

Every chance of our finishing the energy cycle depends on who we allow in and who shares our 'marriage' environment.

A lot of people get drained in this zone, Ed. It's like a the box in Snakes and Ladders, with one of the big snakes' mouth. You get drained here, you're back to square One.

But if you get this zone clean, your inner marriage environment, energy flows into the 8th house, of fulfillment.

EIGHTH HOUSE

The traditional astrology Ed, are crazy about this house as it is said to rule sex, death, transformation and all things occult and mystical. The lore surrounding it is justified, but I feel it isn't really enough to explain actually what happens here.

It's like this, Ed. You have a certain amount of money and you go to shop to buy something with it. (Future generations will wonder what I mean by that, because they'll all be ordering online. So let's replace shop with shopping website.) So you go to a shopping website and you search for the thing you want.

You get a lot of results, and you have to choose one or two to further investigate, before you make your choice.

Then you make your choice, you "Add to Cart," and then you get a page with information with how much the item costs, when it can be delivered, etc. Then you have to click, "Checkout." You click Checkout. That's the 7th house. You made your choice there of who you letting into your close private zone.

The next page, "Pay Now," that's 8th house.

When you click that button, money is going to be deducted from your account, and you are going to be getting something new, something you have not had before, something that is still an unknown.

Even if you order the same brand, same shirt, same color; it's still not the one you had before. It's going to be slightly different; and its energy for sure is going to be VERY different.

But this is the zone in which you actually give your energy, and with it, surrender all that you have gained and become till then. That's the meaning of natural actual sex.

For the fake humans it means death, because they are unable to regenerate or circle back energy through sex. They either drain someone, or they get drained themselves. Either way, every time they have sex and reach orgasm, they have died a bit and will not recover that Jing energy.

But for humans, this is the zone in which we give sexual energy which is all we have become so far in the energy cycle, and receive the unknown thing, because there is no description that will suffice to describe the return of the same love and surrender of our soulmate.,

The only word maybe, that comes close, is Transformation.

That's why this house is traditionally supposed to rule Expenditure as well. Because it is here you spend or give, or invest, however you like to see it.

The older astrologers, Ed, mostly fake human had a view of this house as a place of fate. Like a house where whichever planets are in it; determine whether you'll lose the gamble of your life energy expenditure, or you'll win the toss and get the prize. \

But that's for the fake humans who do not have the soul ability to purify oneself.

Because actually Ed, it is in this zone that one purifies their energy. This is because in fact this is the zone of JUSTICE, where one learns that what you get is what you give.

The purer and higher quality your giving is, the purer and higher quality what you get will be.

You throw some energy out in sex, you'll get some miscellaneous random stuff thrown right back at you.

You chose some random partner with a good-looking face and a stuffed wallet in the 7th house, you going to get equivalent shallow energy returns in the 8th house.

All the deceptions you bought as you progressed through the previous houses, get shown up here. You're getting the product here that your energy is able to buy.

Here you find out, that your foundations in the previous houses are weak. Here you realize you have a wrong idea of who you really are (1st house). Here you realize you have strengths you didn't know you had, and what you thought you did, needs to be developed more (2nd house). Here you realize your energy management methods and hustle, aren't really up to reality standards in adult life, though they might have worked in primary school. Others can see through your ruse. (3RD house). Here you realize you don't really have security in your home life and support system (4th house). Here you realize you don't realize the outer projection you've done of yourself in the world isn't true to your inner soul experience (5th house). Here you realize you haven't really moved according to your soul priorities (6th house). Here you realize if you've made the right spouse choice or home environment choice to support your future progress (7th house).

This is the ultimate energy bottleneck, energy strainer, energy cheesecloth zone.

But when we finally go through the gates of the 8th house, what moves on to the 9th house, is something sublime, our transformed self.

When I found this out, Ed, I asked, "Why would I ever need to be transformed if I'm born perfect?"

God's answer was, "You were born perfect for one time. But as time changes you have to transform to keep being perfect."

Everything in nature keeps transforming energetically; that is what LIFE ENERGY regeneration and cycle is all about. If we stop transforming we will decay and die.

Therefore, it is here in the 8th house that we are re-born.

NINTH HOUSE

This is the zone of consciousness where we are like a baby in a new world. We have grown all the sense organs to enjoy it. We have developed the instincts to keep us safe. Here our energy experiences consciousness outside of the one we knew before. We learn new things, see things we never saw before. We travel and our eyes open up to possibilities, dreams and hopes we never dared to aspire before.

In this zone we first experience ourselves without the limitations and restrictions that came with our birth situation, home situation, and those people we knew in our lives.

Here we spread our wings and go beyond what anyone imagined for us; beyond what we even knew existed before.

TENTH HOUSE

In this zone of consciousness, is what I call the telecast tower. Here our consciousness telecasts out to the world, to others, to the rest of the human consciousness. And our telecast receives responses from places where our telecast has been understood by those on the same frequency.

You could call this the radio zone, the Ionosphere of consciousness.

This is where manifestation begins to happen.

All manifestation starts with us telecasting ourselves out to the universal consciousness, and then the universe sends signals back in the form of the elements of what we need for our manifestation to happen.

Great upheaval and changes in life, can therefore result because of our telecast.

You could call this the house of prayer, because prayer is a telecast, and God often responds by changing our circumstances drastically, sometimes not in ways we like, to answer our prayers.

But this is where we telecast ourselves out to the universe and where we begin to get energy responses from the universe.

ELEVENTH HOUSE

This is where our consciousness expands. Wildly, suddenly, without warning; that's how consciousness expands. You're lying down in bed, just as you do everyday when realization hits you. Suddenly you see something you never could have conceived of before. Everything changes. The way you see yourself, the world, the universe, God, everything.

Just as a man whose land ownership suddenly expands from one acre to 20,000 acres; suddenly you have energy wealth at your disposal like never before.

You didn't even know you had access to so much, and were so wealthy. It was right under your nose all the time, and you didn't know it. Because your consciousness wasn't expanded enough to comprehend this DIMENSION of life.

The keyword is Dimension, Ed, because this is what leads us to the 12th house of Transcendence.

TWELFTH HOUSE

I think the word "Transcendence", says it all, Ed, but I'll explain it for someone who might not know what that word really means.

It's when you're in the same place to the sight, but you're living a whole different life experience.

It's like the caterpillar who grew up on the Mulberry tree, his whole life about eating the leaves and becoming fatter and fatter, crawling up and down the branches and stem and trunk of the Mulberry tree. Occasionally a caterpillar will get adventurous and venture out from the mulberry tree to other trees. On the way as they crawl, they get trampled over by other animals and die. Sometimes they don't know what they're climbing up or down. Many times in my childhood, they'd climb up on me as I played in the place they haunted, and I'd go to bed not knowing a little creep was looking for a leaf to eat.

I would wake up in the morning invariably to find a big red patch on my neck caused by poke caterpillar claws and hairs; with a pissed off curled up caterpillar. I'd throw him or her back outside and they'd be really relieved to smell green leaf and find green leaf after the night long search.

But that's their life, Ed. Crawling about almost blind. Eating whatever. Just getting fat and surviving, not knowing why maybe, just that they got to. It's not like they're even social really, as such.

Then, Ed, they spin their cocoons, and you know the rest.

One fine day, just like that…. WHOOOSH. It's unbelievable, Ed, the magic that happens to those grubby little poky fellas. It's stunning. It's a whole new world for them. The scent of the flowers, the wind in their wings.

Gone is their adherence to whatever will support them. They FLY now. This is called Transcendence.

You're in the same place maybe; there's that Mulberry tree you were born on, and there's the tree you crawled up and down every day, and there's the place you spun your cocoon; but wow, how small it all it, because suddenly you can fly. You see beautiful flowers, fragrant trees and fruit, sunshine, SUCH sunshine… and all around you is a magical wonderland.

For us, Ed, maybe Transcendence is not so simple and drastic; maybe we have to go through many cycles of it; but it does feel that beautiful.

I experienced Transcendence when I saw you in this world for the first time. My life then wasn't as easy as a butterfly's but wow was it on a whole other level or what.

Humans Versus Demons

Ed, something different in my way of seeing things is, I see human energy fields as different from fake human – that I call 'demon' energy fields.

While the force-field of the planets or thrones and the constellations above affect all things beneath equally, the human soul interprets and manifests those influences in very different ways from the demon energy field which is a static energy field that has only pretend of soul and not actual soul.

These days they call such entities "narcissists". That's a wrong thing in my opinion, because a narcissist is someone who loves themselves and these demons do not have the soul to even love themselves. Vampire is a better word, as they live off the energy of others, but demon is the best, because they are simply unnatural to our world and not connected to earth energy naturally.

Some humans will find they have things in common with my description of demons. It is because the human has all those choices at their disposal, to use whenever required.

It is not the action that is good or bad, it is the intention behind the action. A natural human will never find themselves doing something to hurt someone else without a righteous reason for it. There is such a thing as natural justice and we humans are the agents of it, like all natural living beings.

Demons on the other hand, have a core value, which is that they exploit others for their survival. They are spiritually alright with hurting other humans. Some of them are quite open about it, because they are in such a majority in the population that they'll find many agreeing with them and idolizing them for saying it.

I find that in my life, I would have been helped massively, if I had found a book describing the effects of the planetary placements separately for humans and demons; it would have saved me. So, I'm writing this for all my human brothers and sisters who have demons in their lives and are confused about how to deal with them.

One other thing to remember while reading ahead is that, very often when you have a demon in your life, or many, getting rid of them is not the big deal. You can just cut off, block them and so on.

The main thing you need to do is look into what made you attract and host that demon/s in your life.

If you truly take the trouble to give yourself the time to think about it, pray about it, ask God to show you what happened; you will be on a whole other level in your life so very, very, quickly.

I attracted a lot of demons by having the mindset that my being alive was worth God's effort only so long as I was serving, or supporting others. I literally needed demons to prop up my sense of worth, by taking advantage of me and my energy.

From the sort of demons in your life, look at what you're offering for free, look at what attitude towards yourself you're holding and therefore projecting out that's attracting demons to you.

I knew a woman who believed she couldn't live without support – just that. And she was constantly attracting demons who would do things for her and then drain her. Her life turned around very simply when she lost the fear of being alone and living alone. She later found true love and true, life partnership without having to play the damsel in distress game.

Reading my descriptions of demons will do you very little good if you don't fix your attracting of those into your life. You'll just get rid of one, and another will come and take its place.

There's more about demons in a chapter at the end of this book.

Your Boot Camp Zone , Where your Sword is Forged, Warrior Foundations - SATURN in the Zodiacs and the Houses

Ed, we're on hallowed ground here, like never before. This writing I am writing to you, Ed, the intention is to reveal for each human this writing reaches, the strengths and weaknesses in their nature and energy field so they can be the warrior they have to be at this point in time, when the old mass consciousness is finished and we are returning to our primal consciousness of ONENESS with all of nature.

The Life Force of God, the Throne that is Saturn, Ed, is the very foundation of the sense of JUSTICE in each person. Without a sense of justice, we cannot be a warrior, because to be one means we are aiming to restore justice and balance to us, or someone or a situation.

Our **foundations** as someone who can defend ourselves and our loved ones, are shown in where Saturn sits in our birth chart, ie. In the skies above at the time of our birth.

The energy of Saturn, Ed, makes the zone of sky it is in, shimmer with a sort of shivering, as it negates a lot "fluff". Saturn de-magnetizes the area around it as it moves, ie. It breaks energy patterns existing simply because of habit, sending all that was spinning in that vortex back to where it belongs.

In a way it's an undoing, but really it is the return of the zone back to its own nature, and a much required clean-up of the area making it fresh again.

In our lives, Ed, Saturn in our birth chart shows us **the area of our life we need to keep cleaning up and de-magnetizing to keep close to the truth and fresh, without any clutter.** Finding out which area that is, and taking care to keep clean and fresh there, will make energy flow in our lives.

At the same time, Ed, Saturn in the birth chart shows us our primary weapon in dealing with our enemies. You'll see as I go on, what I mean by that.

Now, Ed, I've learned not to shy away from a good fight. God has taught me to be merciless with my enemies, Ed. So I am also writing this to reveal what Saturn in the birth chart of a soulless fake human says about them.

Here we go.

SATURN IN ARIES

The sun is black.

Yes, the sun is black. Look at the sun, close your eyes, you'll see the sun is black. No light body can exist without its dark body, and the dark body is the SOURCE of every light body.

With Saturn in Aries, you need to keep your source dark field close, and focus your energy deep within in your dark field. Saturn will keep showing you your dark side, because that's where the purest light starts. If you spend 10 minutes in the light, you need your 50 in the dark. Your primary weapon is, your enemy sees only your light side.

You are a master of the dark side, unafraid of things that are dark, mysterious, unknown, You are just born with this magical ability. People will try to make you believe you've got weird obsessions that aren't quite socially acceptable. F*** them. Stay in the dark. Revel in the things you like, the ones that have deeper meanings than words can carry. Your enemies can only reach you in the known. The second you slip into the unknown – you're invisible.

For all of your warrior life ahead, remember your strength lies in being in your dark field within. Find it, meditate to go into it. Surrender to the unknown darkness. Trust it. Your energy field will build up, you'll get healthy, and you'll get guidance you could never have in the light.

Your challenges will be predominantly those that can only be solved through exhuming things buried in your subconscious brain, ie., psychosomatic conditions. And your breakthroughs too will come from that. And that will be your weapon as well, because no matter what happens in your external body and life, you will heal and recover and get guidance by consulting your inner dark field. No one can predict what will come out of there. You'll shock people. In there is infinity. You could bring ANYTHING out of there, ANYTIME.

You obviously already have been this way since birth, but now you know that's how you function, you can do it on purpose and enjoy your darkness, your mystery and the power in there.

Demon – Saturn in Aries

The demon with Saturn in Aries is a swindler by default. He has no faith in his ability to actually earn anything honestly, or make anything that is of value. His entire game to survival in life, is swindling. He lies awake late at night thinking of who to swindle next and how to go about it.

He gathers around him people who think he's cool, smart and consider him a leader because he seems to know how to control, manipulate and con others easily.

His weapon is his fake aura as someone who doesn't give a damn about what others think of him. It's obviously fake. As a swindler, he needs to always know to what extent the probable victims trust him.

Some of these demons are of high quality and from good bloodlines. They don't do small swindles. They build up trust over years and sometimes decades before going for the swindle. Unlike the Saturn in Pisces demon, Ed, which swindles drop by drop, this one will do a sudden swindle so huge, it will leave the victim unable to believe it was actually done on purpose.

It will look like a huge accident.

This demon doesn't lie in words. It's very careful to state facts all the time. The deception is done by the demon doing things, actions to make it look like he or she really cares for the victim. They'll be there for the victim, support them in hard times, come around for birthdays, weddings, funerals; pick them up if their car broke down; all that.

One sure sign of this demon is, this demon has a fear of groups and crowds and will always want to interact with people one on one with no one else listening or watching.

This demon develops hand tremors and nerve twitches in the 40s because of being so in control of his or her body language.

This demon's weakness is he or she can't really do math. They will miscalculate something at some point. If someone points out to them that they got the math wrong, it breaks their confidence horribly. What's a swindler worth if he gets the math wrong? "Home Alone" movie type petty thief.

Saturn in Aries summary:

Primary weapon – Time spent in experiencing shadow self

Primary weakness – Not spending time in one's own dark field

Demon Saturn in Aries – Swindler – Pretends he doesn't care – Can't do math really

SATURN IN TAURUS

Lord help the man or woman who crosses Saturn in Taurus. This is a beast of a man or woman, Ed. A sense of Justice like a bullet out of the best marksman in the world. A refusal to compromise on the smallest detail when seeking Justice. Oh, if only there were more of them around, Ed.

Their primary weapon is how they stand their ground. They tire the enemies out. You can shock wake them 3 am in the morning and they'll tell you exactly what they told you in the day.

One problem they face, is the fake humans constantly telling them they're pig-headed, stubborn and closed minded. This can erode their feelings of being comfortable in a situation, as well it should, and they end up moving. Moving from one relationship to another, one place to another; again, as well they should. Because it's no spineless person they're ever going to be comfortable with. They need someone who'll stand for justice with them like they do, or they'll lose respect, interest and move on. That sort of person is rare, Ed, so these people are more often than not loners having given up on love, or in marriages where they've accepted loneliness.

This person needs beauty and a calm environment at home. If ever they accept ugliness, mediocrity, spinelessness, shallowness, for whatever reason, they will fall ill, lose energy, lose their hair and start having bad dreams, weird fantasies that trouble their soul and the like. Till they hit the road again.

They are forced to be travelers, Ed, just to find the person and the place they can be the rock of Justice that they are.

One thing that can greatly help this person, is to establish themselves as a single person and not wait to find love before they decide where to put roots down. 9/10 times their soulmate will love their choices in where to live and even how to live.

Demon – Saturn in Taurus

Ed, When I started to write this, I got so turned off, I suspended writing this for more than a month before I got back. But here goes.

The demon is not very mentally intelligent but has this particular ability. To know where a person's foundations, are. This demon will get to know someone deeply, and this can give the person the idea this demon CARES about them. But actually they're looking for the information about you that will make them absolutely control you. They are control freaks and you will see that in how they go crazy if something in the plan is changed or things don't go according to plan.

They will look to find what a person is absolutely based on, emotionally, spiritually, and even physically. To control the person, they'll mess with those foundational things. Like not allow or provide the person's basic staple food that connects them to their childhood or sense of wellbeing. Like not let them do some activity that they need to keep de-stressed. Like, show them something that shakes the foundations of their faith.

Their warfare on us humans, will be bringing up core beliefs of ours and saying those aren't true. That's the level they play on.

Their weakness is, they're usually not very educated so they have an inferiority complex. In general even if they're financially well off, they have an inferiority complex of some kind or the other. They get absolutely shattered when you so much as know they have an inferiority complex, never mind what it is.

It's because of feeling inferior that they have the need to control others.

They're the kind who'll break up with someone when they know that someone is going to break up with them. They can't handle if they're the one being dumped. So it's not VERY hard to get rid of them.

SATURN IN GEMINI

Holy macaroni. It's the kind of manifestation of God, Ed, where no one knows what the hell is going on, but there is some dead sure purpose being accomplished through the chaos. This is a HIGHLY INTUITIVE person, Ed, whose mind moves faster than his or her own mind. The God force of Saturn here is a chaos creator with a divine plan that the conscious mind and maybe even the subconscious mind cannot comprehend. Because this person is so compelled by instinct, they hurtle on into things and for a while it might look like they've destroyed their lives and every chance of happiness or success; but, Ed, every single time, EVERY SINGLE TIME, they come out on the other side victorious. EVERY SINGLE TIME.

They're bedraggled and covered with scars of course – what can you expect when Gemini is your bootcamp. But my God, the stories and the sheer strength of intuition developed… absolutely amazing. Those lucky people that have a friend like this. Grinning when the rollercoaster of life is throwing you both upside into the air. Absolutely amazing.

The primary weapon here is faith in God. You got to have faith in God who made you, and who guides you on your chaotic path. A SOLID understanding and appreciation of how God has led you through your life so far and keeping reminders of past times when you thought you were done for, but you came out wiser, stronger, realer, will help you on an every day basis fight your battles with even more panache, style, aplomb.

Follow your intuition with style. Face the dragons and laugh. You ALWAYS come out on top.

The primary weakness is self doubt because of comparing one's own life, personality, path, appearance with others. You fix this crap and you're bulletproof.

Demon – Saturn in Gemini
This demon is a hooligan who thrives on making a huge noise and drama and drawing in whoever will believe that and get sucked into the drama. They are unable to get any establishment or base in life that they might actually win any respect from anyone. So they get by by doing these emotional dramas now and then, preying on young emotional impressionable women and children to get them emotionally affected by their drama.

They are most of the time physically violent when they find the audience losing interest.

They use the ability to create shock as their primary weapon and therefore, when a person stops being shocked by them, they will have to move on to a new target. If for some reason, say because the financial condition of their current victim is good, they don't move on, they'll stay and cheat and be a dead weight, cynical, manic depressive, wet blanket sort. But only in private. In front of others they'll be the life of the party, so cheerful, so inspiring and supportive of others and so on. It's because they do need to keep their game going so they can get new victims.

SATURN IN CANCER
Such a beautiful protective angelic force, Ed, is this person. Like the wings of God over all she or he loves.

This person, Ed, is an understated warrior. This is not the sort of warrior who'll jump at someone from the wall in the moment of attack. This warrior, Ed, has a deep sense of justice that goes beyond the good and bad in the moment. This makes others think this person is spineless, has anger-management issues, is passive-aggressive and so on. But actually, Ed, this person is a spiritual ruminant. This person waits and waits and waits till the illumination comes from within showing them what is justice and what is not.

And then, Ed, this warrior begins to do little things. Even their own conscious mind might not know what they're doing. But they begin to do little things. An email randomly mentioning something to someone. A little support shown to someone. A little here, a little there. Often without even knowing it consciously, they set a trap, a net for someone or something who needs taking out.

This person, Ed, nearly always stays in the background because they know where their strength is. No one knows who's the mastermind and therefore they can't attack the mastermind. They keep in the background, Ed, and don't even care that they don't get the credit for half the things they do, being a warrior for who they love.

They are just so wonderful, Ed.

Their strength is in their spiritual vision of circumstances as opposed to what others present to them as truth. So long as they refer to their own insight into the situation and not others' they feel strong and clear. Their weakness is when they give others the authority to tell them what to think. They can go for years in abusive relationships and situations where they're not allowed to hold their own view of the situation. They get drained by people asking them to rationalize what their spiritual vision is. They got to refuse to be with those who need them to logically explain things, because life energy does NOT flow by our thug world programmed logic and we'll just drain out if we keep trying to explain things.

They need sleep, rest and insulation from loud mouthed over-aggressive entities, Ed, or rather, they function best like that.

Demon – Saturn in Cancer
This is a thug, Ed, who'll use the tenderest human emotions to manipulate someone and crush their spirit because they're a pure pain eater vampire. They are utterly remorseless emotional pain inducers, Ed.

Thank God that they usually have something really creepy about their body language that keeps most humans at arm's length. Their voices also are – something off.

The kind of humans they attract are those who are trained to have sympathy for the not very good looking, crooked looking, "people" "because Jesus loves them".

They'll present sob stories for breakfast, lunch and dinner to get their victim's sympathy; cry on their victim's lap, ask the victim and everyone to pray for them; and then slowly after making the victim's guard go down, do things that hurt them emotionally, begin to tell them that the people they think love them, actually don't; and so on.

Textbook emotional manipulation, and when the victim tries to leave them, textbook emotional manipulation. "What will I do without you?"

Their weakness is, they actually have no real support in their evil stunts and at best are only being used by other demons. If the victim stops supporting them, they actually will be destroyed as they well should.

One of ways they control a victim is through subliminally threatening to character defame the victim by telling the entire social circle bad things about them. When the victim realizes that the social circle either doesn't matter, or that the social circle has no respect for this entity anyhow, the victim can let go of the fear and move on.

SATURN IN LEO

There was a carpenter, Ed, working every day in his shop. Night and day, people around could hear the hammering, the dragging, often even his panting. But he wouldn't let anyone in his shop to see what he was making. People wondered what it was. They tried to estimate from the sounds, and from how long he was working at it, what he was doing.

One day, he finished his work and he threw open the door of his shop. To the utter surprise of all there, they saw, it wasn't a chair he'd been making, or a table, or a cupboard, or a bed. It was a SHIP!!!!!!

A whole little ship, he'd made all on his own.

That's Saturn in Leo, Ed. He or she will be making something beautiful, amazing, stunning, but all by themselves and sometimes without their conscious mind knowing it.

They work alone, in secret, powered by a secret passion that maybe only their soulmate knows. They achieve things beyond what their neighborhood or surroundings can imagine. They are extraordinary.

Their strength is in not inviting others' opinions and judgments of what they're doing in life. Their weakness is allowing others to tell them what to do, when to do it and so on.

They have no toleration of any kind of restraints on their freedom.

Their primary weapon, Ed, is how their inner vision is something no one would guess from how they present themselves on the outside. They can follow their dream from inception to fulfillment without anyone else cheering them on.

Naturally, Ed, this ability is most often developed because they don't get the support from others in childhood and youth that others get. It makes them the phenomenon that they are. Self-fueled, self-reliant, steady on their feet.

Demon – Saturn in Leo
This entity, Ed, likes to break others down by pretending to be very logical and forthright and intelligent. There's a difference, Ed, between someone being able to see the mistakes or problems with something and actually being invaluable that way, and someone who is dedicated to maintaining their sense of superiority by finding fault

with everything others do. They don't usually verbalize what they're saying but they'll convey it somehow or the other.

They're actually very insecure, jealous types, Ed. They can't handle anyone around them doing well, being happy, falling in love... They can't even really tolerate the dog running around being happy and even their pets will become morose and low energy around them.

They literally suck the joy out of the air.

But they'll behave like they're so intellectual, Ed, and that they know all they're doing.

Interestingly Ed, these demons are sexually very adept because they literally learn to do techniques and are emotionally inert enough to follow through with the technique without getting carried away themselves in any emotion or feeling. They get victims usually by just giving the victim physical orgasms so the victim mistakes the connection as being a highly emotional one – but actually it's like being in a relationship with an AI vibrator. (OMG Ed, have I got a great idea here or what!)

To get rid of them, a victim might need to learn the difference between actual sexual holistic satisfaction, versus just physical orgasms that keep them feeling good about themselves, because they had the orgasms. The victims of this demon often only wake up to reality when they find they are emotionally crushed, energetically drained and need to get away from the person they became hanging around with this pseudo-intellectual freak.

As friends, Ed, they play the game very carefully, pretending to be a little aloof, like they're not really that interested in you, but you're a general friend of theirs. But they actually wait and wait, till they can get near enough to use their sexual skills – which in the case of the older demons, they can use without even getting you naked in bed or thinking you're in a sexual situationship.

They are adept at covertly making people feel sexually turned on, the victim imagining it's something wrong with them that they're getting turned on by someone who isn't even really into them like that.

Remember this demon follows technique. But that's also how they always get caught out. Because humans always outgrow techniques and patterns.

This demon's weakness, Ed, is the way they can't play their games if they're outside their comfort zone, or one or two of their props and things for their techniques aren't available.

They are a slave to the method, to the program, to the institution, to the way things are arranged around them.

They frequently have severe mental issues and eventually develop dementia if they don't die of something before old age.

SATURN IN VIRGO
Angels who will fight for the downtrodden, the vulnerable and be there despite the stench and the vomit, for the ones they love; that's who Saturn in Virgo are.

They have a deep understanding of the pain in others, natural empaths if you will and they also tend to have the ability to see the causes of the pain. They have meticulous clean and clear minds, and are always following in their lives a plan they have in their minds to achieve something.

This warrior can point out the chinks in the boat, before it's out at sea and sinking. This warrior can tell straight off at the beginning of a project, if it's going to work or not, and if not, why not.

They don't like to mess around being diplomatic when they can be of help by saying things straight out. They can be hated for this, by those who don't want to improve or actually become well.

They are the sort of warrior who'll fight for someone they just met and don't know, but stand by inscrutably silent while someone they know is getting a drubbing, because they have a sense of justice that is deeper than the moment. They have a long term of things, an innate ability to sense things, AND they sense them strong enough for it to influence their choices of who to hang out with.

This person is incredibly sensitive to the energy of the atmosphere and space. Part of their warrior-hood is either cleaning up the energy field and atmosphere of a space, or avoiding having anything to do with a space they feel they cannot clean up because the people involved are addicted to those who bring in the dirt.

They make great advisors for anyone who wants to clean up their act, and find what's blocking their progress in life; because of their sensitivity to energy blocks.

Their primary strength is their spiritual value of purity in everything they do. This makes them win long before the battle even starts. The truth they have built their life on, makes them already very difficult to attack. The many times in daily life they chose, uphold and defend their values makes their enemies think twice before even sparring with them. Only a real fool will attack this person and their loss is a guarantee.

Their primary weakness is thug world programming that sees people as devoted to purity and truth as them as not cool, frumpy and so on. They tend to be bullied as children and even adults. They invariably rise up from that, but in the years before they realize their amazing value and powers they can go self recrimination, even self hatred because of their sensitivity to things others accept as normal, and their inability to accept the evil in the world and work with it.

They are that person everyone laughed at and look down on, but who became the one person everyone later wants to impress and win over.

This person simply doesn't let just anyone get close to them. But those they do, they take care of in every way they can.

Demon – Saturn in Virgo

This demon will cheat you of money, and use you however they can, blatantly believing God make you for them to profit from. These are those demons who'll poison whole populations, burn down whole areas of habitations, just to get the land.

They are utterly without scruples or morality. They do not give a f*** for their own mother, forget anyone else.

Usually they don't even pretend not to be this, making it like they're just being brutally honest about their plans and everyone's like this underneath the nice behavior. This attracts low self-esteemed victims to them, slave trained people; and those who admire open evil.

They can even end up being leaders in thug world enterprises because of their cold, callous, clear headed exploitative nature. Younger demons of all kinds aspire to have the gall to be as open about being evil as this entity.

Humans tend to end up having anything to do with this entity because we cannot really believe anyone is actually that evil.

Very often this demon will have a child or pet they are very, very protective of, and humans will see that as proof that he or she is not as evil as they present themselves. In fact the demon protects its lineage as fastidiously, as their bank account and investments for the future. They will also look after any older relatives so long as there is ANYTHING they are of use for – such as networking with useful contacts.

This demon keeps its dealing all very "legal" and is often a lawyer or working in the criminal justice system themselves. Because of being utterly unscrupulous, they know exactly how to manipulate the justice system and law.

Their weakness is their fear of nature and the natural elements. They need to be in the atmosphere in which everything is controlled. Something like a power cut can shake them, disturb them deeply. They need to see things in order or they start feeling an incredible dread. Drugs, medicines that mess with their mood can terrify them and they keep clear of anything that might take them outside of their usual frequency.

Something that terrifies them is the idea that that they're losing their mental imbalance. They are also terrified of anyone who has evidence of their many covertly done crimes in such a way as can be brought before a court of law. They will quickly disassociate with anyone that they feel could legally get a win over them.

They tend to prey on people who can't afford lawyers, don't have families supporting them, and who seem unable to get their life together. If they find the person is getting themselves together, getting educated on legal issues, human rights and such; they'll usually slink slowly out of the picture.

If they don't, then they should be given the whole whammy of public humiliation and court process because they are utterly cold blooded evil demons who can do ANYTHING to get what they want and they have to be dealt with an iron hand.

SATURN IN LIBRA

This is a most powerful person in terms of power to shift mass consciousness opinion. This person has their ear so close to the ground, no matter which sector of the society he or she is in. They are so close to reality as to be constantly sharpened and refined by it.

Their vision of things is razor sharp and because of this, by the time they reach their thirties they are veritable prophets in their estimation of what will happen next, what someone will do next.

They are incredibly careful and precise with their time and manage their energy judiciously. This warrior will never waste their time on a losing venture, and if they get involved in anything or with anyone, it's for the long haul, and for the win.

They are incredibly closely connected to their grandparents with a strong transfer of racial and family memory in their blood. This is one reason for their grounding in reality. In a way they're seeing things through their grandparents' eyes.

The primary strength of this warrior is their grounding in reality. Their primary weakness is their tendency to expect others to also be grounded in reality. They get shocked by how other humans can't see what they're seeing. They get shocked by the sheer nonsense other humans believe. They cannot believe anyone would want to believe in Santa Claus when we all know there is no, and never was such a person. It was a marketing stunt.

This can cause them to feel isolated, misunderstood, lonely and so on. But by the age of thirty, they stop giving a crap and focus on doing their own thing. If their grandparents believed in it, it's good to go.

They're a pillar of whichever society, family, group, community has them.

Demon – Saturn in Libra
This demon is an incredibly psychically active assaulter. This demon doesn't even approach someone in the physical if they want to talk to that person. They attack them psychically first, make them feel bad about how they're dressed, that they're poor, or ugly or whatever; and then come around casually.

In every relationship of their lives, including their parents, they have one face – the face that doesn't get too involved in others' business but does their duty to family and such; and the other face which is that of the psychic attacker. They secretly control their families by their silent psychic attack of them every time anyone does something that they don't like. The family tends to live in unnamed terror of them because of this.

They have the same attitude in everything. Often they have careers in sports because of their ability to do psychic attacks on the field and break their opponents down.

The primary weakness is, they're redundant. Once you figure out their psychic game, they're finished. Once a victim of theirs decides that they will decide their own self worth and value, this demon has no more power.

SATURN IN SCORPIO
When God made the world, Ed, God made those who would defend its beauty and thereby allow it to keep being pure. A great defender of all things beautiful and pure, is this person. Misunderstood as a misanthrope, a hater more than a lover, someone who has a problem with everything and everyone; this is a true lover of what is genuine and has no toleration for adulterated and fake things.

This manifestation of God refuses to settle for what life gives them; but, like Job in the Bible, has the gumption to expect God to give them what is truly worth having, and not any crap that happens to be in their path.

They are those legendary investigators of old crimes; nothing too deep for them to dig out, nothing too far for them to pursue. They have a strong instinct for truth and will often on entry into a room, immediately know things about the character of those in the room that couldn't be imagined otherwise.

They don't go about minding others' business, but should something stir their heart, they will do everything to restore justice, going out of their way.

They seem stingy as Scrooge, but for those they love, they would give their internal organs.

They have a deep spiritual life, and a keen instinct for prophecy. Their spiritual life is usually completely hidden.

The primary weapon of this person is their ability to work alone and in secrecy without losing passion or needing motivation or support from others.

Their weakness, is when they get overly involved in the financial aspect of anything and start thinking about making money, managing money etc. If they can overcome insecurity and trust God to provide their needs, loosen up and let their energy go towards what really interests them, they will find everything falling into place.

A lifelong problem for them, is finding people who are as intense and committed as them to a cause or anything. Others give up, get distracted, lose interest – and this hurts this person very much.

If they can stop looking for likeminded people and just do what they want to, or can do on their own; hold their own frequency, in time they will attract their frequency of intensity people – who are very, very, rare.

Demon – Saturn in Scorpio

This is one poverty addicted entity. No matter how much money they have, they're poor. They're always trying to get rich or richer, or more powerful or more this or more that. They can't sleep 15 minutes without being disturbed by their own restlessness.

They tend to read a lot, travel a lot, and collect a lot of trivia about all kinds of things. This gives them a benevolent air, but it's just their restlessness, going about looking for some sort of opportunity to free themselves from themselves and their eternal insecurity.

Their sex is a nightmare, with them disconnecting and getting distracted all the time.

They always want to know what's in the other person's mind, and discuss it and make the other person think what they want them to think, or no sex.

I can't even imagine how entities like this ever get a partner, but that's what arranged marriage is for, I guess. This demon usually uses their money or wealth or such to con simpler people into a relationship with them. They come across as very educated, classy, refined people initially; and then the demands start and never end.

They are horrible as children too, never being satisfied with anything their parents provide, picking fights with other kids just because the other kid has something they don't have. They partner often with demons who have Saturn in Aquarius and devise mind games to cause distress to "stupid people".

Their weakness is their dependency on things like their job, looks, money to feel confident in their crimes. When one or more of these are hit, they tend to collapse. When their early youth goes, about the age of 30, they lose confidence and get attracted to shady underhand ways of making money, getting sex by seducing their friends' partners and so on.

SATURN IN SAGITTARIUS
The throne Saturn also has a good sense of humor. Almost no one knows about it, but it's there. This person has a great, great gift. The ability to understand and see the humor of God being delivered through justice and karma. One needs a long term vision and a big heart to even comprehend the workings of God, but this person has that.

This person is a comforter to the sad, a reviver of spirits and a support for the weak. They will lift up every tired human soldier and carry them on the road till they can walk on their own again.

They will give their money to those who have less, and take care of whoever they possibly can.

Their primary weapon is their innate understanding of the big picture surrounding an event. They are prophetic in that way, and able to see how God is weaving a higher justice rather than a lower one. This warrior can foresee events months and years ahead and prepares for them too. They know where the enemy will be a few days from now, or months or years.

Their weakness is their intelligence and astuteness getting wasted on things they're not really into, just because they're good at nearly everything. People tell them, "You're so good at this, you could make a career in it," and they go trying to make a career out of something they're not really interested in.

Prophecy, prediction and long term planning, long term projects are their forte. They can achieve the impossible things, because they can think for that long.

This reminds me of the guy in "The Shawshank Redemption". He was stuck in this prison for life, but for decades, little by little he worked out his eventual escape. People came and went, but he had his long term goal worked out and he worked towards it steadfastly. He achieved the impossible, as a result.

Nothing is too difficult or unachievable for this person, really, nothing.

Demon – Saturn in Sagittarius

This is a penny pinching miser who hides behind a façade of being a person of service to others. A beggar if ever there was. They are unable to actually feel any emotion of service to anyone but find at a young age that if they look like they're service oriented people, dedicated to serving others, people will tell them stuff like, "Do take a rest, you're always working.." In fact they're slackers in everything they do. They never do anything really, well, Ed, just do the basic required and then pout that they didn't get enough credit for it.

They're very slimy, Ed, they can come up with excuses and stories and worm out of being held accountable for things.

Their weakness is that they cannot pursue a target for very long, usually. If you go physically outside of the zone of their influence they'll look to others to live off of. Now and then they'll do their games online but if you block them, they'll most probably go find an easier target.

SATURN IN CAPRICORN

This is your legendary leader of leader's Ed. A warrior with the sharpest mind, the most grounded calm, collected person in the room, and yet the swiftest to act when the moment demands it. This warrior starts young, understanding how demons do warfare, whether psychic or through the various physical means. He's watched adults. She's seen things and remembers them.

This person, Ed, goes through a spiritual crisis young in life, because they see what's happening around them and it is hard to handle. But they come out of that spiritual crisis, a warrior. They actively learn how to deal with entities that come against them. They look for help from books, from others, and they have the guts, Ed, to actually try things and see if it works.

This makes them value people who can be trusted and counted on, and they choose their friends carefully, because they know your weakest link will give it all away.

They fortify their lives, their families, their homes.

Their primary weapon is their observational skill. They can get to the bottom of things in a very short time compared to others. They can do lots with very little. Thrifty, powerful on their feet, and quite fearless once they start; they just need to know they already got all a warrior needs; they just need to keep practicing.

Their weakness is getting influenced by Gemini placements into taking on too many roles, opening too many windows, doing too many things at once. They need to focus on one or two things they're naturally interested in, and not get pulled aside.

They have a tendency to give people the benefit of doubt until proven guilty. This goes against their instinct most of the time, and they usually regret it.

They tend to have pets who help them hone their instinct. If they allow their pet to go from being just a pet, to a partner in their spiritual walk and warfare, they can move even more quick than before.

Demon – Saturn in Capricorn
This demon is almost the most perfect example of perfect relations with everyone. There's never a word out of place or a hair. They made a plan in their childhood or teenage years, a plan for their life and they're going about accomplishing that.

If you know what that plan is, you've understood all you need to about this person. It's usually something to do with marrying rich and owning particular luxury items that indicate status.

In general, they are obsessed with money, luxury items and wealth. They don't enjoy any of it. They just like having it all and watching tv.

They're in a private hell of their own, not even caring about others really, until someone threatens their dreams of their kind of paradise. Then they can do sudden, extremely cruel, horrible things, completely unexpected from them. They can break up happy couples, murder pets, kill trees and plants, break things precious to other people. They can do just anything if they think it'll help them reach their goal.

They are often manipulated by other demons into committing crimes for money, because they can always use more money.

They are then themselves murdered quite often for being witness to crimes and so on.

They have very little real grounding in life and can be tricked quite easily into investing in get-rich-quick schemes. Wealth actually turns them on sexually but they cannot really have a good sexual life, unless they're given expensive things in the exact minute before the sex is to be had. That time keeps shrinking... so they're doomed to sexless relationships with a lot of expensive souvenirs.

They can be gotten rid of by stopping giving them gifts or showing wealth. If that doesn't work, say you've written your will and everything's left to your mother, or some other relative, of the same sex as them (so they don't go trying to seduce them next).

You get the picture. It's all money, money, money for this demon.

SATURN IN AQUARIUS

This is a most deadly, dangerous warrior. This warrior is extremely energy sensitive, has a mind like a super computer, while being extremely emotionally astute at the same time. They almost never have to get into any actual sparring, because they can see conflicts developing way, way, earlier than others can, and if it's something to do with them, they're defuse the ticking bomb way before it's close to exploding.

They are level headed and calm and non-confrontational, till they absolutely have to get into the ring. When they do, it's all over before it even started. Because they've done their homework so well.

This warrior tends to have communication and speech problems in early life, causing them to develop their abilities to communicate non verbally and consequently read others' non verbal cues. They are also sensitive to the atmosphere and can "read the room" so to speak.

Every time I've met one of them, Ed, they were feeling very tired and fatigued. It's because they are high energy bodies and require more of everything than others. More fresh air, more water, more sunlight, more exercise, more everything. If they accept their appetite for life, they'll find they're also that much more productive in every way and have the power to do things others find daunting and can't.

Their primary weapon is their ability to maintain their own consciousness and viewpoint no matter where they are or how much pressure they are under.

Their weakness is not getting enough lung strength that they would have developed if they'd followed their instincts through childhood, teenage and so on, to do exercises like running and cycling. If they manage to do things to strengthen their lungs, they'll find the blood supply to the head vastly improved and with it their entire nervous system untangles and they can become the smoothly functioning deadly warrior they are.

Demon – Saturn in Aquarius
This demon is an enabler of other demons by supplying them with ideas on how to manipulate people. This demon's brain seems to work from early childhood, learning how to trick, deceive, manipulate people. They begin to form patterns really early on and by the time they are a teenager, they are manipulating people all around them. It becomes dangerous then, though, because people begin to realize what this person is up to.

They then begin their real career. Enabling and teaching other humans how to deceive, trick, cheat, manipulate others.

This is often presented as training for success in business or something like that, packaged as survival training or hustling, but it is actually about manipulating people.

You remember that famous book, Ed? "How to Win Friends and Influence People?" By Dale Carnegie? It's an innocent enough title and many innocent people like me thought it would really help me in making friends in a new place and making others happy. In reality it was about making people you like them, when you don't and that sort of thing. It was done real smooth, but it was outright training people to trick others.

This kind of person has a lot of potential in thug world, in the fields of marketing and what not. The whole thug world order is based on trickery and deception anyhow. I knew one of these who was a pastor of a church.

SATURN IN PISCES

This warrior is a fluid, flexible force of nature. You never know where they're coming from but when they reach – BANG – they will do or say something that will change the whole story instantly.

They are emotionally and spiritually always flowing, and as a result they have their ear to the ground like few others. There are very few things you could tell this person that they didn't already know or see coming.

They can be prophetic, they can be far sighted, but for the most part their strength is in their ability to be in the moment. They are able to hold together all the various aspects of the situation and actually deal with the problem fully, instead of one little solution here and one little help there.

They are warriors on a holistic level as they're awake in the physical, emotional, spiritual, at the same time.

They can seem sometimes to get overly lost in doing something; for example, they might do nothing for weeks at a time but one particular activity, like swimming. A few weeks later they could do nothing but painting for weeks. They get immersed in things like that, and that's usually difficult for the people they live with to understand as they mightn't be as flexible as needed to cope with that.

But that's the weapon of this warrior – they immerse themselves in things and see things on a holistic level.

Their weakness is when they limit their vision and their viewpoint to conform to others around. This invariably dissipates the ray of energy forming in them.

Therefore time spent alone and developing their own spiritual body and path is a constant requirement for this warrior.

Demon – Saturn in Pisces
This demon is an escapist, liar. They find at a young age, that spinning a story to engage people emotionally, is a good way to present oneself as valuable, without actually helping anyone or doing anything of substance.

We need our storytellers, to inspire and guide us. But these are not that sort of storytellers. These are the kind who have a warped view of reality and actively spread that warped view, warping it further according to their convenience.

They simply do not get the need to tell the truth, as in their heads, everything is a lie.

They are drifters even when they're managing to hold down a job and stay in one place. They often manage very well to disguise their complete lack of adherence to even the concept of truth, as them being a great Sage, "questioning" everything.

For all this, they are nearly always after others' money or wealth, one way or another. They come up with business plans and ventures, get investment from others, go around town looking like they're achieving this great thing, and then suddenly one day, they say, "This isn't going to work, I don't feel it anymore."

In fact, they can't actually do anything more than for a few months if there isn't a constant stream of money coming in. They're actually living off the energy of the investors. They can't be trusted to do what has to be done without that constant stream of energy and attention.

And even then, they never really intended to do that long term. They did it as long as they felt they looked good around town doing it. As soon as people stopped reacting with, "That's wonderful..." they started losing interest.

This is that kind of demon that can lose interest in his or her own children because others aren't appreciating what a fine mother or father they are. They have to be constantly supervised and pushed.

Once they turn disinterested, they can pull down a team, destroy a business.

Usually, these can be gotten rid of by telling them straight off that the thrill is gone and it's time to move on. However, every now and then, when they're in a relationship for example, it's dangerous to tell them anything directly as they are capable of things like poisoning, sexual assault, hurting the kids and so on.

It's best to take the kids away to safety first, and the pets and anything or anyone they could hurt, and then inform them.

MERCURY – THE SPARK OF LIFE

I wrote to you earlier, Ed, the following introduction of Mercury:

Mercury is the sparking or friction between life energy flowing in opposite directions, giving rise to new cells or formations, causing all growth from primal energy into vibration, life, form, everything really. It is the spark of intelligence or where consciousness goes from being "everything" to "I am THIS," and then back to "everything". Replace "everything" with "nothing" if you swing that way.

Buddha for example is named literally after Mercury as "Budh" is Mercury in Sanskrit.

Imagine a green leafy tree, Ed. It's buzzing with life energy. Maybe not everyone can hear it, but I do, and most humans can, if we go silent enough. That buzz of life energy, Ed, given off by all natural beings in this realm, whether a rock or a tree or a human body; that's caused by the friction of energies that interact to make a "body" out of pure consciousness.

On Youtube, Ed, there are videos where the sound is "Frequency of this" and "Frequency of that." That frequency they're talking about is the buzz of life force, as it creates matter and therefore body.

They have ways to amplify that sound these days and you can see many examples of this online. "Frequency of Moldavite" for example is one I like to play on my computer, because it's very like the energy of one of my favorite rocks. (Note that it destroys energy fields to re-build it according to truth.)

There are these experiments where they put sand on a flat metal plate and then vibrate that metal plate to a certain frequency. That frequency makes the sand particles form themselves into patterns. When we have a pattern repeated over and over, we have an energy field generated, and when we have an energy field generated it becomes a force field and then a thing, or body if the pattern requires it.

All things visible and invisible are basically a force field created by repeated energy patterns. And that spark where the ever-existing divine consciousness, results in the creation of frequency and with it a force field or body, is called Mercury.

It is the God-Force of turning unmanifested consciousness of soul into a manifested frequency, and therefore the root of Life or Being as we know it.

This sparking never stops, and it is what is constantly keeping us alive, generating that frequency our souls and therefore bodies give off. It is transforming us all the time according to our ever-changing consciousness.

All "deadness" therefore can be seen as the result of the force of Mercury in our lives being suppressed or blocked. All confusion can be seen as the force of Mercury in our lives being splattered, distorted, from flowing out properly.

When we begin to use our bodies to walk towards things in life our soul doesn't want, we immediately feel the mind-numbing, the deadness. That's our sparking going out. Mercury can't spark up where our soul is not willing.

So you see, Ed, the very spark of creation, of creativity, in our lives is Mercury.

Traditional astrology does not see Mercury as ruling Fertility but it does 100%. You can be as fecund, as sexually potent as you wish, but there's no use of that lamp, or that candle or the entire fields of oil and gas, without the strike of a match to set the fire off.

In everything in life, Ed, we need the spark. The God-force of Mercury.

The question that will arise at this point, Ed, is how does someone's Mercury force get suppressed and how do we get it going again.

A general answer, Ed, is that **the spark gets suppressed when you're forcing yourself to do what your soul isn't invested in.** It's really that simple. What's not so simple is that we tend to have wrong ideas about what our soul wants. For example, I thought I wanted to earn money to build the fake mother, a house, at one point. My soul wasn't into that, so my Mercury didn't flow and I nearly died. I didn't even know what was going on. I couldn't mentally comprehend that my soul might not want that. Why wouldn't anyone want to build their mother a house?

You see, Ed, at the time, I had a huge misconception about myself. I thought I was the daughter of that entity and that that was my life duty, to take care of her. This was literally the result of holding a FALSE IDENTITY.

When we have a false view of our own selves, our soul is going off in one direction, and our mental idea of our soul is a completely warped idea, because it's not matching our reality.

Therefore, one of the main problems someone with a blocked Mercury force has, is usually having a false sense of identity.

This false sense of identity, Ed, is more often than not, based in false relationships, because it is relationships that give us our soul-honored place in the universe, in the mandala of Life.

Our parents by giving birth to us, give us our first latitude and longitude point in Time, in consciousness. Those who are ignoring, or ignorant of their biological birth identity; they're operating under a false idea of who they are.

This makes their Mercury force skewed. Their intellect is numbed, their intelligence blocked from being rewarding; their learning, their creativity either blocked or not rewarding.

In general, their very life force is blocked at the very root of manifestation and this is going to show up in tons of ways, but most of the time it leads to multiple illnesses, fatigue, organ failure and even death.

My own Mercury being suppressed led to severe heart weakness or Cardio Myopathy and two heart attacks during which I passed out and left my body, ie. I actually died, once for 9 minutes and once for 15 minutes.

If I'd known then what I know now, I'd have not gone on that trip trying to get an education I didn't want, to make money for someone who not only wasn't my mother but was one of the worst, most cruel, cold betrayers in my life, and that's not even getting near it.

My soul wasn't participating in the well meaning but ignorant paths my mind was leading me in.

And it was mostly based in my having a wrong sense of identity at such a basic essential point in my consciousness – my birth.

For anything to exist in this universe, that spark must happen, and that spark is a result of Male force and Female Force meeting. That is literally how every natural baby is made, how every SOUL is created, and re-created.

Therefore, the first way to get back to Mercury force flowing well, is to find out the truth about our birth identity and honor it.

Now, Ed, I have people always telling me that they know their parents are their real parents but there's no love lost between them or they are hopelessly at odds with them and never get any support, and in fact their parents are their enemies, in the sense that they come around destroying their chances for happiness and so on.

I got to say this, Ed. True parents are the energy source of a child. If a child is not receiving that life supporting energy from the parents, that LOVE is simply not there, then those are simply not the parents.

The thug world is RIDDLED through and through like a sponge with false parentage. Sometimes even the supposed parents don't know that's not their child. Sometimes the physical body is made from the physical matter of two people, but because the baby was made either in a lab, or in a non-holistic-sexual way, mechanically; there's no connection of soul or spirit passed into the baby. The baby can be occupied by an angel, a demon, or even just be a blank zombie. Sometimes, an ancestor's soul will occupy the baby, just to be with one or other of the parents who might be a human duped into believing the other parents is actually a natural human when they're not.

There are all these various scenarios, Ed, and these multiply like crazy when you have conceptions that happen along with frequent "check-ups" because implantion of lab-made babies can be done easily enough at these; births that are done in hospitals and the baby taken away from the mother.

There's a fertility clinic near the previous place we used to live in; that had a guarantee or your money back, advertised on the board outside the "clinic". This thug world excels in achievement through fakery and baby making has been a big money business, not just now but for a long time.

But our path is actually simple. If the soul, as evidenced by the heart not being IN something, says that our basic sense of identity is not right, then just accept that, and do spiritual exercises to honor the Great Mother and Great Father of who we all are definitely born. When we want to, Ed, our real mother and father souls will show us how to find them and guide us on. It's real, Ed, living or passed into another time, our parents' souls are constantly giving us birth, making the SPARK OF LIFE happen.

If we're alive, Ed, it's because they are loving each other and setting off the spark. If they withdraw, we end. In all times, we will end just like that.

They are a constant force-field of love and we are living in that spark between them all the time. Just as a baby cries out and immediately the parents' soul is drawn to the baby; so when that call in our heart arises for our Mama and Papa, their soul, wherever in consciousness they are, immediately responds to us.

Their guidance will come; who knows how... But it will come and keep coming at us, pulling us out of the wrong life for us into the one where we're sparking.

Now, Ed, birth identity isn't the only sense of identity we have. There are other levels of identity. Those identities don't affect our Mercury force as drastically as our birth identity being skewed, but they can cause damage enough to destroy our academics, careers, etc.

Those identities are essentially those got through relationships. How often have you seen people getting into a relationship, then losing their ability to progress in their career or art or studies?

"Relationships" also include business and other partnerships. If you partner with the wrong person, the business is going to sink, no matter anything else. If your soul is not in it, nothing's going to be rewarding.

Sometimes we tell ourselves, "We're just going through a rough patch. Things will become better soon."

For such situations, Ed, **to know the difference between a "rough patch" and actual Mercury suppression; the difference is in the nervous system of the person.**

When you're going through a rough patch, the rough patch bit is outside your body in the circumstances. You yourself are hale and hearty. But when it's not a rough patch and your Mercury is being suppressed, you find your hair is limp, you're not as confident as before; in fact, you're not so sturdy on your feet. Your dancing is not as on point as before. You're not so sharp, you need to sleep more than usual. Your brain and nervous system are just not as awake and clear as usual. You feel tired a lot, disinterested in things you usually like, especially music – you're not feeling the spark anymore.

I guess, Ed, a most famous song about this situation, is B.B.King's, "The Thrill is Gone."

I love B.B.King's music, Ed; that music used to give me energy on days I felt dead. But I never got that song, "The Thrill is Gone." At some point, it showed up in my internet feed, with the words, "This song made B.B.King a celebrity musician, and it was published in...." Some year, Ed, like in the 60s. I dimly realized that it was one of his oldest records. And it began to dawn on me, that his facing that the thrill was gone from something in his life, was actually what set off his career. He went from obscurity into becoming one of the most successful recording artists and one of the most vibrant live performing artists ever. His 80th birthday concert was just WOW, Ed. I honestly haven't come across anyone that could spark a crowd like that man, at that age, sitting on a chair onstage.

But it all started with his realizing the thrill was gone.

And I think that's a good point for someone wanting to spark their bodies and lives up again – acknowledge that the thrill is gone, and start again.

B.B.King in 2009, Vienna, Austria.

(Picture Source: Werner100359 on Wikimedia Commons).

In ancient alchemical practices, Ed, such an Ayurveda, the use of the metal, Mercury, as medicine, goes way back. Because it is both a liquid and a solid – because it melts so quickly – its other name being "quicksilver" – it is used in thermometers to give us an indication of how hot or cold the temperature is.

But imagine how powerful it is as a medicine. Naturally, you can't play around with it. There are forms of it you can use and forms that are bad for the body. It considered poisonous as a result. It has serious immediate effects on the nervous system – which is why it is used in vaccines.

I personally, find that one of the best ways to have Mercury, the metal, in one's life, is to get the stabilized form of it, called Parad in Sanskrit. They made beads and various things out of Parad – a form of mercury mixed with Lead – which is a metal with a Saturn frequency and therefore heavy and causing one to go deep into things rather than fly with every wind. It's a good combination to develop stability in thought, in intention while finding out what really sparks you.

One doesn't really need it, Ed, but it can have a powerful consciousness stabilizing effect for someone who's just so confused about everything; and it can make crazy stuff happen for someone who's stuck, so that they can move out of that stuck situation.

Now Ed, this writing is about being a Spirit Warrior, and this bit about Mercury is so important, because you cannot defend yourself if you're not sparking right. And you sure as hell cannot attack someone else if you're not sparking right and your body is dying.

So, this is a major drain-hole to fix if you want to be a Spirit Warrior. You can't even start to hold a sword if your nerves are weak. How will you hold it up, and how will you point it where you want it to point?

Mercury, Ed, in the heavens overhead a person's birth, shows us what we need to do for nerve strength, to hold our nerve in battle. DEVELOPING NERVOUS STRENGTH and with it the ability to hold our consciousness in the face of assault is INCREDIBLY IMPORTANT for a warrior, Ed. So this is something for each person according to where Mercury was in the heavens above when they were born.

MERCURY IN ARIES

Sexually, this person is awesome. But they tend to be unable to convert this sexual energy naturally back into energy for their lives, because they're tuned to a paradigm of life where they were with their tribe, and the whole tribe functioned as one unit.

In life in our times, this is simply no longer the case, and Mercury in Aries needs to do what it takes to learn to keep their energy to themselves and their immediate soulmate and children. They have to learn to invest their energy in their own lives and own business, own family, consistently, rather than dissipating it by supporting some others' grand cause (that hasn't gone anywhere in 50 years) or others' anything.

They must stop behaving like they have a tribe and everyone's "in this together". That's just not true anymore.

When they begin to reinvest their energy in their own lives and business, they begin to develop nervous strength, resilience and the ability to see projects through to completion.

They are a formidable warrior because they're not going to get thrown by personal attacks, character defamation, or even intimidation.

When they speak, their word holds and people respect that. That is money in the bank in our times.

This person will find, that one becomes a true leader in our times and in fact an inspiration for the tribe, when one cares for and invests in his own person, life and immediate family above all.

Demon – Mercury in Aries

This entity is a liar and will siphon off money cunningly, among other things. You do not want to trust this entity with the keys to anything, the passwords and so on. They are crazy for recognition, acknowledgment, and to be seen as a powerful person. But they don't have the substance to earn that, so they get their kicks by doing hidden acts of violence and hurt on people, and feeling real powerful that they could actually hurt someone like that.

MERCURY IN TAURUS

The mama bear or papa bear is not playing hokey with anyone. At any time in their lives this person is busy building a spiritual and energetic nest for themselves and their loved ones. They are a refuge for their loved ones and they know it from early on.

They can hold their nerve easily enough when they're in the same place a long time. Their challenge is holding their nerve when the location, and situation is changing.

Dealing with change therefore, is what they have to work on incessantly. They don't have to worry about building anything, because they're already doing that one way or another all the time anyway. It's the dealing with change, from day to day they have to focus on. Flexibility in plans, adapting to a different environment; that sort of thing.

This warrior is expected by those attacking him or her, to always hold the same opinion, be in the same place and so on. The attackers can be taken by surprise if this warrior made sudden moves very contrary to their usual choices or moves. It is this warrior's special weapon – the sudden change or shift. It's like an earthquake.

And God gives this warrior chances to shift and change just when required.

So all this warrior really needs to do, is stop associating security with the lack of change, and start actively jumping into a different paradigm fearlessly as God brings them into focus.

Their nervous system will greatly benefit from experiencing change in little ways every day, keeping fresh and flexible, trying new things, new foods, losing the fear of what is outside the established comfort zone.

Demon – Mercury in Taurus

This demon is a dead weight and wet blanket, although they can seem quite cheerful, sparky and intelligent initially. You'll find very soon that's all only within a certain circle or environment. Suggest a different restaurant or area of the city and they go flaccid as…. Er…. Never mind finding a simile. They lose air like a popped balloon.

They're always worried about money and aren't really fun long term, because if they get close to someone, they'll start sharing their constant worry about money.

They have a precious few hobbies and if you don't share those, they'll assume you're useless in this world. They are small-brained and near-sighted.

Of course, depending on other placements they can disguise all of this well, but that's how it is beneath.

They're just going to drain and pull down any human that gets stuck with them. You can get rid of them by presenting that you're never going to be financially stable ever because you've decided to go be a missionary, or volunteer for the rest of your life, or become an artist or a professional dancer, or some such profession where the chance of you having financial stability is very low.

If you're already dependent on them, you can get rid of them by spending a lot of their money suddenly.

MERCURY IN GEMINI

Wow, whatta man, whatta man, whatta man, what a mighty man. Or woman. But wow, we're talking the ruler of the sky here, the rider of the winds, the spark of sparks.

This warrior is made by God, to be the one who'll start the fire and get everything actually going. They have the vision, and the anointing.

But this warrior is near constantly under attack for just this power, because the demons can sense it immediately. The very way this warrior stands, their feet almost dancing even when they're standing in one place, tells of their astute ability to get things going.

This warrior has to develop nerves of steel, because that's what it's going to take to fob off the a$$holes going to come at him or her to try and put out the spark of God glowing here.

This warrior is the frontline of God's army marching against the thug world consciousness of doom, pain and suffering. This warrior holds up the flag of Freedom, Love, Joy, and everything good in this world and holds it up right in the face of the demons.

If chutzpah had a placement, it would be this.

But this warrior, who fights every single day, by the way, because the very mass consciousness of the thug world is constantly attacking his or her joy and eternal spring withing, needs constant nervous system replenishment and strengthening.

Herbs for nerve strength – Ashwagandha, Rosehips, Vervain, Borage, Apples. I've written a lot about this on my website Holistic-Treatment.com. Just search for, "herbs for nerve strength" or "nervous rehabilitation".

But these are just for a start. The thing that has to be done, is find what one really truly believes in, whether that's God, or a connection to the earth, or whatever, and develop a daily spiritual practice grounding and connecting to that thing, absorbing all the energy of one's body back into the center and holding that stability for longer and longer periods of time.

Such a person can have a big circle of friends, but it's important, like Gideon's army in the Bible, to sift out all those who are there just because… hanging about enjoying the mood… versus those who believe in what you believe in, who are energetically grounded, who really will have your back.

Everyone wants a piece of this warrior, like his things are a lucky charm. So it's important for him or her to learn to safeguard, protect and own what they own. This right there is serious nervous system defense already.

They will benefit from limiting their exposure to too many books, movies, internet surfing, and focus on one thing at a time.

Learning to identify energy or loosh attacks is an important thing for this person's success. Once they become aware – 'I was doing this, when I got drained'- they'll become able to see who they got drained by, and go further to – "Who was the origin of the INTENTION to drain me?" As this person progresses, they become a veritable storehouse of genuinely useful information on how to maintain one's energy and motivation in the face of assault.

Most of them tend to have life experience that involves isolation, maybe even imprisonment of some kind or the other, that turns them into formidable mentally stable holders of freedom consciousness.

Demon – Mercury in Gemini
This is your TV salesman making you buy that awesome new product which has seventeen additions for free; can do miracles never before done in civilization and that is available to you right now; at a 60% introductory discount, and a further 20% off if you order right now, by calling the number on the screen; or replying to the post with the word "Geronimo".

This is a dangerous demon to have money around, because they have a list of associates in real estate, friends who own restaurants, and shops, and they will take you around to see how much money they can get out of you. They then get "taken care of" by the "friends" they took you around to.

They come off as intelligent, and even sexy, but actually they are incredibly insecure, small minded entities, whose entire lives are a show, like a theater show with no one even knowing who they really are. They are adept at changing identities, one person in church, one at home, one in the park, one in the childrens' school PTA meeting.

Sometimes because of other influences, they can have a relatively stable settled life as a sort of frame, providing them access to many people and a reputation of familiarity to use as they play their games.

It's very hard to actually confront this demon because most of the time he or she has already covered all their bases and thought of what they'll say or do in the occasion of any sort of confrontation.

They tend to even know the police in the town, because they need to keep all these contacts.

Their weakness is that they can't really function without the network. They have certain key enablers, often an indulgent parent or sibling, or old friend who finds them useful.

If you so much as notice who the key enablers are, they'll start feeling insecure, and begin to be careful around you, say and do things to get your sympathy. If you hold your reserve and not show any sign of sympathy, REFUSE TO SPEND MONEY ON OR AROUND THEM, they will smell the coffee and start looking elsewhere.

MERCURY IN CANCER

These people are great inventors of medicine and things that truly benefit and help others. It is so unfortunate, Ed, that the great constellation of the Crab should have been associated with a modern illness like cancer. It is in fact the sign of healing, medicine, rejuvenation.

A person with mercury here is a warrior in the field of healing, comforting and rejuvenation. While they may not work directly in those fields, their energy is in some way or another working towards the healing and upliftment of the human race.

They see a human problem, they want to fix it.

This warrior's strength lies in the ability to divine what a person needs to feel well.

Their weapon is knowing what can tear someone down too. They suppress this ability because of modern conditioning where you're not supposed to think such things. But it doesn't stop them from knowing deep down.

If they want to take someone down, they instinctively know where that one arrow, that one stone must hit.

This warrior is of pure heart and does not gather such information for a feeling of power, but as a form of defense of themselves and their loved ones.

At the right time, they are the David who will come out and take out Goliath with the one stone aimed at the one place without armor.

Their instinctive knowledge of others' strengths and weaknesses is their weapon. Their ignoring or suppressing it is their weakness.

They are amazing cooks and makers of medicine.

Demon – Mercury in Cancer

This demon is an expert in the use of herbs, pills, drugs. It is very unlikely you'll get through a relationship with this demon without being drugged or poisoned at some point. If you find yourself falling mysteriously ill, having a stomach upset, very sleepy regularly, start noticing what brings on these episodes and you'll find out what's making this demon feel threatened. Invariably, if you don't want to end up in the psychiatric ward of your local hospital, or with organ damage due to poisoning, you will have to remove this demon entirely from your life.

MERCURY IN LEO

This is a person who makes a powerful teacher, guide and inspirer of others. However, to become that, they go through a lot of situations that bring their inner wisdom out. As was written on a t-shirt somewhere. "To be old and wise, you must first be young and foolish."

This warrior tends to have a lot of experience getting attracted to the wrong people, getting caught up with the wrong crowd, and getting into one fix or the other, all while trying to do the right thing.

At some point they begin to realize that they've been programmed into all these patterns of behavior and that they have an inner wisdom, which is the only wisdom they can really trust.

Once they start trusting their own wisdom, there's nothing that can stop this warrior.

Their weapon is their inner wisdom of what's right and wrong in the moment, their deep inner sense of justice. They also have been equipped by God to know how to deploy this to advantage.

They know how to use their understanding of relationship dynamics to advantage. This is a potent weapon they have. They can influence the relationships of others, be excellent negotiators and relationship crisis resolvers, counsellors and such.

Their weakness is letting themselves over-intellectualize anything really. Their mercury power is of the heart, and they need to keep that heart mind connection open and strong, and not ever trip off into mental explorations of things leaving their heart behind.

If ever they get into trouble it's because of getting seduced by mental exploration without involving their heart in it. If ever they're rescued, they're rescued by their heart waking up and asserting itself, pulling them out of their trip and back to what's important.

Demon – Mercury in Leo
This demon is an emotional manipulator and comes off like a child who never grew up. People think, "Aw… he/she is such an innocent childlike person…" And then suddenly one day when you do something they don't like, they say something so horrible, so hurting, so shocking, you just can't believe they actually said that.

This demon is an actor from the second they wake up to the second they fall asleep. They are many characters in their head and they will play that character and that role, majestically, with the appropriate amount of pizzazz and style. They have perfected before the age of ten, even, the various emotions humans go through and they have it at their fingertips. Love, pain, sorrow, hurt, forgiveness, anger... they got it all practiced and ready.

When you begin to realize this demon is all one big act, and you want to get rid of them, stop giving them opportunities to play out the characters in their head. Stop giving them drama. They can't survive without drama. They'll lose all confidence if they go a week without a drama in which they could pose and deliver dialogues and all that. They'll begin to think of their mother and father and all those people who tolerated their drama all those years and think about going back there.

Often these entities are spongers, living off your money and that becomes a problem because they're scared to leave even when they want to, because they don't have a way of supporting themselves yet. You'll have to do something drastic to make them leave. It's going to be nasty either way because they're going to make you feel guilty, but you got to respect your own self and value your own life and do what has to be done.

You have your warrior abilities given to you by God, just for situations like this. You can do it.

MERCURY IN VIRGO
The eternal student, the faithful scribe, the one who remembers; that's Mercury in Virgo. A pure mind that values information for what it is and doesn't make egoistic attempts to attain wisdom or knowledge just to be a puffed up "expert". This warrior learns things for the sake of using that knowledge. A true seeker, who absorbs energies from the Moon, that further clarify and reveal their

learnings with this placement of Mercury. The Moon in this person's birth chart shows their area of specific natural expertise. The Moon and Mercury here are in a special partnership. Look up where your Moon is and read the bit in this book that describes that and put that and this together and you got something uniquely special.

This warrior has the ability to clear energy spaces and even as they get more and more expert at it, the ability to weaponize a space, or concentrate the energy so that it breaks down what should not be there.

This is this warrior's weapon – managing space, whether physically or energy-wise. For example, when a group meets online, they are not in the same physical room, but they are in the same space while they're together in the discussion. The virtual room if you will. This warrior has the ability to read and understand and manage that space, that atmosphere.

This warrior's weakness, is thug programming that makes them allow people they don't really like or vibe with, get into their personal space and hog their time and energy. Their nature of valuing everyone, like Emerson said, "Every man I meet is my superior in some way; in that I learn of him," is just not practical for this warrior.

They got to learn to be discriminating, and not start observing and learning and getting fascinated by just anyone. Focus the learning, if possible, don't try to learn everything at the same time. If the mind is fascinated by something, check to see if your heart is in it. If the heart isn't it, don't pursue that.

Demon – Mercury in Virgo
This demon is an intense observer of everything happening and uses it to advantage. It sees the whole world as a chess board in its head and is acutely aware of how the game is progressing. You'd think this demon would be a person of power, but no, this demon has a problem. This demon needs rewards in the moment or they won't

take a step forward. They're chasing rewards every second so therefore their entire life is very small and consists of all those who reward them instantly and immediately for every thing they do or offer. They are "rewards based".

In a relationship they're like a snacks machine. Choose a snack, put in the appropriate coin and you'll get the snack. But in reverse, get the snack and put in the coin. If you don't put in the coin, the snacks will stop coming.

You'd think it's easy to get rid of this demon, but it's usually difficult because people who even get in a relationship with this demon, get in, because they're programmed from maybe childhood, into feeling that all their worth is in what they can give others. They can't believe someone could love them and want them for free, spend time with them for free. So, they keep rewarding those who spend time with them, and this attracts this demon who needs that.

Finding your own sense of worth and deciding to have in your life only those who value you for who you are, and want to be with you because they actually like you, will automatically get rid of this demon for you. Otherwise, they'll keep sending you pics of them looking sad or whatever pulls at you, and you'll go meet them, and reward them and keep the cycle going.

MERCURY IN LIBRA
This a person with a sharp brain that can pierce to the bottom of deceptions and trickery. Their problem is, they get conditioned young by the thug world system to not respect their own vision and intuition.

The strength of this person is their ability to sift through all kinds of rubbish, misleading and distracting things to get to the core of something.

Because of knowing how things are hidden under layers of misleading stuff, they also know how to keep things secret and this can come in handy in our times when a human needs to keep things secret till the right time.

They are family-oriented people who are great warriors because of how they enable the lives of their loved ones and in fact all of humanity by not falling for the lies and bullshit most others fall for.

One human's seeing through lies gets telecast to us all. Therefore, this is one very powerful warrior who is usually completely hidden away somewhere. God keeps them obscure and safe for us.

Their weakness is also their dependency on some substance or the other. This is because they have a brain that is faster than most others. A good exercise for them is to calm the brain through breathing exercises and the like, to not be so cerebral and become energetically stable without depending on stimulants to keep going.

Demon – Mercury in Libra

This demon is mentally sort of loose. They have flashes of great cunning, but because they are unable to keep their mind focused on anything, constantly swinging to the other side, and then swinging back, they end up inconsequential wherever they are.

Their danger to us is in how they give all the impression of being a staid, balanced person that can be trusted, but they actually can't.

They tend to be overly attached to or embedded in family groups and when you get to know them you find out that every choice they make is made because of someone in their family or friend group suggested it.

This extends into relationships where their entire vision of a person is not their own but dictated by their group.

They can cause severe stress and drain the energy of a human just by being such a flaky, untrustworthy entity.

Just say bye and don't look back.

They'll try intimidating you by making it like they're a saint, a Mother Teresa or Nelson Mandela or one of the apostles of Christ you abandoned, but just don't give a crap.

MERCURY IN SCORPIO

This warrior has an understanding of how earth, metal, and other things whose magnetism affects our life here on earth work. They get the inner workings of machinery, of organizations and even of the body. They are a great healer of broken-down systems, engineers of systems that will work well a long time.

Whichever problem they face, or their loved ones, face, they approach the problem with this divine ability to understand all the beneath-the-surface things that happened to cause the problem.

They are the most amazing resolvers of conflict and mediators between people but usually do not go into those professionally because they operate with a sense of divine intelligence that is not understood "logically" by the demon population which is the majority now.

They love to work with their hands and they love the feel of metal of any kind because they're intensely and deeply affected by natural magnetic fields.

Their primary weapon is their understanding of the structure and machinery of things. They can understand things instinctively that it takes others years of study in a university to understand.

Their weakness is not believing what they know, and trying to find proof that others think so too.

They are quite rare and they are great engineers one way or another. God is cultivating an army of human engineers to make a new world possible.

Demon – Mercury in Scorpio

This demon is a glib, but stupid sexual deviant. They can't really perform in bed, but they can talk like they do, especially over the internet. They get hired by thug world organizations to target and seduce and trap people. Once in a while they get into acting and theater and of course, porn. But they don't do really well there because, essentially, they can't perform when their face is being seen. They need to hide their face and identity to do their thing.

In relationships, they present themselves as staid, stable family people looking to have a family. That's because they cannot satisfy someone sexually long-term. They can drive someone crazy for a few months and get married in that rush of hormones, but that's it. So, their plan usually, is to get married and have someone to come back to, but continue their hunting online or on the phone or such.

If for some reason they cannot do their favorite pastime of sexual predating on the internet, they take to drugs and go into writing, advertising or various sorts of media where they can use their ability to load subliminal deviant sex into just any scene and situation.

Their great fear is of actual male sexuality or female sexuality. And of their sexual deviancy coming to light.

MERCURY IN SAGITTARIUS

This is a person with a bird's eye view intelligence. There is nothing that escapes this warrior. He/ She is acutely aware of what is where, who's looking at who and why. Initially they use their intelligence to progress in their career, but through life they begin to use their intelligence to affect changes in their environment that support humans and in fact are life and paradigm changing. They do all this, often without even knowing what they're doing.

This is a warrior who will be the brother you don't have, the sister you don't have, who'll look out for you, and take your call when you're in trouble. They share their knowledge freely, mentor others and shelter others.

Their great weapon is their heart which cares for all around them. You'd think, Ed, that this is not a weapon but it is, because it lifts up those warriors around who are weak and need just a little support to go out there on the frontline and raid the enemy.

Other warriors have just their two hands and their one sword, but this warrior has hundreds of hands and hundreds of swords and weapons of all kinds – all he or she nurtured and enabled, taught and mentored and sheltered and grew up into independent fighters.

Their only weakness – until they reach a certain age – is that they don't know the difference between a demon and a natural human and can get hurt trying to look after demons.

Demon – Mercury in Sagittarius
This demon believes it can buy anything with money or some sort of deal. Their brain is always making deals and then one way or another they try to cut deals in every area of their lives. It's not very difficult to get by in the thug world with that mindset. But they never really go far, because they're usually not born rich enough to have a lot to offer, to do big deals. So they're usually restricted in a particular zone of the economy, and eventually even demons don't like this, "What's in it for me?" attitude.

They tend to use merchandise of sports teams, or props to show they support something or believe in something, but actually it's because they don't believe or support anything. They really are pimps in that way. They just want that friction of feeling they're moving in some direction making deals.

In a relationship, they are either openly or secretly keeping account of everything you do and everything they do, and always trying to see what more they can get out of you or your family. They see the relationship itself as a ladder to somewhere else, so for that reason they might make some effort to keep it going.

But if they find the partner is not going to be a willing player in the deals, they'll leave. If they don't it's because they got too much money, security, status in the relationship. Then they have to be told to get out.

MERCURY IN CAPRICORN

This person is an excellent manager of energy of all kinds. A financial whiz even if they aren't so good with the numbers. It's about energy. This warrior is a thrifty, nimble, highly intelligent planner. They thrive in situations where the resources are limited and the needs many, or where the resources and the needs don't match.

They do real solid networking and can build networks of people truly actually benefiting each other, where everyone wins.

They have the ability to advise others on how to get out of energy and financial messes.

This ability, they get by getting into a mess or two themselves early in life, and then learning all they can about the topic.

They're quick with finding solutions.

The primary strength of this warrior is in how quick they are. They're far ahead of others and when they get confident and learn to move just as fast as they think, they're like magic to watch.

At some point, people are going to call them magicians because of their abilities.

They can take two completely opposite things and make them work together.

The are magic. Made by God to handle the things few others can.

Demon – Mercury in Capricorn

They're stuck to their mother even in old age, because they don't really grow. Their mother is a resource for them, a never-ending one that demands almost nothing back. If their mother isn't alive or they're separated by distance, they will find a mother figure to take care of them.

Sometimes this is not very obvious but it's there underneath everything else as their primary source.

There's a weird personality warp they have where, they seem to be stuck mentally in a place where they are owed stuff by others for reasons that either go back to their childhood or which are too obscure to remember.

They're resentful of people who try to make them go outside of their comfort zone. They don't like change, but will often use it as a weapon to trouble others who they don't like.

You could say they're intellectually stunted, because they do not get simple concepts that others do. For example, if you told them they could get more detergent powder for the same price, they'd ask you why should bother when they've been getting the same detergent powder all those years?

The fact that something has been a certain way for a long time, is in their heads, reason enough to keep it that way.

They're the kind of demon who never tries to see the world outside of their little hole, looks down on everyone who is not in their little hole and believes them to be evil, and ultimately becomes a low life criminal when his mother or whoever was playing his mother figure dies or kicks him or her out.

They often manage to have a child or two as old age insurance and they go live off the child after the mother is gone.

Sexually, they are quite sadistic and can be mysterious for a while. Till you figure out that he has to go see his mother to get recharged. He/she forgets who they are if they don't go meet mother regularly.

It's a case of pure vampirism off the mother and whoever takes her place.

MERCURY IN AQUARIUS

This is pure genius. This warrior is a starter of fires in places no one expected them. This warrior can shoot many birds with one stone. The anointing here is on a human who can anticipate things others can't and have the divine inner guidance to be prepared for things without mentally knowing it.

They also can work with just about anyone, they're so flexible and easy to work with and be with.

Their mental agility shows in many ways, more than I can list. But their most important weapon here is their ability to convince people into doing things. They can if they want to. They never do it unless they really believe in something. And they're the angel of God in that moment getting people to do things they wouldn't do in the normal course of events.

This warrior changes the trajectory of events because they are so agile and can demonstrate to others why they should change too.

If they have a weakness, it's their addiction to eating. Not food, but eating. For some reason they find a sort of meditative security in munching on things, going to restaurants, ordering, or having dinners or going to dinners. Which is very understandable. Most animals do that. But here it can become a problem because the food we have available these days is not pure natural food. Even "natural" food isn't energetically stable. It can begin to hog too much time and energy. It would be a good idea to start finding security and connection through something other than eating.

Demon- Mercury in Aquarius

This demon is an energy thief, almost born a sophisticated thief. They learn at a young age to get others to do things for them, use others' identities and reputations to get by and by the time they're in their twenties, they're a full-on parasite living off others but to the naked eye they look like they're just someone who has to struggle a lot because they got this diagnosis of this rare disease or they had this unfortunate accident that spoiled their sporting career.... All that sort of thing.

They don't really know how to live without stealing and manipulating others' energy one way or another and they tend to believe everyone lives like that.

They tend to always have a lot of pertinent information useful to gossips and people snooping on each other, and perhaps that's one reason the demon families keep enabling and supporting these entities.

Every few years they'll have a good idea, get their friends and family to invest, start a company or such, pop the champagne bottle, take pics; the family feels like, "We're finally going somewhere. We're getting lucky." For a few months it keeps looking sparky.

Then this demon finds people aren't as impressed as they were on day one and the demon starts needing to get fresh energy. So he or she gets into other pursuits and neglects this one, which fails sooner or later. They manage to find a way to blame others for it of course.

If you're stuck with this demon, cut off and cut off anyone who maintains contact with him or his network, because it's a network demon. They'll make you feel guilty forever if you don't take the initiative for yourself and see that they're a proper energy parasite.

MERCURY IN PISCES

This person does not look this way or that, and is an uncompromising and unwavering supporter of what his or her intuition says. This is an extremely powerful warrior who is always however in the eye of attack, because of how uncompromising they are.

From a young age they come under attack to make them give up their strength of belief and acceptance of their own intuition and wisdom. They tend to reach teenage barely surviving. Some of them go into drugs, herbs, medicine as they need help to survive the assault on them.

Their nervous system is highly sensitive and yet mysteriously resilient, because of how keenly in tune with the soul they are.

This warrior's great weapon is his strength of belief in his own intuition. His weakness is sharing his point of view and telling others about it. This kind of gift should be kept secret for the most part and used for sudden drastic action. It should never be assumed that this kind of gift can be shared or taught to others as that is simply not possible.

This warrior might seem to be your average person working a 9-5 job, and not doing anything spectacular as such. But that is because they have been restricted by the thug world, surrounded by fake humans and played with by thugs directly to keep them down.

They are prophets, visionaries and leaders of a rare caliber and maybe God keeps them hidden while they're developing their powers so they don't get killed outright before they reach the time of their destiny.

Demon – Mercury in Pisces

This demon is a very ordinary looking person, who often demonstrates a skill in some kind of academia. They progress very well in academic studies, get along well enough with others and often get jobs in the education system.

Underneath that they have a dark side as all demons do. They are vampires of brain energy. They are like middlemen of intellectual property. They recognize intelligence, genius, in people and they vampirize those entities very cunningly, playing them by complimenting them a little, then tearing them down, then lifting them up again, all while seeming like a mentor; but actually, secretly jealous of natural intelligence and skill.

They can do the same in the musical and arts areas. Identify natural talent and vampirize those entities leaving them confused, weak, lost and no longer able to do what they do.

What gives this demon away is their consistent persistence in details of everything. They will take some topic, shred it into details and focus on each detail like a maniac. Others think, "Maybe he has a reason for this focus on details, maybe he'll reveal that reason now." But he'll never reveal that reason. Because the main reason he does that details thing, is he thinks that shows he's interested in the topic, when actually he's reeling people in to drain their vital energy.

This demon will supply details about each thing he does. It's a ruse. A pretend personality. They will rarely listen to someone else going to details about anything for more than two minutes and even that, only if there's money or something of theirs at stake.

They are very bothered about their reputation and you can get rid of them easily because they'll be afraid, you'll spoil their reputation.

They'll stalk you online, and always try to keep tabs on you because they're so worried for their reputation.

Venus – Primary Life Energy – The Power of Desire

Ed, if ever there was a force of God misunderstood, it is Venus. We have paintings of "Venus" as imagined in the ancient world, voluptuous, sensuous, women. In Indian astrology and mythology Venus, or Shukra is male and isn't of very good repute.

Eons of thug manipulation have suppressed the vision and understanding of this most mighty throne.

This is God-Force in us, Ed, that is at its core, sexual desire.

It is not sexual desire as demons know sexual desire to be. It is sexual desire as natural living beings know it to be.

It is that force in the deepest depths of our being, the core of our bodies, that calls forth from the universe, all those manifestations of God that our spirit exists to enjoy, exult and revel in.

Without this Venus force, life is worth nothing. Without this Venus force life energy isn't life energy. Without Venus force all of the work of the other planets is in vain and useless.

Someone said to me recently, "All my hard work makes sense when I see my sweetheart smile. That just makes it all worth it."

That's the result of Venus in our lives, that's the feeling of fulfillment, holistic pleasure, true joy and comfort in our place in the grand scheme of life; that we get from our Venus force.

Venus force is called "Ichha Shakti" in Sanskrit, which literally means "Power of Desire".

If a warrior has a power, first it is this power.

If you don't know what for you're fighting or doing anything, you will fall really quick in battle.

You really have no place on the field if you don't know what it is for you fight.

A lot of people in our times, because of thug world programming, believe that having something to fight for, means having a family or someone we love, in danger of something, and we must fight for their safety. That's alright, but that is a very narrow view of things.

The thug world teaches us to fight only when under attack, in defence.

But Venus force makes us fight for our pleasures and our joys. If we fought for our pleasures, our joys, our right to love and make love to who we want, when we want, how we want; we would never find ourselves in a situation where we live lives of pain, ugliness and struggle and fight only when we're going to be killed even out of that.

Venus force teaches us to be a warrior long before that final chance to save ourselves.

Venus force teaches us to win our rights to love, life and happiness on a daily basis so that no one even dares come near to mess with us.

A person's Venus Weapon is therefore critically important to develop as if it's weak all the weapons are useless. It is the consciousness weapon that brings in life energy or vital energy into the body in the first place. You get this right, most of the time, the rest will fall into place.

Venus in the heavens above at the time of your birth gives you an indication of how to care for and best allow your life force or power of desire to flow; what can block it, if it is blocked.

Because this writing is about the aspect of warrior-ship, Ed, I'll be focusing on the wielding of the power of desire that each person has. There is so much to write about it and I will in the future. But we will focus on the warfare aspect here.

VENUS IN ARIES

If ever there was a warrior for love, of love, it is this person. His or her love is itself a potent weapon against the thug world consciousness, and love happens to be the area of their lives they give the most attention to, just as it should be.

They tend to have a most romantic and fun view of their lives and even their battles. Laughter is never very far from this warrior's lips.

And yet, when their love, or their right to love, is threatened, this warrior will rise into the most fearsome, the most powerful with divine spirit force, devastating warrior.

This warrior is super-protective and you just need one in every family really because they're so watchful and so quick to protect their loved ones, that the family never really lands in any serious trouble.

Their weapon is how they can launch from resting to attack, like a cheetah goes from zero to 170mph speed in a few seconds. Most people never see it coming.

Their weakness, is getting their heart broken by entities who are not humans, but demons. They love everyone they allow into their lives so fiercely; they get devastated if someone maybe is even slightly chill towards them. So, it's really important for them to know who has a heart and who doesn't.

Someone asked me recently on Instagram -How do I know if someone has a heart or not. The answer is – If you feel with your heart and you get no heart response, they don't have a heart.

A heart response is different from a mind response or verbal response. You can think of someone and they will think of you back, that's psychic, that's mind. That's not heart.

Heart is when you feel free, when you know that no matter what you say, or do; they're going to be sending you that warmth, called love.

If you feel you could lose the warmth by doing or saying or not doing or not saying something; that's a mind connection, a business deal, not love.

In this world, 90% of all relationships at least are mind connections or business deals.

Demon – Venus in Aries
This demon is a sexually violent, insatiable beast. Some people like the sound of that. In reality you get no pleasure out of the brute heartless sex, the brute forceful pursuit in dating and the way you feel you have no option but to accept them because they're so forceful. You could even be afraid of saying no, because they have this glint of intimidation in their eyes, like, "You better accept me, or else...."

This demon is all force but it won't last. You might have to take stern steps to keep it out of your life.

One reason a person attracts such demons, is by seeming easy to get. Because for all its supposed strength this demon actually preys on the vulnerable, those who don't have many family and friends and so on.

A person who is in such circumstances needs to learn to not FEEL vulnerable and build trust in God, because the reality is, every human is surrounded by God and angels of all kinds. That's the fact. You need to fix your insecurities so you don't attract this kind of demon again.

VENUS IN TAURUS
This warrior has a heart that will stay fixed and faithful. Do I even need to say any more than that, Ed? But because we are talking about spiritual warfare, I will go on.

The weapon this warrior has, is their inner security in their own love. On the battlefield of life, a constant weapon used against us humans, is the suggestion that we do not REALLY love others and others do not REALLY love us. But this warrior knows himself or herself well in this department. They know their love is real, and that becomes their proof that there IS love in this world.

They search and they find their soulmate who loves like they love and they are grounded in that love. No storms can shake the heart and the love of this warrior.

They have the ability to create motivation on a daily basis by making the daily routine and surroundings beautiful. This daily motivation is a potent weapon, because great things can be sabotaged if we lose momentum in our projects. We are only as strong as our weakest link, and daily motivation to keep going when the weather is bad, or the funds are low, or the friends are scarce, is a most powerful thing to have. You can achieve almost anything if you can keep motivated steadily.

The weakness of this warrior is their occasional overwhelming feeling of guilt. They tend to take responsibility towards their loved ones very seriously, even in childhood and thug world programming, makes them feel guilty for things quite outside of their control that happen to their loved ones.

They will on some days, go into a shell, feeling regret and guilt and being upset, that they did not do something they wanted to do for their loved one.

They need to understand, really understand that when we love someone, that love energy is itself the power that makes things happen for those we love. It will go into the universe and bring help and sustenance to our loved ones. This is literally and actually true.

I know this because my whole family is no longer is in this world, and yet I feel their love so very really, protecting and even providing for me, perhaps in ways they could not have if they were trying to do when alive and near.

We have to trust God to deliver the right thing to our loved ones at the right time.

Demon – Venus in Taurus

This demon is uncannily and eerily obsessed with money. They are mentally judging the worth of everything in terms of money. Their dreams are about building big things, like stadiums and shopping malls and so on, but it's about a projection of money.

In relationships, they can seem generous, but only when they believe that the return on their investment is going to be good.

They're obsessed with how others view them – do they view them as rich or not. So anyone they're in a relationship with will have to constantly dress and behave like they're rich. They abuse whoever they're with, with their constant nitpicking about how they should improve this or that about their appearance, criticizing any tiny flaw they have and so on. No human can tolerate this very long.

But if you are stuck with this demon, remember that its weakness is it always needs to see a good return on its investment. Tell it, you're getting old and you're tired, and you can't live up to standards anymore. Dress casually and like you don't care anymore what anyone thinks of you. Then watch it slither out of the relationship like that's its idea and not yours.

VENUS IN GEMINI

This human is so full of natural joy and enthusiasm for life. But they are also extremely talented in the arts and have the ability to portray and convey feeling.

Their weapon in spiritual warfare is their ability to keep their chin up no matter what the circumstances, and get energy flowing in the most depressing, hopeless circumstances. Miracles result from this.

They can revive a dying effort, a failing team; and for this reason often find themselves in the business of motivating others.

Their weapon is their vision. It is not that this warrior looks only on the bright side of things. Maybe in their childhood it is so. But this is a warrior who the demons will try to break from when they're very young, to steal their joy and stop their happiness. So they end up stalwarts of faith and vision very early on, and this sets them up for a lifetime of the one thing not otherwise expected of them – stubbornness.

They will not give ground.

You can do what you want, the world can stand in front of them, but this human has been trained from a young age to hold their own. They will listen to all the bullshit, smile benevolently and then go out and do just as their inner guidance says.

This is their weapon, against which nothing can prevail, because it forged out of real experience in battle at a young age.

They are psychically so tough – it's impossible to believe someone so quick to smile and quick to kindness can be that impermeable too. But that's them. A creation of God that withstands the storms, a heart that will rise again and again because their spirit vision shows them divine love and divine order ruling through and despite everything.

Their weakness, is their energetic speed, which requires them to become experts at something in a matter of weeks or they'll lose interest in it. They are not attracted to the way of the tortoise – slow and steady wins the race. They want to see the results of their actions quickly, really quickly.

A good result of this is, that they let go quickly of things that they are not really that interested in. That saves them time and money. But one bad result could be that they do a little of many different things and then never actually become an expert of anything. This can depress them, because they are creators and artists and they really need to be able to fully express the beauty inside in some way or the other. So they really need to work out what REALLY grips them, and then go at it regularly.

Demon – Venus in Gemini

This demon is one of eclectic tastes and "passions". If ever there were a wastrel of money and squanderer of the family wealth, this is him or her.

They will make anyone they hang out with, financially and energetically depleted. Friends, romantic partners, wives, husbands. Even their pets die early because of the constant drain.

They speak and talk like they're extremely learned scholars, high thinking, highly educated world travelers. Actually, they're full of imagined incidents that never happened and spinning a fake life story that has all the elements of whatever sort of movie formula is doing well at the time.

They're able to entertain and engage people with this, especially the young and vulnerable types, and much of their sustenance comes from these interactions.

Most of them are either unemployed or employed irregularly now and them. Usually, they start businesses with other peoples' money, which they shut down sooner or later because it didn't do well. The friend becomes someone who then has to chase them and hunt them down hoping to get some of the money back. Obviously that's not happening.

However you look at it, this demon will destroy you financially and energetically. Just get away and don't even say hello.

Get your entertainment somewhere they have one monthly payment and nothing in-between.

VENUS IN CANCER

This beautiful person, Ed, is the very essence of that beautiful quality of love, that makes beautiful things happen in hidden places. They fill the every day lives of those they love, with beauty and goodness. They are never too tired to do the little things that others depend on them for, to keep going in this hard life.

But they have a weakness, Ed. They can get myopic, look inwards and refuse to see reality. This often gets them stuck enabling absolutely evil demons, who they simply are so devoted to, they refuse to see the reality of.

The river of their heart love, Ed, it flows with such force and it's so difficult for them to ever stop it. They were born to love like that, unconditionally and faithfully. In the ideal human environment, with no demons in existence, it is fine.

But in our current world, this warrior needs to learn to hold back their unflinching loyalty and faithfulness and wait till it is WON; not bestow it on anyone available to bestow it on.

This warrior's Venus weapon, is their ability to care for something that's weak and vulnerable and take it safely across the river, plant it and nurture it and grow it into a big tree again.

They are those humans who preserve things for the children of the future. They are those humans who in the worst of times, will bring out something they've been keeping safe from a very long time ago, that everyone thought died out or finished.

They are financially good at budgeting and saving for a rainy day and their loved ones are secure in this.

Demon – Venus in Cancer

This demon is a chronic betrayer of trust and stealer of little things that you'll find out only very later on were even stolen. They tend to give off the aura of someone dependable, relatable, and trustworthy.

They tend to be embedded in large families, or communities, or such; I.e. They have social proof. It's very hard not to trust someone who has a big social group around them.

But they are not trustworthy and their social group is as evil as them. They don't really give a crap for anyone.

They'll behave like you're someone so special and they're so happy to have met you, and you're going to be part of them now; and all that. A few weeks or months down the line, you'll find that they want you to do things for them in exchange for all that "love" and "acceptance".

Drip, drip, drip, drip.... They want this, they want that. Just a little favor here. Just a little help with that. Soon you find out that they'd like you to quit your job, your career, and even your own personality, to be their full-time help-around and employee.

When you say you won't you'll be accused of never loving them, being ungrateful and so on.

You'll have to move away from this crowd and just not give a crap. They're not worth even a bother.

VENUS IN LEO

If ever there was a "Lionheart" this, is he or she. The love this human is capable of, and shines on all they love, is like the Sun itself. And it's not just surface love. They are dedicated, there for the people they love. They look into the details and truly take care.

This warrior's great Venus weapon is that they do not tire easily. However, the thing about this is, they must invest this love in something worthy of that great energy of investment, long term energy; or they will burn out.

These warriors routinely invest their love in shallow demons who are attracted to this warrior for his or her magnetism, sexiness and flair for life. They get incredibly disappointed to find out that all that's really required for them in that relationships is to keep putting on that show of flair and style and sexiness. They can be hurt deeply, turn bitter, caustic and begin to no longer be able to do the things they're supposed to do for survival even.

They have to believe that there is a love in this world, made to receive the kind of love they give, and return that back in equal measure. That person is rare, but they're there.

This warrior must sit down and list the things they feel they are able to invest their energy in fully without feeling like that thing is not really worthy of their energy. They must withdraw from everything but those people and those activities in which they feel there is long term reward. Short term things – are just not their energy style. Shallow things are not their style.

It has to be deep, and every bit worth the long-term effort and dedication, or it's not for them.

Demon – Venus in Leo
This demon is a head turner as far as looks go. This is one seductive demon. They may not always be good looking to the eye, but they are experienced in making people want to look after them, pay for them, buy things for them.

They tend to have a backstory of how they didn't have a very good childhood, and how unfair life has been to them. It makes people want to take care of them.

They have little wiles and tricks to make a person's heart burst. Like a little drawing of the person, they're seducing as a cartoon – or buying them a balloon as a gift and saying, "This is all I could afford".

They pretend to be childlike and innocent and vulnerable and helpless.

In reality, they have no independent thinking at all, well nearly none, and are completely controlled by some handler – maybe the mother, or elder sibling, or such. These handlers use this demon's looks and ability to come across as innocent and vulnerable to reel in people in relationship after relationship to see what they can get from them.

Very often, the whole family is supported financially and otherwise through this person's string of boyfriend or girlfriends, or even "just friends".

They WILL dump you if you stop the providing, OR they find a better prospect to go after.

This is a gang, not a person. Frequently if a human escapes from this person; their sister or cousin will contact them and fleece them of anything the previous one didn't rob the human of.

It's a gang, not one player. So, you'll have to cut off altogether.

Be careful NEVER TO ASSUME THAT ANYONE THAT IS PART OF THAT PERSON'S FAMILY OR FRIEND CIRCLE IS NOT PART OF THAT GANG.

If someone has this entity in their life more than a week or two, they're part of the gang.

VENUS IN VIRGO

Imagine if your tailor fell in love with you. Or your plumber, or your cook, or your gardener... This warrior loves like that. There's nothing they won't do for you. They will do whatever it takes to make you happy.

This great and holy love is what the entire universe is made of. It is why the heavenly bodies turn so steadily in their paths above us; why the sun rises every morning and the moon at night.

This warrior's great weapon in spiritual warfare is the ability to see what's coming before the enemy even knows what they themselves are up to. This warrior's heart is fierce in detail, in protecting their loved ones.

This warrior's weakness that comes with this ability to foresee things, is that because they end up preventing things from happening, they can end up thinking that they were paranoid before and there was no real danger.

These are in fact the most not paranoid people because they have such powers of instinctive recognition that they know who and what to be wary of and who not to.

It's only when they start telling themselves they were paranoid that they start numbing out their senses.

Demon – Venus in Virgo
This demon is very precise in his or her appearance, gait, behavior. You'll almost never catch them out. Their crimes are well thought out, precision laid and they will make a person start doubting their own existence. That's the kind of mind games this demon can play. They don't pretend to be affectionate or needy; most of the time, settling for coming across as somewhat critical and cold in relationships. They attract people to them by seeming like that coldness is because they have standards or because they're too scared to love again.

Actually, they simply are cold and they don't even play the game of love to the extent other demons do, for even the pretense of having the warmth of relationship.

When they're accused of being cold, manipulative and selfish, they're the sort who'll say, "I'm sorry you feel that way, after all I've done for you." They then guilt trip people for years and decades psychically, without even meeting them.

They're also the kind who'll use your own philosophy and affirmations and such against you. They keep record of what you say, specifically to use it against you some day.

They are terrified of being considered mentally unwell or imbalanced. They also tend to be afraid of small dogs and unpredictable little animals. Anything that could shake them out of their icy composure terrifies them.

There's a part of them always anticipating disasters like earthquakes and tsunamis and floods. Anything outside of their set routine, established paths about town; scares them.

VENUS IN LIBRA

This warrior has a gift with money. They have a primal understanding of how the energy of value works. Often, they are born into a line that has generationally dealt with things of value and developed an instinct to manage value well.

In any place where someone is needed to correct the overall energy or financial workings, this warrior will instinctively know what to do.

A lot of people go to university and all kinds of internships, to learn what this person knows instinctively.

You'd think they were destined to be millionaires, but more often than not, this warrior will be found living quietly and simply, a life of true quality, supporting in many ways the things they truly believe in.

They have a flair for the beauty and fashion industry but rarely are stuck in those as they gravitate towards real beauty rather than the superficial.

They are developers of potential in fields like human resources, nurturing sports or artistic talent in children and so on. They are happiest building something from the ground up because that's so much more likely to do well than something whose foundations are mired in energetic slime.

A powerful weapon they have is their ability to correct and balance broken energy fields. They only get to show this however when they give themselves the chance to try out their natural skill.

Many of them are so good looking they're treated like they're empty heads and good only for posing around or doing similarly shallow things. Or their voices are so beautiful, it's believed that's all they have. That's good for their twenties and thirties; but after that they start yearning to express their natural talents at healing energy fields.

Demon – Venus in Libra
This demon has that "damsel in distress" or "man who needs rescuing" vibe that makes people want to help them. They do this show of being very pithy and "this whole world is shit" while planning how to loot everything they possibly can from whoever tries to rescue them.

I knew one of these demons. She was a model at one time, got into drugs and lost her job. She ended up living in a slum on money old friends sent her now and then. There was this man who owned a fabric store– one of those old-time affairs where people who still go to tailors to get their new clothes, go to buy fabric.

The shop wasn't very rich, big or posh, but the owner thought the lady's good looks and her experience in the fashion world would result in sales, so he offered her the job.

It came when she was nearing dying of starvation, and she took it. In a few months she got back to health. She began to socialize with the man's wife and sons. She won their trust, got close to them. One day, she a 35-year-old woman ran away with their 16-year-old son who was convinced she was in love with him. For the next few years, she contacted the family from different places asking them for money for her and the son to live on. When they refused to send money about five years later, she dumped the boy, and ran away without even leaving him money to go back home. He was narrowly saved from committing suicide – he couldn't believe she didn't love him and had done it all for money. She'd already anticipated his parents would stop sending him money and started working on another "channel of providence".

It's hard to believe someone could be so consciously cruel, but that's how these demons are. They really don't have a bone of feeling in them.

If you're with such a demon, one who's always "needing" your money or help or whatever; just get the hell away. Don't even stay in touch with their friends. Their poison flows like the green goo in the old horror movies, going from person to person.

VENUS IN SCORPIO
This warrior has the acute ability to smell energies and remember places, people and incidents through smell. They are very good with non-verbal communication and also have an excellent instinct at naturally knowing if someone they care about isn't well and what the problem is.

Their energy fields tune instinctively to water fields beneath wherever they're standing and this makes them able to tap into the consciousness held by water under the surface. This makes them tap into consciousness memories – whether of past lives or "what happened in this place before" and so on.

They tend to have problems socially, because in our current day society, people are very disconnected from the earth and reality. This warrior being so affected by what is beneath the surface of the earth, or what is beneath the superficial layers of life and society, finds it hard to play the relationship games and social games others do.

The weapon of Venus this person has, is their unflinching commitment to knowing the truth and holding the truth. They are often in situations where they are suppressed and unable to speak the truth or express it out in any way. Years, decades, even a lifetime might go by, but they will keep holding the truth inside, never letting even their own selves, deceive their own selves, just for the convenience of it.

Their inner fire burns on, oblivious of the assaults on them and their independence of vision and thought.

Naturally this warrior tends to be lonely for a while; but it is all made up for, when they find the person who admires them for their resilience of vision and commitment to truth. This person is a leader whether they are acknowledged as such or not, because they silently drive the consciousness wherever they are.

One of their weaknesses is their self-criticism. They can be overly demanding of themselves and then criticize themselves for not performing according to their own expectations. Some unconditional, mad self-love would really help them keep their nerves already under so much pressure, cushioned and calm. In fact, they are always in need of appreciation, cuddling and admiration. They deserve it too.

Demon – Venus in Scorpio
This demon is mentally hyperactive, the sort that will tear anything to pieces in their heads. They are slow to talk, slow to judge, but once they've analyzed the situation, the person and so on, they can be quick to act.

They are among the most unpredictable predators in the thug world, because of how they can suddenly and unpredictably attack someone, whether verbally, or physically or sexually.

They tend to look like they're somewhat down and out, and "harmless". But actually, they nurse grudges inside from decades, and they will suddenly take something that happened to them in their childhood, and use the anger they felt about that; channel that stored emotional energy in a hit against someone in the present who is most probably not connected in any way to that old incident.

They do this all the time, and in relationships, they get away with a lot of aggression and violence – whether of the subtle passive-aggressor sort, or direct violence; because of how they connect up old anger and old incidents to the present. It makes people believe they are such traumatized souls that needed to "get it out of their system."

But they never get anything really out of their system. They're always finding new things to hold grudges about and store up that anger emotional energy inside to bring out later when they want to attack someone.

Their attacks are launched when they feel their stock in society or a relationship is falling and they need to drain someone of emotional energy to replenish their loosh. They get refreshed by the attack they did and will present themselves as the most dependable, "normal" people on the block for some days or weeks or months, depending on how far on the path to degeneration they are.

They get very perverse as they go along, because shock is how they get their attacks to bring in energy. They tend to keep record of what sort of shock, would shock someone the most, to use.

They usually get into relationships by presenting themselves as "the provider" if male, or the ever ready to have sex, female. After a certain period of steadiness, the partner begins to trust them, and then they begin their shock attacks.

If you have anything to do with this demon, you should know, they know what shocks you. Just don't play the shock game with them.

VENUS IN SAGITTARIUS

This warrior is a gregarious, laughing, cheerful person. Their mirth and childlike excitement at the fun things in life are contagious. They ae always happy to help others and make the atmosphere a jolly and optimistic one.

This warriors Venus weapon is their ability to read the room. They instinctively know what the mood is and what's more, as they get experience, they begin to be able to pin-point where the ominous energy is coming from. This is actually not all that easy for others to do.

Very often in a gathering or group, the person who is overtly spoiling the atmosphere is not the source of the intention or the energy that is spoiling the atmosphere, just the channel. To know who is really the source of the heaviness, or the volatility or the bondage, is very important to really put it out.

This warrior has that rare gift and it is so rare that there are companies who pay people, counselors to do "conflict resolution" in an organization, who are able to figure out who the real source of the tension is.

This warrior also has the ability to start a revolution if they so please.

Their weakness tends to be, in early life, "just wanting everyone to be happy." As time goes by, they realize that to keep all who they love, happy, they have to find and remove the bad apples. Sometimes ALL the apples are bad. But they get there sooner or later.

Demon – Venus in Sagittarius

This is a most entertaining demon, often with a face that can go from imitating a devil to imitating an angel, in seconds. They are quite popular and often considered very lovable for their entertainment.

They are however, underneath all that, consumed by low self-esteem and addicted to things that make them feel better, lift their mood, enhance their personality and so on.

They present as someone who watches the world, current affairs and all of that, which they present in their entertaining conversation. However, they are actually focused on their own selves, their needs and how they're going to meet them.

They spend huge amounts of money, then land in penury and take to either conning whoever will meet their needs, or marrying for money.

They go from one addiction to another, with bouts of clarity in-between, during which they can seem adorable, intelligent, astute and a someone you could expect to hold a job down, turn up on time for meetings and such.

Their high consumption of energy is simply unsustainable and they end up living on others' money or taking to whatever crime they can to keep getting what they need.

Many of them end up in prison for petty crime.

In a relationship, even in the golden period they energetically exhaust their partners and sooner or later the people near them learn to somewhat ignore them as they go about their lives, because you can't really engage with such a high energy drainer and continue on with a stable life.

VENUS IN CAPRICORN

This warrior is a communication wizard. This is because they have a sense of what is actually important to a person. They will sell you the thing you need and want; because they can sense what you want. They can help and counsel others extremely effectively to do the right thing for them.

They can deliver the right message to the right person at the right time.

It's not about just information. It's about understanding someone's practical needs and meeting those needs in a way that actually satisfies them.

They do well in any field, but if it includes meeting people and working with people they shine.

A lot of them end up working with children and people who are communication challenged, because of how good they are at divining the needs of others.

They also are good at organizing events like weddings and functions; complicated projects involving networking different companies or teams.

This warrior keeps it simple and that's why they're so good at whatever they do.

When they take to art, dance, music they produce things so true to the heart, that says exactly what has to be said, nothing more, nothing else.

The talents of this warrior never end.

If they have a weakness, it's allowing people jealous of them to still be counted among their friends. This warrior often sabotages their own best interests and holds themselves back from shining, because someone they consider a friend is jealous and they try to not upset the jealous friend.

It doesn't do the jealous fake friend any good, and wastes the time and years of this human. But it's all good in the end because even that is a learning experience that will come in good use in the future.

Demon – Venus in Capricorn
This demon is sadistic and presents it as a sort of fatalism. They have a selection of lines like, "From dust we come and to dust we go." And, "In the end we all die alone." That sort of thing. They build up

this aura of someone who faces the rotten side of life and is in their own pessimistic, cynical trip.

Actually, they take pleasure in being a wet blanket and puncturing the joy of people living in hope.

They never actually help anyone, but my God, will they describe the hopelessness of their situation to them.

If this demon isn't an open wet blanket, they're even more sadistic and will be into actually sabotaging people around them, just to revel in and suck up the atmosphere of sorrow and despair they created.

They're the sort who'll pretend to be ill when someone close to them is studying for an exam the next day, or going for an important interview, or going for their driving license test.

They're so well played even as a child, that it's near impossible that they're doing it on purpose.

They tend to provide for themselves quite comfortable by having a steady job. The job is just foil for their various sadistic activities. It's hard to point the finger at someone who goes to work 9-5, pays his or her bills and has all the right cable subscriptions; who everyone in the neighborhood has seen regularly doing the same things year after year.

But as sure as night is day, this demon fuels itself by doing sadistic things causing sorrow to others, sorrow energy it lives on.

This demon can get theatrical when you try to escape it, while doing the most disgusting, betrayals of you to stop you from escaping, so never tell them you're leaving. Just do it suddenly one day and don't look back.

VENUS IN AQUARIUS
This warrior is sharp as a knife, intense and at the same time very quick-footed in emotion. You cannot deceive this person. They are

emotionally able to move so quickly, they can meet someone today and experience being in love with them ardently enough to marry them by tonight and tomorrow morning, experience that they've run out of love because that person isn't who they presented as the previous day.

For this reason, this warrior gets right in and right out of situations and careers and relationships very quickly.

They are always getting a crash course in life.

Their weapon is their emotional nimbleness. They don't sit around crying because of how bad their dreams shattered yesterday. They learn their lesson and move on.

This gives them the ability to acquire in a few years or decades, the experience it would take others lifetimes.

When they do find true love, they know it because they don't run out of it like they did before.

Their weakness is their hanging out with people they already know are betrayers, and don't really care for him or her. They have these people and places in their life, they have simply to give them a sense of stability or peace while they're doing their emotional trapeze swinging. Those end up draining their energy, often their money and more.

When this warrior learns to find their stability in their own selves, honor their intensity and emotional nimbleness, they begin to find they have super powers others don't. They can heal people, inspire people, put people in confusion back on the right path.

They've made all the mistakes, so others needn't.

When they find true love, they are stable as the rock of Gibraltar, because they've experienced what isn't love, or friendship and they're living a real love now.

Demon – Venus in Aquarius

This demon is a gambler. In everything in life, this demon behaves with disrespect for everything. They find people who are already desperate and hoping for a miracle and get them to invest in losing ventures.

They are somewhat theatrical and have in their minds always, something like a stage set on which they are rearranging various props, characters, to create an atmosphere that will make people take utterly crazy risks.

In modern times, movies and books have greatly promoted the taking of risks and this demon lives in an unreal cloud of imagining that they are going to be one of those people who suddenly get lucky. They are constantly, involved, Ed, in games of luck.

They'll hurt someone who's always been there for them, if they think that person is bringing them bad luck.

They're into all the arts and science and whatever you want to call the occult that is low-brained and focuses on "getting luck" by doing things like blood sacrifices, seducing women or men of a certain type and so on.

The population of those into these is HUGE, Ed, more than we could ever know by looking at world media.

These demons, Ed, are curiously completely sedate when they are outside of the territory they usually operate in. Remember the stage in their head? That's the only world they really know. You take them off the stage, or you go off the stage and suddenly they're cut down to size. Too long there and they'll start making a new stage.

VENUS IN PISCES

This warrior has an intelligence that is something like the unfettered natural intelligence of a baby seeing the world for the first time. They see things very simply and value things for what those things mean to them.

If you give a baby a shiny ball made of rubber, Ed, the baby won't care how much money you paid for it, they'll value it for the joy it brings them. They won't care for the gold coin you try to give them instead.

This sort of intelligence is incredibly important for us as a species to survive, Ed, because it is based in natural reality and not the perverted false reality the thugs have us living in.

In the end, even in the thug delusory matrix, energy flows according to reality and not delusion. So this warrior actually has their finger on the pulse of human mass consciousness.

They don't preach much, Ed, or share with others what they know naturally, as they don't know that others don't see everything as simply as they do.

They are amazing artists and the things they do and make, even if it's just how they dress or keep their space, communicates to all humans, some simple truths.

At some point in life, Ed, people start realizing they are true leaders because of how they hold their own consciousness despite the tossing and turning of the world's mass consciousness, existing in a world of their own, as if cushioned and kept safe away from the turmoil all around; except that world of theirs is all of our childhood and eternal home state of simple faith in God.

It's important for this warrior to learn ways to express themselves – like language, painting, the arts.

Demon – Venus in Pisces
This demon is a charmer and sexual vampire. They present themselves as exactly the opposite. They are at the forefront of religious and philosophical groups, presenting themselves as

servants of humanity. In their heads, many of them actually think they're saints because of all the "Service" they do for others.

But everything they do is for sexual energy draining and to build their profile. In youth and middle age, Ed, they fool a lot of people; but as they reach their fifties, the inner reality starts coming out on their face. They stop being able to hold their eyes off their targets. They stop being able to be as smooth as they used to be before. They stop being as cautious as before and they often get caught and told to leave places.

They spend the rest of their lives defaming the characters of those who found them out and told them to get lost. They make up sob stories and even believe them. About how they were cheated and done wrong. And how they lost their money helping someone and all that.

They end up employed in thug organizations that need people to do dirty and dangerous work, like spying, befriending and kidnapping kids, grooming young children and so on. They manage to glamorize the crimes they do in their heads.

MOON – SOUL AIM, FOCUS

Dear Ed,

So long as there is the moon up over us in the sky, we will not really need the word "magic". It always fascinates me, how that one shining light in the sky, unchanged through the time, never fails to inspire in generation upon generation, all those things we try to have words for but fail. Beauty, magic, dreaming, miracles.

Always, the Sun shows us who we are, but the Moon shows us who we can be.

For a warrior, Ed, there is no greater guide than the moon. From ancient times and across all species; it is under the empire of the Moon that insight into the enemy's weaknesses and strengths has been got; and ways found to achieve the impossible revealed.

When the warfare is spiritual, this is even more applicable, because it is the Moon that sharpens whichever weapon we use, and shows us how best to deploy it.

The Moon, Ed, in a person's birth sky, shows the person's ability to deploy energy at a point.

For example, in the case of an archer;

The Sun shows the basic life energy available to the archer. Can he lift the bow or not?

Mars shows the force or speed of the arrow.

Venus shows where the arrow will be aimed.

Mercury shows the operational skill with which the arrow will be deployed.

Jupiter shows the quality of the bow and arrow.

Saturn shows the ability of the archer to use the available arrows judiciously, and for how long the archer can keep shooting the arrows.

The Moon shows your ability to AIM.

You see, Ed, how very important the moon is in our lives? Whether physically or as mental intelligence or as spiritual or emotional intelligence; it's the Holy Grail of AIM, Ed.

There is no point of having energy, force, speed, desire, good quality equipment, ability to keep shooting; without AIM.

The mount of the moon in a person's palm, Ed, shows a person's mental well-being. Mentally affected people are called "Lunatics" after the moon. They cannot AIM. They cannot FOCUS.

This ability to aim and focus, Ed, shows up in every area of life, and makes life itself possible, because without it we're just a blast of energy that doesn't particularly BE or DO anything.

The Sun causes our energy to flow out from our center, thereby starting our life itself. The Moon however, causes the energy, to turn back in and flow back towards the center. This return back of energy is therefore what makes us BE a person, a FORM, an entity.

This return or inward flow of energy, is possible only because we know the source of our energy. Our primal simple first aim, is therefore, not any point on the outside of us, but our own inner source.

When a baby is born, Ed, we don't go aiming to climb things, or even eat things, first. Our first instinct is to touch and hold our mother, from who we have just come out, our source, our origin; and latch onto her. We know that this is how life can move forward.

When we stop physically latching onto our mother for sustenance, it is because we are now energetically established in contact with our mother or mother field. I.e. Our Moon energy processes are stabilized so we can work directly with Moon energy in our bodies.

Those who do not get a smooth transition out from being fed by their mothers, Ed, tend to right there have a problem with how they manage Moon energy, that helps them focus, aim, in life; and they spend a big part of their lives then trying to get back that balance. Not that that's difficult, because we are always in touch with our Moon mother, just by being a living being.

Our SOUL is never not being sustained by our Moon. So our soul guides us to energetic stability.

The soulless bio robots do not have this advantage, so they become controllable by guides other than the mother. So you see now, why breast-feeding and separating babies from the mother is a critical part of the "State", programming the population and directing energy.

So in actual practicality, Ed, our ability to translate into mental and physical expression; the mandates and Being of our SOUL; is our Moon weapon.

In other words, our ability to connect to and stay connected to our soul.

Now, Ed, you might wonder why this is even a thing. But think about it, Ed. If a person's soul and body are not properly connected;

1) They'll die easy. Leave the body anytime. Not a good thing on the battlefield, where it's precisely your ability to stay in the body that's going to decide who wins or loses. The one who leaves first, loses. So long as you're in the body, the battle is not finished.

2) The body will be chronically energy deprived, because no matter how much energy is coming in (the Sun), you can't focus it without your soul. It'll just go wherever the thug world pulls

your attention to. You'll not have your energy available for what you want it.

3) Because of energy being pulled out in directions others want it to go, your body itself is not going to develop or be well and all the illnesses caused by constant energy drain – which can be summarized simply as "aging" are going to be present. Your physical longevity is compromised right there.

4) You're going to feel lost, depressed, upset, displaced etc., because you can sense that you're not doing what you want to do in life. You end up looking for spiritual guidance outside of yourself and in today's world that opens us to exploitation, because very few spiritual guides will turn you unconditionally towards your own self. The vast majority of them will teach you to aim your energy at them, their causes, their beliefs.
That might be refreshing after your energy has been skewed about so, but it is still draining your energy away from you.

5) Sexually, you're not going to go very far, because your energy isn't aimed or focused at your soulmate. You're likely to be mentally destabilized by orgasms, unable to recover strength or vitality after ejaculations; and lose any sense of identity you have as time goes by; then go sexless in an attempt to regain and hold your sense of identity.

6) Mentally, you're going to find it very hard to know what's real and what's unreal, because it is our soul that makes us able to know this, not our minds. This can make us believe anything we're told, be deceived by exploiters, played and manipulated.

7) Intellectually, we find it hard to actually put our learning, knowledge, training to use as we find it hard to keep at something till it is done. **We keep getting distracted** away.

As someone whose mother passed away soon after birth and feeding me the one time; I have grappled with these all my life, myself, so I have a deep understanding of this topic, Ed.

A warrior needs to be so damn waterproof, windproof, soundproof, earthquake proof, in connection with their SOUL at all times.

The primary aim of thug world "education", Ed, despite all the ways we humans actually have benefited from it, is to teach us to override the voice and leading of our SOUL, with mental view of the world and rationale which we are taught in the impressionable young years.

Our soul, Ed, each of us, has a unique way of viewing the world and thinking; a beautiful intertwining of emotion and thought. This is us.

But our education trains us to think like them, Ed. Not like us. It teaches us what we should and shouldn't feel, instead of just feeling what we're feeling.

THUG WORLD EDUCATION BLINDFOLDS US, ED.

Luckily for us, our unconquerable soul rebels, breaks through, and some humans go right back and take all there is to GAIN from the thug world education system and use it advantage.

But our Moon weapon, Ed, is our ability to be connected to our SOUL in the heat of the battle, so we don't lose focus.

Let's get straight to it.

MOON IN ARIES
This warrior is able to deploy huge amounts of energy whenever he or she really wants something. The problem is actually finding out what they really want.

Because of being a radiant high-energy body; they are constantly attracting those who would like to direct that energy towards their needs and causes.

This warrior tends to be programmed quite early in life, that they should use their energy to enable others and support others' dreams and desires instead of their own.

They go through several crises in life when they realize that no one comes for them when they need support.

The critical point of change for the better for this warrior is when they come out of the deception that they were born to serve others. They have their own soul reason for being born, whether others understand or accept it or not.

They're going to be a bit of a loner, then, Ed, for a while, because they'll be throwing out of their lives, all the leeches and scavengers who'd been living off their shine and glow.

They're not team players, not because something's wrong with them, but because the team is full of energy leeches and suckers.

These warriors, Ed, take time to reach a point where they listen to their own soul and instinct, but when they decide do, they quickly become expert at it, often using methods of divination like the tarot cards, rune stones; whatever… they can use anything; and when they develop the connection, Ed, wild horses can't shake them from their goal.

They are an utterly formidable spirit warrior because they do not flinch in battle; will NOT abandon a loved one no matter how bad things get, will not turn a hair at whatever drama the enemy might throw at them, and in fact, Ed, they begin to find it all hilarious at some point and start laughing at it all as they lose the fear of being swept away into deception as used to happen to them in childhood and teenage years.

They are intensely loyal, Ed; I feel so honored that God has given me this view of this warrior. They remind me of the Bible verse – "Like Hind's Feet on High Places" (Habakkuk, last chapter). They are that mountain goat, that climbs the high places that others dare not dream of.

When they get in touch with their soul, Ed, they're going to win, win, win.

Demon – Moon in Aries

This demon is a headstrong attacker of all that seems in contradiction of his or her belief system. They are used by others to do full frontal attacks on people, whether online or offline, because they can be trusted to be hard-headed and embedded in a way of thinking so stubbornly, that they actively seen anyone challenging that paradigm as a personal enemy of theirs.

They can be intelligent and comprehend high levels of thought, but only within the boundaries they were programmed to be in.

Once outside that territory they're trained to fight in, they lose mojo, become confused and start lashing out in any direction they can imagine will hurt you. Mindless hurting means that they're out of their territory, threatened and trying to hold on to you.

Don't engage with this demon in places they're familiar with, in fact don't confront them at all. It's not worth the bother, you've probably heard their entire rationale many times already.

Don't try telling them there is life and sense outside of their belief system or zone; because they cannot comprehend that.

Just get out of their territory or comfort zone. If you can't get out of their territory, make your own space within it, and do not allow them, or any of their allies or representatives in either. They'll keep attempting to get in your space, cross your boundaries. Learn to say No over and over.

It's precisely to teach you to do that that this demon has been allowed in your life.

MOON IN TAURUS
There's no fool like a young fool, they say. Meet eternal young fool, Ed. I use the word "fool" in a sweet way here, because they love like it's their first love, every time. This is a most sweet and lovely thing about them.

Unfortunately, as you can imagine, Ed, it does cause them some horrific emotional ravaging before the find the ONE for them. Another sweet thing is, they actually tend to find the one they love, quite early in life. In our times, when our frequencies are skewed because of thug world programming, they can take longer to find their love, but they often find them very close and almost right under their noses.

They are just among the sweetest people, Ed, the sort that remind you of a cute cuddly soft toy to hug and kiss.

But they are also a formidable spirit warrior, Ed, because they have spines of steel when it comes to what matters to them. Their core values are tight, Ed. This is not a warrior who can be bought, blackmailed, tricked, conned or even taken for a ride.

There was this mafia guy in Mumbai; he was all heart, buying his girlfriend roses every day, making an album of their pictures together to carry with him; and his enemies laughed believing he could be honey-trapped so easily. They let him get powerful, Ed, because he entertained them so much. He bought property all around his girlfriend's house so that one day her father would be willing to let her marry him. He got a car with her initials on the registration number. His rivals in the underworld business he was into, bootlegging basically; laughed at him. They waited sadistically to let him keep going, because they thought it would be such fun to break him later on.

All this time, Ed, they didn't know where the money was coming for the investment in his "business". This happens to be a big concern, Ed, because the mafia don't want foreign players on their turf.

So at a time they thought it would be hilarious to break him – as they'd always intended to do, as they didn't know who his sponsor was – they tried to honey-trap him.

And Ed, they got such a rude shock, because that guy they thought would be so easy to play around with, was a granite wall. He was impossible to get through to, Ed. They could not kill him without knowing who was behind him, because they wouldn't want to offend certain people who might have been behind him; but they couldn't get him to reveal his secrets either.

They never expected someone who was so loving and emotional to be so tough at the same time.

That describes this person, Ed.

Such amazing emotional resilience. Loyalty isn't even word enough to use here.

This warrior, Ed, is deeply affected by the weather, emotional atmosphere, and the use of subconscious triggers like symbols.

This is a weakness, until they decide to stop suppressing their ability to read the room, sensitivity to the weather, and how they're affected by the symbols around them. This becomes a special weapon, Ed, for them when they begin to develop it and use it to make decisions.

The symbols the enemy once used to subconsciously intimidate them, can become the warning and trigger their defensive systems; it could also become what our human now uses to intimidate back their enemy – because the enemy obviously already fears that symbol, or why would he use it to intimidate others.

You see what I mean? The powers of this warrior are mind-blowing once they start developing them.

I would keep the whole thing as secret as possible, though. You don't want people to know what you're noticing and so on.

This warrior gravitates towards herbs for healing.

Demon – Moon in Taurus
This demon is often seeing shivering, and therefore wearing a lot of warm clothes, as their nervous system is usually vulnerable to every wind that blows.

They are quite hyper-emotional, irrational and demanding of other peoples' time and energies.

You don't need an enemy when you have a cry-baby of this sort in your life. They just never stop having some horrible problem affecting them and their nervous systems.

It reminds me of Mrs. Bennet from Pride and Prejudice. The mother, in the story. Her entire life, she was in bed most of the time, calling for everyone to wait on her, and listen to her sob stories and how her nerves and bones and what not were being affected by the weather and every letter that arrived and so on and so forth.

They're actually quite terrified of all things good health, robust and cheerful, because it goes against their life paradigm of fear, illness, doom and need for everyone to support them all the time.

This does attract humans who like to sort others out though, and if you're a human with a demon in your life, you deserve it for always trying to sort everyone else's life so compulsively.

This demon is NEVER going to change. They'll probably even outlive you after draining you to death.

If you want to save your life, come out of the idea that you have to save everything that whines and save your own self for a change. Your lesson for attracting this demon into your life, is that an interaction with another real human is always rewarding one way or another. When you're being drained, you're not in an equal relationship, you're being exploited. That's not normal and that's not want God or the creator made you for. You're meant for better things.

MOON IN GEMINI

The emotional energy of this warrior, Ed, is simply amazing. You know how in older times there were open to air theaters? And when people sang, they had to sing so loud that their voice filled that whole theater and more?

That is the sort of emotional energy of this person.

When they walk into the building, the sensitive can feel it. The atmosphere changes according to their mood.

Whether they're down in life or up in life; they are always in love. And that love atmosphere is carried everywhere by them.

Everywhere they go, hope begins to spring forth in the hearts of those around. Everyone feels much better when they're in the building, without even knowing they're in the building.

Those who attack this warrior, Ed, attack them because of the love consciousness and atmosphere of hope they carry. That is obviously a direct enemy of the parasites that farm us humans for trauma energy. They cannot tolerate someone like this human walking around carrying love and hope.

From a young age, Ed, this warrior is attacked by demons trying to cut them down. All the better, because this warrior develops more and more faith as the years go by. They read a lot, and they get very educated in various philosophies and mythologies. They will shut anyone up that dares come at them with doom and gloom philosophies.

We are talking, Ed, of the very energy of SPRING, here.

You can do whatever to the earth, Ed, but when spring comes, spring comes. This person is that force of nature, Ed, like the flower Aconite. It starts blooming in the snow, Ed, because it already feels spring; it IS spring.

This remind me of the Aconite flower fairy from the book, "Fairies of the Flowers and Trees" by Cicely M. Barker, 1950. It comes with a cute poem.

The WINTER ACONITE Fairy

WINTER ACONITE

Deep in the earth
I woke, I stirred.
I said: " Was that the Spring I heard?
For something called!"
" No, no," they said;
" Go back to sleep, go back to bed.

" You're far too soon;
The world's too cold
For you, so small." So I was told.
But how could I
Go back to sleep?
I could not wait; I had to peep!

Up, up I climbed,
And here am I.
How wide the earth! How great the sky!
O wintry world,
See me, awake!
Spring calls, and comes; 'tis no mistake.

This warrior, Ed, Moon in Gemini, tends to feel unexplainable fear now and then. It's them sensing enemies of their consciousness of hope. The homeopathic dilution of Aconite is a huge help in this, as it helps them come out of that "blanket of fear" feeling and focus on whatever it is they have to do.

It will help them a lot, Ed, to understand that the energetic assault on them is because of their ability to change the atmosphere.

There was this character in the "Twilight" movies and books, Jasper. He was supposed to have that ability to change the emotional atmosphere of the surroundings. He could make people suddenly start feeling happy.

That's the ability this warrior has, but it's way more than just emotion, it's consciousness and energy.

This warrior is outright a consciousness warrior and should not waste time on things other warriors can deal with, like discussing philosophies and what's right and wrong etc. Those are all tempting distractions for this warrior, but they ARE distractions.

This warrior needs to focus on communication of a higher level; BEING and HOLDING the energy that they are born to be.

It would be good to weed out the thorns in the flesh that hang around this human constantly trying to pull them down. If they were of the same soul group, they wouldn't try to pull down the creation of God. These attacks are usually disguised as "I'm telling you this for your good," or "for your safety," and so on.

This warrior should stop investing money, time and energy that does not hold or uphold the consciousness of love, hope and joy in a way they can clearly see.

Demon – Moon in Gemini
This demon is full of s***. I hate to use language in my own books, Ed. But really this is a fount of bulls***. It reads a lot, or has many

books at least, and is constantly engaged in presenting itself as a learned high thinker of great and lofty thoughts and ideals.

In reality it is dependent on others for basic things in daily life and is an energy cripple, in the sense that it would feel lost if whoever is their domestic support didn't turn up to make their bed and find their underwear and iron the right shirt.

Its most common way of draining others is requiring others to help them through the day in "little" things.

This demon can sing, dance, quote poetry and do all the things to appear cute, entertaining, charming and make one think they're an asset to their lives; but they're an energy cripple and will drain whole houses and building of loosh by just being there.

They tend to keep contact information of people and maintain contact through phone calls or online, so that they have a subtle intimidation effect on those who say no to them, subtly threatening social defamation of them.

They have an act of being good with children and pets just to keep up the personality of being a really cute, nice person.

This demon causes nervous system problems in those exposed to it long term, because they're actually very high strung, psychotic and ungrounded.

Never give them any reasons for cutting off with them. Just refuse to make contact. If you start talking to this demon, it will take that as a sign that you're available for energy draining.

It loves to do emotional dramas so just don't give it the chance.

And look into self-worth issues you could have that make you feel you need to do things for others to be allowed to live in this world. You have a right, as a child of this earth, to live just as you are.

MOON IN CANCER

This warrior is a extra sensitive inhabitant of the ethereal realms of the earth consciousness. Of the frequency of unicorns and other beings now excluded from public consciousness as those who never existed, this warrior's constant struggle is to prove he or she even exists in this world — because they are a frequency that is so high up above the razzle dazzle of every day life in the thug world.

They are not interested in the stock market, or how rich the people around them are, or aren't. They aren't too bothered about how they or others around them are dressed or who's seeing who.

They are tuned to the music of the spheres above; the breezes of changes others scarcely know are blowing. They look into the soul of those they meet, and if they ask you how you are; they really want to know how you are.

This warrior is made by God as a sentinel and weather-vane for all humanity. When they withdraw, it is because there is danger. When they move forward, it is a good time to move forward. When their hackles are raised, indeed a deception or crime is happening.

They are emotionally aware always of the emotional state of people around them, and can therefore predict with a high level of accuracy, what is going to happen next. They can tell to what extent someone can be trusted.

This warrior tends to have deep emotional anxiety over being loved and accepted, because of how different they are. Their love is all encompassing and unconditional but of course that gets exploited big-time by demons. So they end up carrying anxiety and even withdrawing from all relationships when they're feeling vulnerable, just to protect themselves from being hurt again.

This anxiety can cripple them if they do not develop a way to either find faith in those in their lives, and/or remove those who keep them anxious and tossing and turning, wondering if they're loyal and trustworthy or not.

A key issue in these, is the fact that this warrior is so protective that they can get attracted to anyone and anything that seems to need protection and then expect the same unconditional love back.

This warrior needs to be aware of when they have someone in their lives simply because they feel that person needs protection; versus having someone in their lives as an equal energy interaction; not someone who is just taking their energy.

In an ideal world, we could just put our arms around every lonely person we meet and love them without wanting anything in return. But we be in a time of demons right now. And demons particularly are out looking for this kind of human, who can't resist helping or comforting another.

Learning to be alright with turning away from someone who seems in need, but is most probably an energy vampire is this warrior's huge challenge because it's like training oneself to go against one's own nature.

And yet, it is the key that will make this warrior able to survive himself, or herself in this world and deliver their gifts, to real humans, use their gifts for their own and their loves ones' upliftment and establishment.

Self care is another ongoing challenge for this warrior as they tend to focus their attention and spending on their loved ones, often ignoring their own needs. This warrior being so sensitive to frequency, requires a lot of care and support in a world full of vibrational assault to say the least. This warrior requires life long extra care to deal with vibrational assault; and needs an environment as far away from city noise and frequency pollution. A semi-hermit lifestyle would be best.

This warrior is deeply connected to his or her mother, and this brings in constant feminine energy to the home and projects and groups this warrior is involved in. Everything takes on spiritual refinement, the frequency of love and nurture of others, as a result.

You cannot have this warrior on the team and expect things not to running in a spiritual direction, and spiritual significance of everything being done being brought up.

In the right team they are a most wonderful motivating and energizing factor. The wrong team will get offended by them very soon and they'll be out sooner rather than later.

But the constant inflow of feminine or matrilineal energies through this warrior isn't simply about protectiveness and nurture; it can also be wild preternatural rage, anger and destruction. The Goddess's rage is no small matter, and this warrior's rage when awoken causes a huge effect in the spiritual realms, changing the atmosphere of the place all around, affecting animals, plants, other humans.

An organization or group or family that awaken this warrior's rage is bound to doom and it would be well for people to get out of there immediately.

This warrior's curse is never earned without deserving it many times over and it never fails to destroy those it is on. Their anger is always hard won and once it is gotten, it rarely ever ends.

This warrior's anger is fueled by their love for whatever was hurt. As eternal and unending as their love is, so is their anger.

When this warrior leaves, a place, an organization, a project; it is doomed to failure. It becomes a black hole draining the energy of all involved.

This warrior tends to have issues with memory being blocked, trouble recognizing faces, places and getting lost while traveling, sometimes even in familiar places. This is because of the dissonance between thug world frequencies and natural frequencies. Once this warrior begins to follow their inner soul instinct, this dissonance reduces and they instead have super powers of memory, remembering past lives vividly, including places and paths and faces.

They are able then to tap into the memory in spaces, rocks, walls, trees, animals. You get the picture.

Demon – Moon in Cancer
This demon is a gnawing drain on anyone's energy because of their constant overthinking and nitpicking and engaging a person to examine their guts out. They are suspicious about everything and everyone, and not in a protective way like the humans who have cancer placements; but in a way where they feel others' private business is somehow their right to know.

They tend to find religious or such, reasons to justify their constant obsession with others' business. Sometimes this shows out openly and they become known as a gossip, but most often, they present themselves as a "Well-wisher" and helper of everyone and "keeper of secrets". They let you know that so long as you keep them in the loop, telling them all the stuff about you they want to know, they'll give you social validation to make your life easy.

But if you don't keep them in the loop, they're going to start rumors to make it like you're a criminal with secrets.

You'd be surprised, Ed, at how these characters, who can go about seeming to the naked eye to be like some sort of free hospitality service, can wreck, drain and destroy the atmosphere of a place.

A sign that someone is this demon, is their asking about your personal items like your jewelry or where you bought some particular item of clothing or something about your person, you would normally expect only someone very close to you to ask about. It's one thing to be complimented by a stranger on your dressing or looks or jewelry or hair or whatever; It's quite another thing to be asked a personal question about those. That's them announcing themselves.

If you answer, soon they'll ask another question and so on.

Now, the human Moon in Cancer is also curious, will compliment strangers and ask for things like "What does your tattoo (in a foreign language) mean?" But you will know the demon by how they immediately being to classify you as a "type" and start judging you for it. With the human, you will feel a pleasant high that someone noticed something about you and you will like that about you more as a result. With the demon you will feel devalued, brought down, slit open on an operating table to forcibly expose your internal organs.

This demon collects information, data, about people. Don't give it to them anymore.

You've attracted this demon into your life, most probably because you need to learn to draw boundaries and keep what is sacred and precious to you safe from the prying eyes of energy vampires. Take this opportunity to draw a line of protection around you, your life and your loved ones. Do not allow someone who isn't your immediate family, very close friend, into that inner circle.

Your every day life, your person, your presentation; this is sacred stuff, not "data". You do not expose your inner life and sacred home space to demons.

Learn to keep your home space sacred and free of demons and you'll solve like 80% of your health problems immediately because of your energy no longer being drained.

Take advantage of this situation to learn to defend and protect all that is sacred and holy to you. Never let it be treated as "data".

MOON IN LEO

This warrior is like that person who goes walking on the beach, stopping to pick up something every few seconds, then tossing it back down and moving on. They are constantly in the search for something precious, always on the look out for it, so that a large part of their life energy and hobbies are actually about searching for that something precious. They are the ultimate connoisseur of energy perfect beauty as their soul constantly searches for that perfect frequency of truth, honor, nobility and purity that is in their own heart.

Because of the frequency of purity of their heart, they are nearly always slightly uncomfortable in surroundings where there are many others with chaotic energies.

They are drawn to stable energy fields, whether places, or people, as a base from which they can do their searching for the frequency of their own soul.

They become able at a young age, to filter out filler material, surround noise, and fluff; to look at the nuts and bolts, the core structure of a thing, a person, an organization.

They move quickly through places, relationships, fields of philosophy, religions and even cults.

Their search for the perfect frequency makes them non-judgmental because they know that what they're looking for could be ANYWHERE. But once they've dived deep into something or someone, and searched, and not found what they were searching for, they'll be off and away, not even leaving their tools behind.

This warrior can remove from their consciousness at will, things that hold them back in their spiritual quest. They will not look back. They will not emotionally engage with someone they have no intention of keeping in their lives.

Their face is ever pointed forward to the jewel of frequency they are searching for.

This warrior is most often alone in their daily lives; but should they have a family, woe betide anyone that dares to sniff around them with intent to exploit.

This warrior is unpredictable and the methods he or she might choose to defend themselves is unpredictable. This is their greatest strength in battle. Even they themselves don't know how their own spirit is going to lead them.

Their intelligence and guidance come straight from spirit and you will never find them ungraceful, "thinking twice" or confused on the battlefield. Their allegiance is not to a person, place, organization; but to their own higher self, their spirit.

The chance of this warrior being poisoned is very high as the demons around usually find no way to negotiate with this human or manipulate him or her into complying with things.

There are jealous demons all around, whining and wriggling about, trying to get this warrior's attention, compassion, friendship and loyalty – such a great prize.

This warrior's weakness in early life and youth, is rushing headlong into situations to protect the people they love. It takes them decades to figure out that not everyone is a human, not everyone deserves their love and loyalty; and that most people too weak to defend their own points of view, or take a stand for themselves, are actually spineless demons whose game is to attract warriors like this to use their energy for them.

More than once, this warrior gets accused of over stepping their authority, and even impinging on the freedom of others, while being protective.

Eventually this warrior learns to start recognizing other warriors and gravitating towards them, instead of towards those who seem like wounded warriors but are actually spineless entities who never did believe in anything enough to actually invest in and take a stand.

This warrior gives everyone a chance. If they don't behave, they're out for good.

This warrior needs to regularly check their house like an army checks every corner of the fort to make sure no one can get in who doesn't come in at the front door. They do not want parasites living in their house, their consciousness, their fort; living off them quietly, draining them.

This warrior is great at dealing with attacks at the front door, and on the battlefield. It's the parasites that creep in and hide under the carpet, live moderately quietly, looking like they're doing no harm, just sharing the warmth of the warrior's fireplace.... Maybe the edge of their blanket... maybe some crumbs from their table.... Maybe just a little water... just a little this, just a little that.... That's this warrior's Achilles heel.

They cannot find it in themselves to begrudge others some small comfort or small help or little shelter; and they don't realize till they have grown the parasite into a demon that makes their very own house unlivable; what they were feeding and growing all along.

Very often this warrior then abandons his own house and goes and starts all over again somewhere else.

Moral of the story – Dramatic threats are not a big deal to this warrior; being aware of individuals that do micro-energy draining and stopping those is important. It's they who become the big threats later on.

In an ideal world, this warrior would offer free protection, care and support to all around. But this is a demon infested world and you do NOT want to feed that which ends up feeding on you.

Demon – Moon in Leo
This demon is a stickler for discipline and disciplining others. They get their kicks out of always trying to set others right. They might hide this initially but very soon it becomes obvious.

Other tend to think that it's because this demon cares for them, but actually it's this demon's way of imposing authority on others and thereby increasing their territory.

Their favorite game is to do people favors, by helping them, and then psychically or subtly ask for a return of those favors in various ways.

When they want something from you, something you cannot give them, they will suddenly turn into a debt collector, holding back things of yours as if they earned them, often even character defaming you as someone who took advantage of them and their generosity and helpfulness in your life.

You will recognize the difference between the human Leo moon, and the demon Leo moon by how the human will not poke into your private space as if it's their right because they helped you; but the demon will. The demon will behave like they own you and your life, and can come and go as they please, because they helped you.

The demon basically wants to own and command people. When you blatantly disobey them, doing what you believe is right for you, they get challenged, threatened and will start working behind your back against you. They will try to put you in a spot where you look like you're of low character, or you're unprofessional at work, or you're not as good as you think you are at your skill; in an effort to make you devalue yourself and submit to their authority.

Just don't. They're not worth even a bother, because in reality they're just energy vampires from bloodlines that used to be able to throw their weight around because of their wealth or property; but no longer can. They're on the way out, their DNA is degenerating fast.

But if you have this demon around you and you can't get red of them, be constantly aware that they're seeing everything you do as either submission or stalling. Don't let them believe that you're one of those people they can count in their kitty as one of theirs.

Maintain a formal distance, address them formally, and behave formally. Even when they behave informal, keep behaving formal. Let it be if it looks like you forgot that you were informal two days ago. Let anyone think what they like. Just keep behaving formally.

Don't let them believe they have any rights over you outside of your work description.

They have stamina to keep circling and making attempts at you for a long time, but you will develop stamina and spine as you learn to consistently hold your own and uphold your independence of your thought, your right to allow who you want into your life, and who not.

MOON IN VIRGO

This warrior is God's answer to the prayers of those who are unable to find out what the problem is that's holding them down, what that illness really is that saps them of strength. This a healer of energy fields who can by instinct locate the central problem in a situation or someone's health or well-being.

They have the intelligence to unwrap layers of various deposits covering wounds, crimes and other consciousness and frequency changing events and happenings.

They have a scope of vision that enables them to see things that might be outside of their experience in this lifetime or ever, really. It can comprehend things that they themselves have never come across.

This warrior's spiritual weapon is this ability to comprehend the hitherto unknown, so nothing can actually be hidden from them. They WILL figure it out.

The weakness of this warrior is an overly sentimental attachment to home and homeland, an attachment born in these times out of trauma. Some demon found out in early life that this human could be controlled and kept down using their attachment to mother and home and homeland. So, they made them feel that if they stray out of bounds, their mother, home; could be hurt.

This, makes very little sense in real life but when such things are placed in the subconscious in childhood, they sit in the subconscious and drive the person's decision-making processes. They don't know why but they sabotage their own attempts to rise up and away from the place their mother lives, or who they considered their mother figure lives or lived; somehow irrationally believing that their staying around, their subsisting financially and living a life of struggle will somehow appease the gods that hold their mother's life and well-being in their hands.

Like I said, it's not rational; it's just placed there to control them, by someone who figured out that that was their weakness.

This warrior's abilities are unlocked by leaving their place they were suppressed in, their gifts defamed, mocked, kept down; by surrendering their mother, ancestral homeland, home or such to the care of God.

The secret of this warrior, is that the earth mother field itself travels IN this warrior. This human is born an actual embodiment of the earth field of his or her birth and this has happened BECAUSE that earth field WANTS to move from that location to another.

The earth moves her energy fields about like that regularly. Just as human souls leave the body and move another; just as the plant soul leaves its body at the end of a season and moves on, so earth fields themselves leave their location and move on. This is why you can go to some famous legendary places and feel nothing of what they told you, you would feel there. The place could have moved.

Very often the place moves sideways on the surface of the earth and there are trackers among the demons who have established temples and such at ley lines and particular points on the earth's grid to tap into natural energy there; who track the movement. This is why temples, ancient cities are abandoned. They no longer sat on the grid they were established on.

A new city is established over the place where the energy is found moved. Other times, the embodiment of the energy of the earth, a human or other animal manifestation carries the field away somewhere else.

The thug trackers of energy fields go where they are and re-establishment their ritual fields over where the field has settled. This is the reason for places named "New" this and that. New York, New Jersey, New Delhi and so on.

Not all the human embodiments of earth fields have their moon in Virgo, but every moon in Virgo person I've come across was an embodiment and with them their earth mother field traveled to a new location.

Their crisis in life was coping with this. They were not allowed by their own energy to settle in the land of their birth; and they could settle down and prosper only upon traveling to the place their birth field wanted to go to.

Demon – Moon in Virgo

This demon is a dealer in antiques and things that carry intrinsic energy value, things that people will want to buy even though those may not have value in the open market. If they are not this officially it's because they haven't had a chance yet, or they're doing it in ways not noticeable, such as peddling information between people or groups and so on.

While this is also something humans can do, the difference is, this demon vampirizes off the energy of those buying or selling the things of value. There is an element of abuse that they slip in in each transaction, very subtly, playing on how much a seller needs money, and playing on how much a buyer wants to buy something.

They get their kicks, power trip on the helplessness of people as they let go of things of value, and as they try to acquire things of value.

They are constantly practicing this on those in close relationships with them, keeping them all in this draining loop of always feeling they must either sell something or buy something to be of worth. Their sense of worth is tied to constantly buying and selling and it constantly drains the very atmosphere. It is a horrible atmosphere to be in, and this demon is at the heart of it.

If you have this demon in your life, and you can't get rid of it; stop transacting in any way with it. Don't exchange gifts. Don't look at anything they show you or tell you about (a dream is also a product they can sell).

MOON IN LIBRA

This human is a great appreciator of the arts and upholder of the rights and dignities of humanity. They have a pure mind, capable of looking with clarity into situations and things and comprehending things with a simple clarity.

They are however incredibly gullible because of their childlike simplicity and it takes them many years, even decades before they are able to understand that there are people who WANT to deceive them.

They find it so hard to comprehend this, because they themselves would never want to deceive anyone.

Their money dealings are a way they get duped most often, and this is the main area of energy draining for this warrior. They just take forever to understand that a person can tell them one thing, and then use their money for something else.

Of course, the grace of God covers them, but we are on the battlefield here and I'm writing this because this warrior is also required to step up and be the warrior they are now. Because when they awaken to deception, they are the cutting edge of knowing who's lying and who's not.

This warrior can recognize a liar before they open their mouth to start lying. This warrior can smell the truth from miles away. They can do TRUE justice because of this.

This warrior ends up holding immense power because they become the sentinel and spine of their human communities and families and wherever they are, because of how they can find out deceptions and therefore find the truth.

This warrior can get depressed by how many lies we're surrounded by and being told all the time; but it will dissipate when he or she finds a nugget of truth – and they will, because it is their destiny.

It is their destiny to find truth and point their families, communities and us all in the direction of it. They are that lantern holder in the dark, leading humanity back home to safety, back home to our own happiness and place in the circle of life.

They are beautiful and can come under sexual attack a lot. This warrior needs to take special care not to be deceived by those using every day transactions to covertly sexually harass or abuse them. They also are the subject of peoples' jealousy and would do well, to simply face that someone is jealous of them, instead of imagining a situation can be resolved by "talking things out". You cannot make someone jealous of your good looks or sexiness, stop being jealous.

If you can't get rid of jealous people, and the atmosphere is too tense; you can just bring up the word "jealous" somehow. For example, tell them something like, "Are you trying to me jealous, with that amazing ---- of yours"?. It will prick the toxic build-up and release the tension for a while as their attention turns back in at themselves instead of you.

Be careful not to let jealous people make you start dressing down, putting yourself down, not presenting yourself as your beautiful self and so on.

You'll have to work on dealing with jealous people so that your energy can flow out right. You'll have to pray or meditate or whatever you do for divine guidance and get up the courage to fully express your energy and your beauty, and develop your defense systems, because as sure as night and day, this thug world is an enemy of all things beautiful.

This warrior is the very beauty of God walking the face of the earth.

Demon – Moon in Libra

This demon is a skillful manipulator, liar, and twister of facts. This demon starts off deceiving his or her own mother and then father and family and so on. No one really knows who they are and what they're up to.

They weave a covering of lies all around them from a young age, often developing multiple personalities to use at different times.

They can come across as delightfully surprising, engaging, charming and even romantic as a result.

It would all be wonderful and such fun, if there were a heart beneath all that. But the difference between this demon and a human who can be charming and enchanting, is, this demon does it to get things out of you; while a human does it to adore and enjoy you.

Ed, this demon disarms people emotionally, gets close to them, and then power trips as they demonstrate that they know how to really hurt a person. When the person doesn't do as they say, or shows independence of thought or action, they will use their knowledge of what really hurts the person, to suddenly deliver a lethal blow to their very personality, or sense of identity, or grounding.

They will insult or slur the most sacred thing in the person's heart; or destroy or break something most precious to them or such.

They are masters at emotionally isolating their victim away from all that gives their victim strength of independent thought and action.

They will destroy the career of their partner, just to make them financially dependent and control them.

Their reality is that they are utterly merciless when their ego and power tripping is challenged by someone. They're only nice so long as you're clapping for them and saying "Wow, wow."

They are an ego maniac and there is no pleasing them really, as they keep wanting more and more pumping up.

They become utterly vindictive and toxic as they age and can't perform and look as they did before. They try to control younger people to prey on their youthful energy. They are miserable as patients in bed – which they become in an attempt to continue getting attention from people. They play people right from the bed, trying to break up marriages, spoil careers, just do anything to make themselves feel powerful again.

At the early stages you can get rid of the demon by walking out of their lives and maintaining ZERO communication; but once this demon gets into the ill and helpless victim stage, it can be difficult to leave. You'll just have to choose between your life and that bottomless hole.

MOON IN SCORPIO
The grace of God shines bright on this warrior, for this warrior will go where others fear to tread – whether the heights or the depths, this warrior will go there, not thinking of the price to be paid, for love, for loyalty and truth.

This warrior's very guts are moved by the forces of the earth, showing them the way to mysteries whose time has come to be revealed, to things God has decided to reveal.

They are the revealers of the mysteries and therefore a great light in the dark for humans held captive in the dungeons of deception.

These warriors do not fear darkness, nor light; in fact those don't affect them at all. Their morning is when their instinct starts leading them to the unraveling of an arcane sacred mystery; their night falls when they find their satisfaction in the search.

They have immense stamina on the search, immense stamina when rescuing others from the pits of hell; but that stamina can disappear when it comes to their own selves.

Because this warrior has been attacked from a young age to drain them of their preternatural ability to focus and hold their gaze on what matters to them. This is the very enemy of the thug matrix. And one of the ways they were abused shows up in them not taking as much care of themselves as is required.

They frequently abuse their bodies with stimulants and drugs that keep them awake long hours doing things; putting aside that those harm their longevity.

Their attitude is, "Just do whatever now, and worry about the future later." This means this warrior very rarely has thought about their needs and well-being beyond a few days or months.

My message to this warrior is that, they have not been sent to this realm for small things, small revelations; they are here for big revelations which change the paradigm of humanity's consciousness and that is not something which can be uncovered or excavated in one week or month or year or decade.

If this warrior will start to focus their amazing gaze on their health and well-being, even matters like a home to live in long-term; they will be putting in the foundation for their destiny – which is something beyond which can be described right now.

This warrior's relationships with others are a cause of frequent conflict. The demons want to keep them down because demons can sense this is their natural enemy. Other humans get hurt by them because this warrior tends to think everyone is like the demons they've known.

So one of this warrior's great challenges is to develop a base of only actual humans who actually love him or her, and absolutely no one else. All the allergies they're prone to, are their own histamine system reacting violently to the demons in their lives trying desperately to keep them down. They develop auto-immune allergy type problems when they're unable to build trust when they actually find someone who isn't a demon, who really loves them.

So bringing out old trauma of betrayal, facing that and then learning to trust again, is critically important for this warrior.

They will find, soon enough, that the greatest glory, the greatest mystery, that was shrouded and hidden that they uncovered during their life, was actually the God light person they themselves are.

Demon – Moon in Scorpio

This demon is a Mata Hari seducer no matter how they look. The aim isn't sex but domination. It's important to remember this, because in our times, seducing people is not so easy, given how we're exposed to naked flesh and all that in the media anyway.

This demon's method of luring someone into their net of domination, is by doing things to make it like they have an "ancient deep connection." Already, Ed, you can get the picture.

They'll demonstrate that they have some natural god given ability to make you feel special, wanted, and then orgasm. But it's just nearly always simple tricks learned from the thug media and books about how to con humans.

This demon tends to have read up, and/or often are born into families where they have a parent or uncle or aunt or such from who can they can acquire generational methods to seduce, lure and dominate others. Every single one of these demons I've encountered so far has been born into such a lineage. This lineage gives them the subconscious confidence that comes across as a sort of aura that makes their victims believe that God has sent them to their lives.

The word "God" comes up often around this demon as they directly or indirectly invoke divine authority, divine this and divine that; to make their victim orgasm like they never could or did before.

A human will do this same thing, but the difference is; this demon won't orgasm themselves. To orgasm is to surrender, and this demon will consistently NOT surrender. They will expect their victim to tell them all their secrets, take them to all the places they go, introduce them to all the people in their life; tell them about all their finances and investments; hopes for the future, everything.

But they themselves will keep their secrets, except for a few things here and there, required to be revealed for operational efficiency.

They will paint you one nice pretty picture of their life, usually featuring lots of pets, the great kind and philanthropic things they've done for others; great service done to the country; and that's it. You'll have to work with that picture of theirs they've given you. The rest is a secret.

If there is any part of them they hold away from you, know that you're being deceived. It's that simple.

Sexual draining is one of the worst kinds of draining and can literally make a person bedridden as a result. Actual sex is not required to do sexual draining; it can be done by just general sexual acts, even online sex and so on. It's about getting permission to enter the human's sacred space. That demon and all their lineage and communities can feed off that opening, and they usually do.

If you're a victim of this kind of sexual draining, you already know it.

The way this demon holds onto you is through divine intimidation. Divine intimidation is actually mentioned in the laws of most countries as a form of controlling a victim by subliminally or otherwise threatening to cause hurt – by physical or spiritual means – to them or those they love. They make it like you'll be going against God, and you'll be causing hurt to your loved ones by provoking the demon or not submitting to them anymore.

You must pack your bags and get the hell away from this one.

This is a one woman or one man cult you must escape from. Their birth family is their enabler and co-feeder on your energy. Never trust anyone who is connected to this demon, because they're either an accomplice or a victim.

The reason a person attracts such a demon into their lives is because on some level deep inside you feel that you have fallen and are not longer covered by the grace of God; that you have compromised on your purity and therefore God has doomed you to suffering.

You need to deal with these very demonic thoughts very seriously. The grace of God is NEVER removed from a human. NEVER. It wouldn't be grace if it were removable.

A real mother or father will NEVER EVER STOP LOVING AND PROTECTING their child, EVER EVER EVER. If yours did, they're not your real mother or father. Even if they were the biological producers of your body, they are not the parents of your soul. In our times, angels and human souls have walked in like that all over the place, because we need our human army here like never before at this time.

God is your real parents and there is nothing you can ever do that will disqualify you from being the beloved, cherished, protected child of God. Your life, your body, your sexual energy are sacred to someone, and you must heal and protect and nourish yourself for when you make love to the love of your life. As a human with a soul, it's a guarantee they're out there.

You've gotten mauled by this demon but you can never be destroyed because your body and life are generated by your soul, and your soul is a piece of God, indestructible eternally.

MOON IN SAGITTARIUS

No one knows this but their mother, I guess; how they're always watching, observing and collecting up this database full of deadly information, that they know is deadly and will come in hand, someday, at the right time.

This warrior has the amazing ability to always be in touch with the time. The right time to say something, the right time to do something. The inner clock of a living being is so much more than something which clocks the hours of daylight and night. It literally keeps us in our place in the universe, as the great forces of nature move around and over us.

This amazing gift of knowing the time, makes this warrior be able to take a stand for the things they believe in, and complete what they started. They are amazing in a team, or alone, because they have the timing right.

They have a very "Shepherd" instinct towards others around them, always trying to look after everyone and see that everyone's safe and so on. This can make them come across as minding others' business, by those who cannot recognize love. But this warrior really doesn't care for others' opinions.

This warrior has an excellent head for numbers and the progressions of time. It makes them able to estimate and predict many things.

He or she is a natural magician; able to take a little and make it a lot, take one thing and use it as another.

They have an intense inner urge and longing to set the world back to balance, and they are constantly, in one way or another working towards setting things right for the people they love, their environment and so on.

They have a fiery temper that flares up whenever they perceive injustice or even imbalance somewhere. Justice is such a core value to them that it pretty much dictates their personal ethos in relationships and their lives in general. For example, they will not continue to be friends with someone who has done an injustice.

They instantly take up the case for the downtrodden and the underdog. They will go to great lengths, do what it takes to help someone they believe has been wronged.

This warrior's great weapon though, gift of the Moon in them, is their immense psychic and other extra-sensory consciousness reading ability. They are quite unlimited in their abilities; only their fear of being exploited ever actually limits them. Being exploited is something they have to contend with a lot, because it is very clear from a very young age, to abusers and exploiters all around, that this is human is an old soul, a magus and has the power to change consciousness around them.

They will literally change the energy of a room the second they enter, simply because of how potent and huge their energy field is. They are like a strong wind moving about. I know about this myself because my son is this placement and when he comes into the kitchen even silently, I tend to drop things, because it feels like a huge energy wind entered. The magnetism is huge.

Whatever this magus decides to do, they will do well. Their challenge is their home environment. Unstable emotional environment – where they are not sure of who loves them can drain this human. They need emotional stability and security.

They do not usually find it though, not as much as they need, and this fuels their search for spiritual stability – a lifelong pursuit and one which brings them reward upon reward.

They are the sages of humanity who hold the consciousness of justice, peace and stability for us all.

So long as they're moving on their spiritual journey, they are happy. Staleness and shallowness tire them.

Demon – Moon in Sagittarius

This demon is always calculating things. Their mind is forever awake and calculating and quantifying and weighing this option versus that option. They rarely ever show this or share this with others though. This demon has a lot of secrets and keeps them.

They are manipulative of others from a young age, in the sense that they notice what motivates someone and what breaks or demotivates them, and they can use this to turn people on and off like switches.

For example, if someone in their sphere of control – everyone around them has to be controlled by them, by the way – is going on a date with someone they don't approve of them going out with, they will say something or do something just before the date, to completely psychologically and emotionally shatter the person.

They are extremely dangerous to have around even as a housemate or friend, because they want to control everyone and everything, and they have no scruples or limits to this, no matter how they present themselves as upholders of justice and helpers of those in need.

They have the personality profile of someone who is "rock solid and dependable" but that's because of how they perform when people around are in trouble – like they're the father figure or mother figure alpha male or female, who'll pick up the fallen and "tough love" them back into shape.

They poke their nose into everyone's business and will get very insulted when left out.

They come with a lot of "benefits" like free stuff they're always sharing, finding solutions for others' problems; but it's all really about control.

People imagine that this kind of person is good for them; but in reality, they find themselves drained, underperforming, having anxiety attacks, falling ill regularly.

This demon is a regular user of poisons and black magic to control those who are defiant of them, ex-partners, partners and even their own children. The chance of them using sedatives, aphrodisiacs, drugs to control others is very, very high.

And that is why you should not stay around this demon.

They CANNOT have an equal or fair relationship with anyone. They will want to be in control and constantly demonstrate that. If you're looking for a sexual abuse dominatrix, here's your candidate.

One reason a person attracts a demon who wants to control them into their lives is because of being abused by a controlling parent or authority figure in their childhood. There was covert or direct sexual abuse, that locked the child into a pattern where they need to be dominated and abused to feel turned on. The child attracts demons who want to control and dominate them, because these bring up subconscious memories that are hidden, and provoke the child into finding his or her release from that cycle of sexual and energy abuse.

Letting go of this demon might not end the cycle of attracting such a demon. You'll have to break the cycle, and it is broken by experiencing your sexuality fully without feeling bad that you need to be tied up or restrained or forced to orgasm. Love requires surrender. Always does. The demons use that to dominate us and we innocently get programmed, in a world where we cannot trust anyone, i.e. we haven't yet found the one we can trust; robbed of our faith that such a one even exists; we get programmed to needing to be dominated and forced to get turned on.

Take some time off and think about cultivating trust and believing in love again. A love in which you surrender completely. You might find the wrong person again, but don't give a f***. The right one, your eternal soul's other half is out there and your love is always going to them. That's your only real sexual relationship. All the others are just try-outs. Your real sexual relationship is existing from before. It is spiritual, and you are always connected to your Beloved. Cultivate trust in that sexuality that honors every part of you – mind, body, soul – give that love and know it will come back.

Believe in the miracle of it. Remove art and things that are anti-love and anti-miracles from your walls and devices. If you can find love in your heart, it means it exists. Surround yourself with all that reminds you of the reality of love.

Break the programming of "love is not real" in your life once and for all.

MOON IN CAPRICORN

This warrior is a perceiver of seasons and times and has an emotional calm and resilience where they are aware that the season or time will pass. They are emotionally the spine and backbone of the family, their team and so on, because of this.

This warrior has a keen and fearless perception of evil. They are simply unafraid of the depths of evilness. This makes them powerful judges of character and as they go through life, they become able to know things about a person very quickly as they refer to the database collected up in their memory.

An issue this warrior faces, is a deep-set criticism of themselves. This naturally is simply their ability to look at their own selves critically, without sugar-coating things. But because we are in the thug realm, outside influences can warp that powerful ability into something that holds this warrior back, instead of empowers him or her to be the best version of themselves. They can go into depression because of this.

The good news is, this warrior also rises like a phoenix after going through the darkest inner times. They rise, shaken but forged into a weapon that is able to see through mind games and trauma programming. They develop crystal clear mental ability to see through thug emotional manipulation tricks.

This warrior will protect the ones they love from emotional manipulation. If you recognize emotional manipulation, you can stop an abuser from progressing further and save yourself much harm and time and energy.

Therefore, this warrior is able to save time and energy and drastically increase their own efficiency and quality of whatever they produce. They are an absolute whiz.

Their love is a strong, steady love that builds things from ground up. Slow to start but established forever. Pets love this emotional grounding and stability they have.

Demon – Moon in Capricorn
This demon is a mental pugilist – or attacker. They develop the ability to use facts and figures and do sudden compelling hits. This is greatly prized in the world of business and commerce, but surprisingly it's main use is in the world of religion and politics which is religion's illegitimate baby. This demon finds a place wherever they need someone who can attack verbally, or write speeches for public speakers and so on.

They are quite heartless and often don't pretend to have a heart either. But once in a while, if they get mentally enamored by the prospect of a relationship, they can absolutely have someone eating out of their hand, and then trap them with sudden and expected mental violence.

The danger of this demon is the mental assault. They aim to make you doubt your very foundations if you so much as question some small thing they said. Once they believe someone is their mental enemy, they will quickly make the home, and wherever, the battlefield because they cannot tolerate ANYONE being mentally superior to them.

If you're in a relationship with this demon, and you're more "educated" in the world than them, know they will at some point punish you for that. And it's rare for them to get into relationships with anyone who challenges them mentally, but if you are such a one, know that if you don't get out, you could be driven to breakdown because this demon is not ever going to let you be an equal. They WANT to be the mental or intellectual superior. They cannot relax or feel safe until they are. And don't imagine you can fool them either. They know when someone's more intelligent than them. They can get dangerous, so I recommend you don't wait to find out to what extent they can go. It's not about their pride. It's about their basic feeling of safety. If they're not the more intelligent one, they won't feel safe and that can drive them to do stuff they wouldn't otherwise consider.

MOON IN AQUARIUS

This warrior is a artist that can bring out the most complex deep emotions in a surprising simple way. They are able similarly to penetrate through much and understand emotionally layered and complex people and situations very simply and effectively.

They are constantly pulled towards escaping the world where their experience of life is dictated to by others and the mass consciousness. They want to experience life in its raw form, like they're the first man or woman to experience it. That want to experience the raw first truth of everything drives this warrior into a search that sometimes goes outwards into the world, and sometimes inside into their own depths.

Their search for this basic pure experience has then trying out many different things, passing them over and then maybe even returning after a long while. There's an inconstancy in their lives when seen from the outside, because of this. But in fact, they are like the waves of the ocean that go out at low tide and then surely come back at high tide. It's just a different rhythm from others. But in their own way they are as dependable as the tides of the sea.

They are passionate about what they love and passionate in love (like all humans but just a tad more crazy). This means however that if someone doesn't match that passion, they will find themselves suddenly and unceremoniously cut out. As this warrior's level of passion is rare, they're more often than not nursing a broken heart.

And this is this warrior's greatest challenge. Getting over the fact that they are very rare in the way they love, and that their soulmate or the one for them is equally rare. It's not their looks, or whatever that made someone love them less, it's that they just didn't actually love them. It's a rule of nature, that when person A loves person B, if person B really loves person A, their love reaches the same level of passion in both of them, because their love is joined into one. If person B's passion level is different, it's because they are not IN love together.

That's all this warrior needs to know and remember.

This warrior's greatest weapon in spiritual warfare is how they know instinctively who's the driving force and emotional stirrer up and enabler of someone attacking them. They are able in the moment to not get so carried away by an attack itself as to not notice where the emotional energy and intention to hurt came from.

This warrior is constantly being attacked by enemies who hide behind others; a feature from his or her childhood; and this has trained this warrior without them even knowing it, to always know who's the real enemy.

Holistically this warrior's brain develops over time to look for the root of the problem in everything. Others may not understand how they solve a problem, but they do. They are the magic of God, that God brings into people's lives just to carry this consciousness that uncovers and reveals hidden things that carry the secret to real solutions. In other ways, they are the answer to the prayer of those who are stuck in stalemates, unable to get a breakthrough and so on. Just this warrior's presence makes things happen.

Demon – Moon in Aquarius
This demon comes across as someone without motivation and a rather accepting of everyone and everything type. Someone who'll be friends with whoever is around, doesn't judge others really and just really gets along with everyone.

But it's a false ceiling. This demon is highly judgmental, critical and can tear someone down in a matter of seconds. Only they reserve this for those who they are sure are absolutely unable to hit back or defend themselves.

This demon nurses deep grudges against his or her parents, family or caregivers. They believe themselves damaged and their lives spoiled because they did not get a head-start at life. They are always cankering after the past inside, and it's sometimes like their heads are screwed on turning back, because that's where they're always looking. Their decisions are based on the past.

Anyone in a relationship with this demon should really leave before their spirit gets crushed and their very body's vital energy gets drained by the toxicity of this demon.

They are very anti-life in every way, to the point where they can actually murder and not really feel anything.

Their weakness is compliments and they can behave like an adoring puppy around people who give them compliments for anything.

MOON IN PISCES
This warrior is essentially a spiritual warrior first and last. From childhood, they become aware of the flow of emotional energy within the family and between people. By the time they reach their twenties, they are already experienced enough to be very emotionally mature and know how to comfort people and relieve the atmosphere of tension.

They tend to have an excellent sense of humor and be able to make everyone relax.

They are extremely intelligent, quick to understand things and also quick to know what a person is interested in. They are often led to helping people deal with trauma, find God and so on.

The most amazing thing about this warrior is their unshakeable faith in God, based on a relationship with God. These are words thrown around a lot, but they are actually true for this wonderful person.

How I would love to meet this warrior in person – because what a lighthouse they are for those on stormy waters... Surely God even brings such a person to others, as a sign that they have reached a safe shore.

I must have had close family and friends with this placement, Ed, because I am close to tears remembering the radiance of their soul, their embrace of love and the sweet comfort of their presence. I don't believe anyone could be lonely in the presence of this person.

And I don't believe this person would not be able to heal anyone from their most terrible wounds and set them on their path again.

They are a natural repairer of broken things and maybe God gives them experience in that – as their lives tend to have been broken a lot. They find their own way to God, forging a path made up of bits and pieces of whatever God brings them on the waters.

They have a deep and great love for humanity. They can take it to heart and be seriously depressed when they read the news. So it's very important for them to read my writings and know that humanity's heart is well and in the right place as usual. Demons in the guise of humans are doing those horrible things.

When this warrior takes it upon themselves to actively face demons, they are utterly formidable, because few HATE evil so much as them. They cannot be bought, manipulated, coerced, blackmailed. They will hunt down evil and save their loved ones, and in doing so save the world.

It is their destiny and nothing can change it.

Demon – Moon in Pisces

This demon is a low-down money grabbing miser. They've got a map in their head of who owes what to who, who's doing who a favor and for what in return. They're constantly watching the power struggle between people as one gets the upper hand and the other goes beneath and then the one beneath comes back up and the other goes down.

This demon turns to all kinds of spirituality, magic and so on to understand the working of fate and therefore develops quite a good understanding of how energy works on the basic psycho-physical or psychosomatic level.

They are adept in using herbs and other substances to control people, lure people and even heal a little – enough to make someone go back to them.

They are – in their heads – the king or queen of an empire and they steadily cultivate through various means, the trust and esteem of people around them, very carefully building a network.

The aim in doing this, is to collect emotional energy and deploy the whole network against someone they're jealous of. Because jealousy is their constant companion. In fact, you could say, this demon is the personification of jealousy.

They will walk into a party, walk around looking to see who is the one with the most power in the room; then they will feel jealous of that person; and then they'll start cultivating their network or empire, to leverage to hit and bring down that person.

They often use blackmail, and quite openly too, to get people to fear them and be in their network that way. Ultimately that network itself one day turns against this demon and then this demon ends up having to leave that place and go somewhere else and start all over again. They end up having lived in many places and had many marriages, as a result.

They don't keep their promises or even try to. They're all about what they can get from every relationship, even with children. They frequently use children and pets to control the parents.

One of their common ruses is pretending to be really passionate about music, or art or books – of which they tend to have a large collection depending on how much money they've had access to; but it's a smokescreen to attract high energy individuals into their network.

No one really takes this demon seriously though, in the long term. And you shouldn't too. Because they WILL cheat on you.

SUN – AWARENESS, ILLUMINATION, MANIFESTATION

Dear Ed, I almost tremble at the prospect of trying to put into words the magnificence of the light body that rules life in our realm the most directly and powerfully. To say we are, each of us, little pieces of the Sun is an understatement. It is true of all the heavenly bodies above, Ed, but none is so close to the manifestation of us as a unique separate individual as the Sun.

The Sun, Ed, is the lifeforce of our father that began our lives, both physically and as a soul. It is the life-force that has continued to cycle within us and will for all eternity though we might change our bodies many times. It is our eternal first force of existence, Ed.

Demons might make "babies" for all kinds of reasons, Ed. But natural living beings are secure in the circle of Life, every single one of us emanating from the pure Love of God and nothing else. It is that, Ed, which reason itself fails to describe, because it is simply something we can only experience.

Only someone who has loved can understand, Ed, what is the Sun.

Not only are we made from the Soul of the Sun, Ed, He sustains us all our lives here in this realm, and all our existence in every realm. We can never be cut away from Him – not in the darkness place, as the great light that moves over us is just the brightest part of him.

He is also the darkness and the darkest part of the darkness is also full of his love. We are IN the Sun, Ed, forever and ever.

As this writing is about our spiritual weapons, Ed, that we're born with, I will focus on that.

The Sun, Ed, gives us our vision specifically, and awareness in general. If we are awake to anything, whether to the visible world of frequencies around us, or in the dark to the subtle forces; or awake with the cells of our bodies to frequencies and magnetism; or awake to our deep subconscious as in meditation; that is all simply the function of Sun in us, as that is the function that has made us awake in this realm – otherwise called Birth.

This Function of Awareness in us, or Illumination, Ed is directly equal to our Life energy or vital force. The more spiritually present we are in our bodies, the more vital energy we have in our bodies. This we get directly from the Sun.

As our awareness or presence in the body increases, our Sun or life force increases and with it, automatically all the other heavenly body's functions increase. So, when we increase our Sun function – or Awareness or Presence; we activate all of our other functions, all of which require and are triggered by Sun.

So our very basic ability to know who we are, and know our place in space and time, know what we want in life, are all Sun function.

In plants, the Sun makes a plant know, "I am a rose plant. I must make green leaves and red flowers." Every living being knows itself and manifests itself according to its own nature because of Sun function.

That function of Awareness, IS Manifestation, is Sun function.

In spiritual warfare, Ed, the first point of attack is always our sense of identity, because that's the key to ALL of our powers.

Identity is the key, Ed, to everything in the universe. The universe has all this stuff available and you get whatever you need based on who you are.

It's a big supermarket, and you can take whatever you want based on who you are. If you're a camel, you can come in and get all the grass or hay you need to grow up as a camel and be a camel and make camel babies.

If you're a whale, you can come in and get the ocean and all the life forms of the ocean that keep you a whale.

If you're a dragon, you can come in and get all the things you need to be a being of fire.

As a human, if you are AWARE or AWAKE to the experience of being an artist, you can download all that you need to keep being an artist, all that will help keep your fingers strong, keep you envisioning beauty and then expressing that out.

Whatever you believe yourself to be, on a core deep level, you will manifest that, and all that enables that.

Is that not a high magic we are all doing all the time, Ed? We are taking the memory in our DNA which corresponds exactly to our SOUL memory, and we are manifesting that in this time and place – literally creating our bodies, so unique each one of us.

Now, Ed, as this writing is about spiritual warfare, I'm going to focus on how each Sun placement relates to spiritual warfare in particular in our times.

To do this, Ed, I have to explain two things;

1) Loosh or manifested energy in the human energy field, and how it is drained out
2) How the Sun works with Mars in each warrior's field to give them an advantage that cannot be resisted or stopped.
   Knowing this, Ed, will make a person be able to sharpen the very tip of their weapon and achieve pin-point precision and devastating results.
   To do this, we will first have to do homage to the great Throne, MARS.

MARS – THE ABILITY TO TAKE ACTION; RESIST, PREVAIL

I think this heading says it pretty clearly, Ed. You know, my love, the more I look at myself and others, I see how we get so much training, in our times, in daily life, to do violence. The tv shows, and even just the language in daily life is full of violence.

This, Ed, is because the thugs need to make us the population constantly release trauma hormones into our blood and be in the trauma frequency – because that's the only energy they are able to work with anymore.

I've written a book called "The Pain Eaters" which explains this even more.

But essentially, Ed, we are constantly subjected to violence and violent language – violence from radiation assault, from poisoning, in the media we watch and even in relationships – whether that's emotional or physical or sexual.

I follow an account called "Liberty Beans Coffee" on Instagram and it's run by a sports team coach, who pretty much posts sports team motivation posts thinking he's promoting the coffee. It just comes out. And he says stuff like, "Crush it," and "Kill it." And you know, Ed, that is Mars.

In previous times, sport- was about fun and relaxation. It can no longer be that, because the population is now adrenalized and in trauma. Sports is now spiritual warfare, whether we like it or not; and a human coach has to get his team up to spark with that.

"Get out there and have fun," will not win a sports game, or any game, these days.

If you're playing for fun, that's great. But if you want to actually win any game now, you'll have to "Crush It".

In fact, to be honest, we have to have the "Crush it," attitude, even to get through the week in our times, because we are all under such severe assault, even if it's just from the mass consciousness.

But that's where Mars, comes in.

This great manifestation of God, gives us to the ability to TAKE ACTION THAT CHANGES THE SITUATION. Taking action, isn't about just getting up the energy to do something about our situation or problem; it's about the intelligence to know how and where to focus our energy to achieve a result; and then prevailing or repeating or defending that first move, with move upon move till we achieve a lasting change.

This great power to change the very forces of the universe is Mars.

It is also therefore the power to resist forces pushing us in directions we don't want to go. It is the power to be resilient, when times are bad or when we're under fire for our choices, under pressure.

And the great God force of Mars, Ed, gives us courage.

SUN AND MARS COMBINATIONS – SEXUAL ENERGY STABILITY, ENERGY FIELD DEFENSE AND ASSAULT, SPIRITUAL AND PSYCHIC AWARENESS

Why I'm combining the Sun and Mars together, Ed to reveal a person's spiritual warfare weapons, is because they intrinsically reveal a person's ability to withstand energy field assault, do energy field assault, and very importantly, reveals their sexual energy force.

This sexual energy force, Ed, is very simply the sexual energy stability they have. In our times, Ed, nine out of ten assaults of ANY kind are aimed at breaking a person's sexual or hormonal stability. And if we want to defend ourselves, we must be able to defend our sexuality, sexual force, and maintain sexual stability.

All the time, Ed, all the time, when demons are interacting with a human, they are interacting with our sexual force. We humans very rarely like to face this reality, because most if us meet and engage with a lot of people and it is an incredibly unsettling idea, that the people we are engaging with, are actually engaging sexually with us.

It is not our intention, and perhaps not even the demons' mentally. But a demon in our times cannot engage with another, not even their own mother or father without sexual engagement; because they are massively energy drained right now, and they cannot go get energy from an emotionally charged environment like a sports game, or concert or a memorial to a tragedy. Those days are gone.

They cannot get energy that will truly sustain them, from simple emotional interaction, or mental stimulation, anymore. They try and it helps them a very tiny bit. But they need sexual energy, desperately. That's the only energy they can actually feel fed with, enough to help them get out of the mind-slump they go into as their energy levels drop.

So, if you want to actually protect yourself, forget being more proactive as a spiritual warrior, you will have to first learn to become aware of your sexual energy, which is your root, or basic vitality, that's centered in your deep abdomen and pelvic zone. You'll have to become aware of how people affect your vitality levels, because you'll know immediately from your own sexual energy level if someone tried a steal on you.

A lot of people, Ed, have friendships and relationships where, after the interaction, they don't feel sexual; they've numbed themselves. After the interaction they feel non sexual for days, out of sync with their own selves, tired. There could be mental motivation and excitement but it doesn't translate to physical energy, like REAL motivation should.

That's because they've been sexual energy assaulted.

Most people in our times, have to live and work in environments that are sexually and energetically assault environments.

Those who do will know immediately what I'm talking about. You feel you have to sexually numb out, or emotionally numb out just to be there, to function there. You can't be yourself in all your beauty there – because it's coming at you from the mass consciousness that you don't qualify to be beautiful. You're not the right color, shape, size, race, income level; to be beautiful.

I am writing this from the Spirit of God, to help humans understand and negotiate these environments and interactions.

A HUGE function of spiritual warfare is psychic or spiritual awareness.

In the following readings, Ed, where I have written separate descriptions for Sun in Aries (for) example, with Mars in either a water, fire, earth or air sign; ALL FOUR DESCRIPTIONS will be more or less true for the person; only the one that matches where their Mars is, TENDS TO BE the one that's most accurate to them.

If for example they have other planets in majority water signs, or other signs, that can influence them too.

So I would recommend that you read all four descriptions for your Sun Sign and follow your instinct to pick up what your spirit needs to hear.

The same with the demon signs. Read all four descriptions to understand how they do their energy draining and what sort of psyche or ethos you're dealing with.

SUN IN ARIES with
MARS IN ARIES, SAGITTARIUS, LEO – THE FIRE SIGNS

This warrior carries tension around the back of the neck, from all the things they sense but don't allow to come through into awareness. They have strong clear psychic vision and instinctively know if someone intends harm for them or their loved ones.

They are trained in spiritual warfare from past lives and instinctively know things about energy defense and assault as a result.

They have a problem with how they communicate, as that's the one thing that's different between past lives and now. How people communicate now, is different. Communication is also the frontline of assault in our times, where the majority of assault is done via words. This warrior needs to learn to follow their instinct about what the person MEANS rather than what the words they're saying or have sent through mean. They get into energy knots because they suppress their instinct, and tell themselves the words don't mean that. Forget the words, believe your instinct.

Learn to communicate what you want to say, and know the difference between what you mean and what you want them to think you mean. This is not always deception. For example, if you want to tell a teenager that the boy she's infatuated with is a loser, a bastard and a criminal, you can't tell her that in those words. You need to know that you're trying to tell her he's a dangerous boy who could get her into trouble too. You'll have to convey that to her in gentle language.

Very few people are this warrior's level of energy or forthrightness, or willingness to see and stand up for the truth. Very, very few. Ok, almost no one.

This means, this warrior has to stand alone, or stand down most of the time. The sooner this warrior learns to stand alone, the better, because they'll fall ill and have energy blowouts if they keep standing down.

At the same time, this warrior is sought after by all and sundry to use this warrior's energy for their purposes. This warrior needs to choose his battles for himself. It's difficult because when someone loves like this warrior, he's there, she's there for all the battles the people around are facing.

A lot of the "people" around are unfortunately demons and energy vampires and so this warrior ends up fighting battles that can never be won and just drain them endlessly. It's time to sign out of relationships and involvements where the person themselves doesn't fight as hard as you. In fact, stop fighting others' battles. Let them go down. If they really want something they'll come back up and learn to fight their own battles.

You need to be with warriors of your caliber. They are those who personally actually really value truth, freedom and beauty; who walk the talk, practice integrity and don't give you bullshit to keep you engaged. Most importantly, they fight their own battles.

Demon – Sun in Aries Mars in the Fire Signs
This demon is intellectually stunted and actually acquires his or her worldview from whoever used or demonstrated the most force in his life. He is a worshipper and follower of whoever is most violent and can make an impact on others. This is can be disguised in many ways, even presented as a sort of intellectualism where they promote the "survival of the fittest" mantra as the reason why they worship violence so.

If this demon doesn't do physical violence, perhaps because of being in a situation where they cannot get away with it; they will turn to other forms of violence to control people. They are themselves critically insecure and they will notice and collect up information about people, what makes a person scared or insecure; and they will use that information to directly or psychically attack and control people.

They hold on to money, collecting a lot, to use as an intimidating factor, because people are scared to mess with those who have a lot of money. Their every move is about increasing their covert and subtle intimidation of others through having money, showing power over others and so on.

This demon will never be able to be in an equal relationship with anyone at all. And there is no amount of submission you can do to satisfy them. "You cannot stoop low enough to please the devil." Life for others will be a constant string of either submission and humiliation, or defiance and punishment. You'd have to go sadistic and like master-slave bondage games to keep alive.

Humans who have been abused in childhood and cannot remember it or have pushed it to their sleeping memory, will frequently get attracted to this demon, to try and exhume the buried memory of abuse. It can be a life changing experience for a human to rise up and take a stand for their own dignity and human rights and throw this demon off. It's not difficult because this demon is an insecure coward, very worried about his or her reputation and the money really can't go VERY far these days.

SUN IN ARIES with
MARS IN CANCER, PISCES, SCORPIO – THE WATER SIGNS
This warrior is an incredibly powerful psychic and spiritual visionary, with the ability to transmute or change energy from one form to another.

An example of this ability, is the ability to record a beautiful song and then make a video for it and produce this confluence of vibrations of different kinds that's breathtakingly beautiful and affects you on so many levels.

In every area of their lives, these warriors transmute energy from one type into another. They change money into happiness, sound into song, words into poetry; they use whichever kind of energy they have available to make the lives of those they love comfortable. Liquid sunshine is what they are.

They are amazing motivators of those who are emotionally destitute or wounded and will often take up careers where they lift up or buy that which is unvalued and discarded or broken; which they will repair or restore and re-introduce as a working, effective thing or being.

They are wonderful with plants and gardening.

This warrior's weakness in terms of spiritual warfare, is their innate unwillingness to call a spade a spade, because they're so used to converting things to use, restoring the broken, that it's very hard for them to actually ever believe something is not fixable or usable.

They could end up collecting a lot of junk in their lives because of this. They find it near impossible to let go of things or people who they have the slightest hope for change in.

They get trapped in cycles of despair for this reason.

It's important for this warrior to upgrade their energy sensing and powerful psychic powers to where they begin to look into the future and see what their instinct tells them about a person or project. WILL this person ever change? WILL this project turn profitable?

Note that the word is, "WILL" not "CAN". Everything is possible in this world but not everything WILL .

So go prophetic and ask, "WILL this change?" And believe your answer. Keep asking yourself this, and keep asking for a sign from God till you get your answer.

If this warrior learns to distinguish between what CAN change and what WILL change or WANTS to change; they can seriously up their game and keep their amazing energy and so such magic.

Demon – Sun in Aries, Mars in the Water Signs

This demon is a good for nothing loser. I don't know how else to put it, Ed. This demon has zero money sense and only knows to spend it. The demon cannot manage money and only a fool would ever, for any reason let them manage their money.

They have bouts of conscientiousness where they pretend like they're not going to waste their money, they're going to think of the family and children, but it's just a temporary fling.

They cannot be depended on for anything. They're basically spineless.

One deception they have that makes people think they're dependable types, is that they tend to have lives that look very stable. They'll be visiting the same neighborhood bunch of shops their whole lives, listening to the same music, have the same books on their table, generally watch the same genre of movies.

But it's not stability, it's clinging on to these things to give their spineless lives structure, so others think they HAVE a life.

Their greatest game is getting the sympathy of people who are kind hearted. They give them this story of their life where they're just an ordinary person who is trying so hard to beat the system; but they got broken because someone dumped them, and their mother had cancer, and their dog died and their foot got run over by a car... You get the picture.

They are spineless, say bye, no hope here.

SUN IN ARIES with

MARS IN TAURUS, VIRGO, CAPRICORN – THE EARTH SIGNS
This warrior has vision so sharp it could cut you. And they're very rarely afraid to speak up for it too. They are not very popular because of their ability to see things and people for what they are.

As a spiritual warrior, they can be sent to the very frontline of defense because they are a wall that can't be climbed. The phrase "the buck stops here," applies to them. You cannot bullshit this person.

The weakness of this warrior is their utterly unhinged kindness and mercy for all that is small or vulnerable and needs nourishment and love. Their heart just opens like the sun and shines on whatever needs care and love and they'll go down on their knees and look after someone or something they feel this fatherly protectiveness for.

They will fight for the right of those, put their all into it and hold nothing back for themselves.

This beauty of theirs is exploited much in our times and this is precisely why I am writing this, Ed, so that people like this will stop getting swept away by appearances and learn to spiritually discern between what's a solid actual natural living being and what's a thug world simulation or fake natural being.

This warrior, so very real and capable of seeing the truth like an XRAY machine, needs to use that to look into the very soul of every being and see if there is indeed a soul, or are they a cloud of matter being pushed around by an egoic entity with no actual soul of its own.

This warrior will begin to withdraw 95% or more of their energy spread – which is huge – when they filter out the fakes. This will result in them investing in their own lives and in what truly will return energy to them in one way or another, completing the energy cycle.

Humanity needs them to do this, as they are our heroes and heroines. The unconquerable great souls of consciousness who inspire us all to be strong and courageous and dream the impossible and do it too.

Demon – Sun in Aries with Mars in the Earth Signs

These demons are capable of sudden destructive violence. They have a rather pleasant outlook and personality. However, they are capable of great evil and trickery in relationships. They store up information on how to play people against each other, from childhood, and they begin to experiment doing this, very early on. They can be devastating when they're a trusted third person or family member in a couple's life. They get their sense of power in controlling relationships between people. If they're acknowledged as a power, they keep their interference to a minimum; but if they're not paid obeisance to, or they sense that two people are getting so close their energy field is closing around them; they'll pull out their database and consult their various sources (which can include astrologers and black magicians and even private investigators) and find out how to break those two up.

They develop an aura of "power" around them because of the violence inflict on people through their maneuvers.

This demon however is intrinsically an utterly powerless person, because no one really gives a damn for them emotionally. If they died no one would miss them. They know this because from childhood, they haven't had any real connection with anyone. They're a demon. They don't want love, they want that feeling of power a person in love has when they know someone wants and needs them. They believe that if they break people up, they will take that power from them.

This demon has a horrible hellish aura underneath the superficial "positivity" they might telecast. They are frequently in the media business.

One reason a human might attract such a person around them or into their lives, is because they quickly break up the relationships of whoever threatens their control over you; and this exposes all the fake relationships in your life. You don't want those anyway. The relationships that survive this demon are most probably good solid ones.

SUN IN ARIES with
MARS IN GEMINI, LIBRA, AQUARIUS – THE AIR SIGNS
This warrior is a surveyor and purveyor and taker of values. They have an inbuilt mechanism to know the quality and value of things, people, everything.

If a feather is more valuable than a brick of lead, even though the brick of lead is obviously so much heavier; they will know it, and they will say it too.

This is essential for warriors who are in lives where is a LOT of deception around them. And these warriors are surrounded by it.

They tend to have grown up in near complete confusion because of people around them not being either stable emotionally or upfront about their dealings. This made this warrior start at a young age to start figuring out and weighing things for himself or herself.

It's a long lonely road when you're surrounded by deception like this warrior has been.

Frequently this warrior has tried to put aside their instinct and search for loyalty, truth, faithfulness and steadfastness; to try and find some happiness and companionship in a substandard friendship or love. Their body is scarred and seared by that injustice they did to their own spirit.

They learn the hard way that a person has more strength, health and dignity, searching for the needle in the haystack, than calling hay a needle.

They become loners at some point and focus on standing up for themselves, expressing their own selves and accepting that the kind of quality of soul they seek is very, very rare. They give up their gregarious dream of big crowds of friends and all that; deciding that they'll just be single or be friendless or whatever, until they find someone worth their time and their heart.

The good news is, they always will. I just know this from my soul and that's why I'm making this statement. Because this is how it is for all true lovers and friends. You stop settling for second best or replacements, and you start being yourself; your frequency becomes your own and that gets telecast into the consciousness and brings your true love and true friends to you.

But because we're supposed to be talking about spiritual warfare; the thing is, this warrior's great ability is the ability to resist emotional manipulation and sexual seduction. This warrior can go into the pit of hell, with the most cunning emotional manipulators and seducers, and some out without having even gotten turned on or affected in the least.

That's because they have already seen so much deception even before they reach adulthood, that they can't be fooled that easy anymore.

When this warrior wants something from someone, they walk right in that person's door, straight up to them, eye to eye and asks them for it. 9.9/10 times they get it.

That's this warrior. Quality.

Demon – Sun in Aries, Mars in the Air Signs
This demon is a razzle dazzle kind. They've got all the various profiles on all the social media; and if they're the previous generation, they've got all the things used to seduce and engage people – books, music, knowledge about history and all that.

No matter what age they are, they have multiple romances or sexual engagements going on, and in fact they cannot have a relationship with even a rat without trying to see if they can push in a bit of sexual innuendo there.

They are capricious, undependable and shallow. They are obsessed with their looks and personality – which they imagine is irresistibly attractive and alluring. They have a circle of friends who agree with them and they definitely do not hang out with anyone that doesn't agree with them.

The danger of this demon is the way they can put in an attitude of disrespect of love, of life, into a person to where the affected person actually can go into depression because nothing feels real anymore. The affected person can stop investing in their own selves, in their health and lives, because of believing it's all not worth anything in the end. They can lose years of their lives in that feeling of un-realness, never know who the source of that is. Because this demon will never openly go against love or life, so it's very hard to imagine they're a negative person or spreading such anti-love consciousness.

This demon should be gotten rid of, even from one's thoughts, because that's where they do the damage.

SUN IN TAURUS with

MARS IN ARIES, LEO, SAGITTARIUS – THE FIRE SIGNS
This warrior is a collector of true value in their lives. Their strength is based on well thought out and well exercised and proven principles. If anyone is a man or woman of principles, this is that person. Because they have build their house upon a rock.

This warrior is a shelter and strength for many but very rarely is this warrior supported in their own life. They tend to be surrounded by people who need a lot of support and this one warrior often ends up supporting so many others.

This can drain and distract this warrior from their own life battle. We are in a time when we ARE fighting a battle. This warrior's battle is for the destruction of mind patterns in the mind that keep him or her feeling locked underground and away from beauty, hope, happiness.

They experience life in this world as a rather depressing affair, when deep down in them is the memory of such joy, freedom, and purity.

They want as children and young people to pursue those dreams of emancipation and personal freedom; but get weighed down by supporting others.

This warrior is a light in the darkness even in the deepest hell, but if they would prioritize their own pursuit of beauty and freedom from restriction; and let those people and projects go from their lives that they're entangled with, believing that those are somehow mandatory; those drains that have become habit; then they will flower in the human consciousness with the sweet smell of hope and beauty and happiness to support their real mates, us humans who need that light in the dark to guide us too, to beauty and happiness.

Demon – Sun in Taurus with Mars in the Fire Signs

This demon is a regular energy drainer. They know just how to stimulate people and get them excited about something. They work people up. After all that, they go missing for some days, or they say something that deflates the balloon of excitement. They do is very subtly as they grow older and get smoother.

These are very dangerous for children and young people to be around as this is serious emotional energy abuse.

These entities are very often involved in sexual abuse, of people of all ages. They stimulate and turn a person on, and then turn away or disappear and such, leaving the person hanging in confusion and not knowing what to do. This can be destroying and therefore this demon simply a very dangerous one.

Humans tend to attract this demon, to force us to face attitudes buried inside us, where we are antagonistic to our own progress in life. For example, like a parent or caregiver who made us believe that getting rich would be the end of our true relationships with family; or that if we became the head of a team or business, we would become proud and lose the people we love.

That sort of thing. Deep set beliefs that make us sabotage our own progress.

SUN IN TAURUS – MARS IN CANCER, SCORPIO, PISCES – THE WATER SIGNS

This warrior has a childlike ability to find his way, no matter where he or she is, because of how in tune they are with nature. They love rocks and all natural energy fields and a large part of their life's learnings come from interaction with natural energy fields.

They are incredibly perceptive of truth and lies, but most of the time they do not show when they know someone is lying. They are beings like the soul of animals in nature. They don't want unnecessary confrontations about philosophy or whatever. They seek peace, clarity and beauty above all.

This warrior's special weapon is their ability to escape traps set by predators, to get their natural energy that's so in tune with the earth and nature. They don't go around showing off much, but they are incredibly intelligent. You cannot catch this escape artist, either with cunning words, or philosophies or trickery of any kind.

They'll just show up as usual, when you thought they'd be out of circulation after what happened; but they'll be there, calmly continuing on as before never betraying that they know someone tried to con them, trap them, but failed.

These warriors can follow unconventional paths to self-realization, but something they all do invariably is buy or own land and other assets that enable humans and natural life to heal and just be natural.

These warriors often are sought after by secret services and investigative agencies, because of how they can walk in and out of anywhere safely, get information other more dramatic people can't.

These warriors won't stick around to say goodbye to their abusers or someone they don't want in their lives.

They have a deep love and connection to the physical earth and that shows in every area of their lives as time goes by. Stable solid love, prosperity, peace.

If anything is a weakness of this warrior, it is the way they can end up grieving for loved ones they have lost. Those who want to exploit this warrior, and force him or her into work or service with them; often organize the illness or death of someone close to this warrior, to try and get them in the aftermath of the shock.

Most of the time, this warrior cannot believe that that has actually happened though they know it is so deep down. This makes the whole thing be unfinished business and drains them.

So an important thing for this warrior to do is be very aware of how valuable they are to others.

Demon – Sun in Taurus with Mars in the water signs
This demon is incredibly sensitive to the emotional make of people and the emotional exchanges happening. This makes them able to imitate the art and other energy expressions of humans very well. They are great actors as a result. However, they are such great actors that almost no one knows they're acting.

They present themselves as angels of tranquility and peace. Their entire life is a performance. Only those very close to them ever realize that underneath the façade is a very jealous and actually bordering on lunatic person. They tend to believe that they are spiritually connected to "gods" and such, and they are, in fact aware of connections to disembodied demons.

Their ability to drain people of emotional energy makes them valuable to disembodied demons who need huge amounts of emotional energy or loosh, to survive.

Only, this demon is not the kind that can supply loosh regularly. It's the sort that takes years to set up a character profile and get close to a target, and then suddenly one day say one little thing, or do one little thing that emotionally devastates them.

In our times, the disembodied demons are dissipating fast and don't have time to wait that long, so these demons are being killed off.

SUN IN TAURUS with

MARS IN TAURUS, VIRGO, CAPRICORN - THE EARTH SIGNS
Ed, this warrior is a formidable one who cannot be shaken out of his or her position. They are incredibly intelligent and take their position or stand after a lot of inner questioning and looking at things from every angle. When they take their stand they're unshakeable.

These are that pillar of human consciousness that refuses to budge no matter what assault or attack you throw at it.

They are hell-bent on their aims, Ed, persistence like I cannot describe it. So long as it's what they want. Woe to the person that tries to control or drive this warrior towards something the warrior doesn't want. The energy of resistance of this warrior will destroy the one attempting to control it, and quite quickly too.

The very physical body of attackers will go weak because of the magnetism of this warrior.

If they have a weakness, it's that when they get into a rut, they don't get out quickly. I can't really call it a rut, because their soul has decided to take full advantage of studying and learning all there is to learn about a hell before leaving it; but it is something that troubles them. They get frustrated and even depressed.

The key to their getting out of ruts is to cut off from people who are depending on them to be in it, and because of who they got in, in the first place. These warriors get into trouble for helping out their friends. They'll try out new things just to cheer a friend up or be loyal to someone, and then they get stuck in it.

Invariably they begin to supply energy to a lot of so-called friends, projects, partners, while they themselves are frustrated, stuck and getting more and more depressed by the day.

The key is misplaced loyalty. When they withdraw their support from those who are using them, their energy gets released.

Demon – Sun in Taurus with Mars in the Earth Signs
This demon destabilizes people's foundations of belief and support, as a way to control them. For example, when they make a new friend, they'll quickly find out what the foundations of the friend's stability and faith in life are; and start hacking away at those. The friend finds themselves increasingly demotivated, but cannot figure out where the attack is coming from. Actually, they're being made to distrust and question some core beliefs of theirs, which connect them to their family and friends.

In daily life, we all go through those questionings as part of growing up. But this is different. This is done covertly, so the friend doesn't know it's happening so he or she can face it and discuss things and so on. All they experience is a sense of confusion and isolation from others.

Humans attract this demon when they are in false families, i.e., either they have been placed there through adoption, or are an angel that occupied a lab-made baby for the family, or they are an angel taken birth for some particular reason, in a demon bloodline.

This demon makes the angel question the core values they've been brought up upholding, and they end up leaving the fakes in their life and pursuing their own truth and their own spiritual core values. The process however is not very pleasant. Once you've read this, you know what's going on, you can move on without this demon hacking away at you.

SUN IN TAURUS with

MARS IN GEMINI, LIBRA, AQUARIUS – THE AIR SIGNS

This warrior's great weapon is his or her ability to quickly compare things, and notice the difference. It seems like not-so-important ability to have but in fact in daily life it is very important and in spiritual warfare is life-saving.

A foundational method of demons' spiritual warfare on us humans, is their hijacking human DNA and hijacking just about anything to get us to accept their evil.

Take the trojan horse for example. It looked like a big wooden horse toy. Most people have seen children's wooden toys of horses. Worldwide, kids love rocking horses and horses in general. But this 'Trojan Horse' was no normal horse. It was a big wooden horse toy that was hollow inside, and a whole army was in there. The people of the city let in the horse toy and wheeled it to the center of the city. There, suddenly the army inside the horse toy jumped out and took the city.

Now if this warrior we're talking about were there that day, they'd have known something was very wrong, because it's their God given gift, to remember what something is USUALLY like, including its magnetism and energy emanation; and know that what's in front of them is different. This would have opened their eyes and mind to look for clues to show what's different. And in a matter of seconds, they'd have known what was going on.

In every demon attempt on us, hijacking something acceptable and familiar to us, is a part of the game.

If demons for example, presented is some evil thing directly – like, "Let's go kill everyone in this country"; of course humans would refuse that. But if they work us up, calling on our love for our own country, calling on our loyalty to our country's "leaders"; then it's easy enough to get us to agree to wars upon wars.

But this warrior has the ability to compare things, and they are constantly doing that, so they become aware of the difference between the chocolate they ate of that brand last month, and the one they have now.

They know when someone is behaving different, even if ever so slightly, compared to yesterday.

They know when a child is being abused or bullied but can't say so. They know when someone's giving them lesser, or more, or a different quality of something compared to before.

This warrior therefore is incredibly powerful and effective spiritually. They become the voice for those who cannot describe what's happening to them. They feel someone's hurt or confusion before that person knows what's troubling them.

There is just no end to this power this warrior has.

If there's a weakness this warrior has, it's their fondness for sweet stuff. They find such little true stuff in the world today, that they look to the simple pleasures of food as something that connects them back to the times when they didn't know so much or see so much.

For most of them, this means sweet food. This can become a bit of an escape from reality, in times when they know something is not as it seems, but they have lost self-value because of some abuse; and so they look to sweet stuff and comfort eating to shut out facing what they know. The sweet stuff then begins to cause them various problems and it might come to them having to quit sweets.

The real problem is not the sweets, but the loss of faith in themselves that leads them to block out their own insight and vision; accepting stuff they know is not what it seems. If they fix this, they fix the sweets problem.

I am not this astrological placement, Ed, but I have the escapism into sweets problem. HAD, anyhow. I can bear witness, that once I decided that I was worth the battle, and faced my own powers of insight and knowing and accept my own version of reality; the sweets stopped causing me the many problems they were.

Demon – Sun in Taurus with Mars in the Air Signs
If ever there was a demon that constantly tricked one, while somehow getting away with it, pretending like they didn't do it on purpose and it was a misunderstanding, it's this demon.

It reminds me of the devil in the movie "Bedazzled". The devil gives the man (Brendan Fraser) who was desperate to get this girl to love him back, a wish, and he asks to be poetic, but the devil makes him so cheesy and boring as a poet that the girl he wants to fall in love with him gets bored. The man then asks to be rich; the devil makes him rich, but as a Mexican gangster, whose wife hates him and runs away with her English tutor. The man then asks to be a successful sports star; the devil makes him that, but with a very small d***. The man then says he wants to have a big d***, be very eloquent and good looking; the devil gives him all that, but now he's gay.

That's what this demon is like. They give you what you want, say all the right things; they're there for you when you want, but there's a price and it's not a small one. It ends up being the taking away, or holding away from you, of the most important things in your life, the things for which you go through all the struggles you do. This is this demon's form of feeling important and in control.

They keep stringing you along, and often make you feel bad for considering cutting off from them after all they've done for you. But you have to, because they're never going to be honest with you or anything. They're just playing you like a cat plays with its food.

SUN IN GEMINI with

MARS IN ARIES, LEO, SAGITTARIUS – THE FIRE SIGNS
This warrior is intensely curious about the working of energy and interactions between people. They have a love of making things

happen that seem impossible and it is what motivates them to get on through days of monotony and drudgery. They are fascinated by the magic of life that transforms what seems dead and useless, into amazing wonderful things.

They are very social and often have younger siblings or friends, who they mentor and take care of. They are emotionally very protective of everything sweet and gentle and pure because they know that this is the power of the universe.

They can be altogether ignorant of the evil side of life, even when growing up in an abusive environment; simply because they are so entranced by the magic of life in this world.

This warrior's great weapon in spiritual warfare, is their unfailing connection to the benevolent reality of God and nature, as GOOD. They have the faith and vision of a child no matter what their age, and this is something that demons find absolutely frustrating and unputdownable. You torture this warrior and he or she will be singing something the next day in his cell, fully sure that God is going to rescue them.

What can anyone do with an angel like this? They just win, win, win.

If they have a weakness, it's their reckless rushing out to help anyone with a cause; getting emotionally involved with people who need support and encouragement, and trying to mentor demons who only want to drain their youthful energy.

Keeping emotionally closed to all but those who are their true soul group is the challenge this warrior faces, if they don't want to be drained. It's difficult initially, but it becomes easy if they train themselves to look at people from their spiritual instinct, rather than their mind which is programmed by the thugs to like everybody, or almost everybody.

Demon – Sun in Gemini and Mars in the Fire Signs
This demon is one snake. It wriggles up close, with cute giggles and jokes and cute hair and cute chin and makes you feel like childhood again. And then, like those evil wives in the mythologies; like the wife of King Herod who asked for the head of John the Baptist; they ask you for something that's most precious to you, in exchange for them being in your life.

This demon does relationship terrorism covertly. They behave like a piquant child, and say, "If you really love me, you'll give me this." Or give me that, or do this and do that.

And you'll realize at some point they don't really care about you at all. The sooner you do, the better, because this is an emotionally manipulative demon and they will make you feel guilty for the rest of your life for abandoning them, if you're not careful.

SUN IN GEMINI with
MARS IN CANCER, SCORPIO, PISCES – THE WATER SIGNS
This warrior is a wonderful dancer and experiencer of the rhythms of the earth, and earth fields. They have a preternatural ability to feel earth fields to the point where they embody the earth energy at the place on the surface of the earth, where they love.

They are sexually very expressive and it shows in all they do and say. This embodying of the rhythms of the earth field wherever they are, is a wonderful and powerful source of healing for themselves and others. With it comes fresh eye-opening, fresh direction, fresh guidance.

They can change the lives of people with their ability to see things differently, as they're in the flow of the rhythms of the earth. They are amazing problem solvers as a result. Breakthrough artists.

This warrior really can find a way almost out of every bind, and will, too.

If this warrior has a weakness, it's his or her problem with fixing things that break. Because their energy is so fast flowing, they find it very hard to stop long enough to repair something that's broken. They're most likely to believe it's not for them and move on.

In fact, it's actually stress that makes them move on when there's a part of them invested in something broken. A lot of their life lessons are hidden in things they do that fail initially, perhaps because their passion seems too much for such an ordinary thing.

But they will save a lot of their energy and be a lot less stressed, if they learn to let themselves stop and linger and not be unnerved by slowness and stillness. A little more attention and the broken thing could be fixed, or if not fixed, a deep lesson can be learned.

Demon – Sun in Gemini with Mars in the Water Signs

This demon is a litigator or lawyer, whether professionally or not. This demon is committed to, from a young age, using words and the law and philosophies to justify whatever it is they want to do. They do not like living according the morals, or rules of the world and they are always finding ways to say things and finding ways to twist scriptures and sayings to get their way.

One of the first things others notice about them, is how they find ways and shortcuts around anything and everything. This makes them very valuable in the thug world.

This demon however usually does not get rich on his or her abilities because they mess with the wrong person at some point and be seen for the criminal they are.

Humans attract this demon to show us the beauty of faithfulness, loyalty and actual love – all of which this demon pretends to have but certainly doesn't. Humans learn to recognize real emotion from fake emotion from this demon.

SUN IN GEMINI with

MARS IN TAURUS, VIRGO, CAPRICORN – THE EARTH SIGNS

This warrior is full of dreams and wishes, but feels woefully under supported and restricted because of his or her circumstances. Every time this warrior tries to fly, tries to rise up and set themselves free, something or the other happens to pull them back down.

This is because this warrior, is a warrior first and everything else later. As children their peculiar magnetism is noticed by many, as the child shows they're different from other children in their pursuits. They always want to experience the feeling of freedom and joy without end; spiritual bliss.

They're happy for the toys, and the yummy things. But what they really want is to feel free as a bird, and joyful without restriction. They want to stand in the rain and let tears of joy pour down their face. They want to climb mountains and smell the air of freedom at the very tops.

But this very longing of theirs seems to trigger restrictions in their lives. Because their soul does not want to experience bliss as a form of escapism; where they'll have to come back down to hell after a few moments of joy.

It is for demons – that trip to the top and back.

The destiny for humans, is to actually change life itself so that those things we believe we can experience only at the tops of mountains or in the deep of the sea, we can hold and experience in our daily lives too.

This warrior really wants that. A life of true joy and happiness, infinite in every direction. This opens up to them all the things in their consciousness that stop them from experiencing that joy and living it and holding it. Their life feels like one long counselling session, where they're the counselor and the counselled.

They learn more in one month of their lives than others in many years.

They learn a LOT just surviving.

This writing of mine is just one of their many books on stopping energy drains and manifesting their own inner power.

This warrior just needs though, to learn to keep their secrets. Not everyone intends good for them. It's just that you save a lot of energy not having to deal with psychic attacks of jealous people, if you keep your plans and secrets to yourself.

Demon – Sun in Gemini with Mars in the Earth Signs
This demon is a spendthrift and carries the consciousness of poverty. They are glib liars and can come up with all kinds of stories to draw out emotion from listeners. This demon has a connection to his mother and a strong inherited build-up of how to manipulate particular sorts of people. This stops working when this demon is taken out of their home ground and to another environment. For this reason they will keep going back to their home ground, even though it destroys their career, marriage and so on.

This demon doesn't give a crap for anything or anyone. They just want the ego rush of an audience that thinks they're a wonderful person. Their real aim in life is gathering young people to "impress" and drain. Young people because God knows that anyone past a certain age of maturity will know that this entity is conning them in some way or another.

Every now and then they will have brilliant ideas, literally got from sucking up energy of the young people they've drained; someone else will implement that idea and this demon will then forever talk about how it was their idea but someone else somehow got wind of it and used it.

In demon hierarchies, they're all clones of clones of clones, so if one has an idea, there will be many getting the same idea at the same time. This is different from human consciousness, where what one human experiences, is available for all humanity to experience and build on, in real time.

If one human experiences peace and happiness, or anger or joy, all humans do not experience that surface emotion at that same time. Because we are not the exact same energy field or the same soul.

But what one clone carrying a demon experiences, all clones carrying that demon, experience that emotion, that idea and so on.

So this demon you know is actually in many bodies at the same time. You need to know this, and you will understand many things about them.

This demon will financially and energetically ruin you, so escape.

SUN IN GEMINI with
MARS IN GEMINI, LIBRA, AQUARIUS – THE AIR SIGNS

This warrior is mentally extremely adept at finding what is of substance in a piece of writing, or a movie or a book; and building a rock solid idea of what the reality of the environment is, based on that.

They have a strong brain that is capable of exploring all kinds of extremes, and extracting what is of value from those.

This warrior does not reveal their true self to others because from a young age, they have been exploited by people trying to take advantage of their talents – of which there are many. They become very cautious with what they reveal as they grow older and with very good reason.

They go through a period of life during which they are like wine that's aging quietly becoming more and more refined and pure. They develop into fine warriors through this process, their intellect becoming sharper and sharper.

This warrior has strong affinities for the uncles if he's a man, or the aunts if he's a woman. If this warrior is displaced into a family not his or her own then the connection builds psychically and in the consciousness. They are the inheritors of the uncles and aunts' anointing and consciousness, because those did not have natural children or did not have children.

As such these warriors are born with a great destiny and anointing.

Their own exact path might always be a little obscure to them, because God only shows them one step ahead at a time, as the actual height they are going to climb or their actual destination has to be kept completely secret at this time.

This warrior needs to be careful of children being used as a channel to drain them. Not all children are human children. Demons as children are easily trained to snoop, get information and do energy draining. Demons know this warrior's weakness for children and babies and often attack them through this.

The isolation this warrior goes into for survival is right and required. There are very few people worthy of this person. True love finds them though, even if they're in a cave far from everyone else.

That's a guarantee.

Demon – Sun in Gemini with Mars in the Air Signs
This demon is reckless and loose mouthed. They simply love to pretend like they're carefree fancy free overgrown kids just having a good time, hanging out with everyone free as a bird, singing songs, clapping and dancing and all that.

In reality they are somewhat mentally disturbed, in the sense that they do not follow the logic routes that others do. For example, if most people see a black heavy cloud and think it will rain; this demon sees the black heavy cloud as a sign that they should attack someone today. I cannot explain it as I don't understand it either, but their brain is tuned in some strange way, where they get triggered into doing evil things by this sort of "sign" and imagine that it's God or angels leading them.

They have a severe spiritual deception, often imagining themselves to be a great king whose harem is spread among the population waiting for him. Or queen. And they actually have multiple affairs with many people at the same time thinking it's their spiritual calling.

They're in a simulated hyper emotional state even if they don't show it all the time. It's very tiring for others around them. They just are in a mental zone of drama that's demonically arranged to attack several people, emotionally accuse people of things, sexually drain and dump people saying "I made a mistake, you're not the one," and just all that sort of thing.

They present themselves as emotional but actually they're heartless cold-hearted psychopaths.

SUN IN CANCER with

MARS IN ARIES, LEO, SAGITTARIUS – THE FIRE SIGNS
This warrior is an extremely calm, lucid person who is able to keep their head for a long time, until they see that something they want to achieve has a chance now. It's about timing for them. They are able to wait patiently for the particular time when they know the shot will reach the target. Something like David and Goliath, Ed. David let Goliath do his yelling and prancing about, waiting till Goliath was exactly at the right point and position, for the pebble to reach its target.

This warrior has this particular ability. To know the timing.

This warrior's weakness is hanging out with people, women mostly, who aren't focused in their lives. When you keep company with people who are shallow and unfocused, it holds you back too. This warrior hangs out with this sort of person because they aren't too charged up and going out and getting into fights and all that. In an ideal environment, this warrior would be with real humans like that. Chilled out, calm, people. But in our environment, with demons, this warrior gets stuck with shallow entities that actually drain him or her of energy on a slow, steady drip.

This warrior is deeply passionate and keeps it a secret, as well they should. Whether they know it consciously or not, they are the warrior who will come out of nowhere and shoot the final bullet or arrow. People take them for granted, who don't know how deep this warrior's heart, and with it, strength and even knowledge go.

They might not be the fount of knowledge about trivia and current affairs, but the things they care about, they've gone deep into. When they talk, they know what they're talking about.

They often suddenly discover or invent things that were under everyone's noses all along but couldn't see.

They are also excellent negotiators between warring or disagreeing parties.

For some reason, they have a tendency to slip, and should wear shoes or slippers with grooves underneath; keep away from very shiny "mirror" clean floors.

Demon – Sun in Cancer with Mars in the Fire Signs
This demon is an imitator of whatever they feel wins the trust of others. Their game is winning people's trust, finding out information about them that others would not, and then psychically attacking them.

Their warfare is mostly psychic because they're too cowardly to confront anyone about anything ever. But they can do real damage psychically, because when we trust someone, we open our energy field and consciousness to them.

A sign that they are this demon is, they tend to wear threads around their wrist or ankles a lot. Not once in a while like most other people. They tend to always have something tied, like thread is knotted – not like a pre-made bracelet of beads, but something they or someone tied, around their wrist or ankle. It's just something common to this lot.

They also are quite focused on how they look and practice delivering dialogues in front of the mirror. They have this game where they pretend they're looking at themselves in the mirror but are actually looking at others, who think they're too absorbed in themselves to notice.

They get a lot of private information from people while talking about themselves. For example, they'll be talking about what happened to them that day; this will make the other person think they're mentally absorbed in that and put their guard down. Then suddenly this demon will ask the other person a pointed personal question and the other person will blurt out the answer as they're not on guard.

This demon cares for no one, not even their mother. They just like to have a lot of broken people around them, broken by them psychically, who they can pretend to feel sorry for and so on.

They cannot know anyone personally without trying to break them emotionally.

SUN IN CANCER with

MARS IN CANCER, SCORPIO, PISCES – THE WATER SIGNS
This warrior is no stranger to the fact that people aren't what they seem on the surface. This warrior has the ability to constantly be in touch with the subliminal and subconscious triggered body language and vibes of people.

They like to spend time with children and the older generations who do not have much of a difference between the subconscious and the conscious energy telecast.

They find it tiring to constantly have to negotiate the contrast between what people are projecting consciously about themselves versus what their subconscious is projecting.

This warrior needs quiet, privacy and much rest for this reason. They should not numb out their great gift of being aware of the undercurrents beneath what's happening around them. This is their great gift from God. Instead, they should retire to their safe space as much as possible and slowly train themselves to consciously be aware of what they're sensing, and accept what their instinct is telling them.

This warrior's way out of every problem is destined to come by way of their inner knowing based on the subconscious telecasts of people around. They know what the other person is thinking deep down, that the other person doesn't know themselves, that they themselves are thinking.

This is huge.

This warrior shouldn't tell others what they know. Keep it secret, and trust God to show the way to work with this ability.

This warrior's weakness is trusting people they know from their childhood, just because they know them from childhood. Childhood for them is a magical place in memory – no matter how hard it was – they believe the world was in fact what they believed it then to be.

This is simply not true. And in fact a lot of the people this warrior knew in childhood were demons and many of them secretly were jealous of this warrior and looking down on them behind their back.

This warrior needs to clear out from their life, people who don't respect their gentleness and their forbearance and toleration. Keep only those who treasure you, even if that's one or two. And if there's no one, well, good riddance to them all.

Demon – Sun in Cancer with Mars in the Water Signs

This demon is incredibly astute in finding out what hurts people, what motivates them and so on, and then using that extremely cruelly, to sadistically watch them be in pain. This demon's self confidence is rooted in their ability to make people say "Sorry" to them. They constantly create situations where they come across as the angel who was just trying to help, but others misunderstood their innocent attempts and now they're hurt and Sorry should be said.

They do lots of energy draining by sitting down with people and having long drawn discussions about who said what, and how it felt, and what it meant, and why it meant that, and how it feels now, to know what it meant before versus what we now know it to be.

This bullshit will never end, because this demon feeds off this.

Just get really far, really quickly, there's nothing of value here to any human.

Humans attract this demon when the human's life has gotten so full of bullshit, they need someone to drive them over the top and make them cut off from society and go seek real meaning in life instead.

This demon is always giving gifts and expecting others give them back gifts. Be really careful not to engage in the gift giving thing, because they use those things to energetically and psychically access you later.

SUN IN CANCER with
MARS IN TAURUS, VIRGO, CAPRICORN – THE EARTH SIGNS

This warrior doesn't beat around the bush or like those who do. They are incredibly straightforward people, who value things between them and others being clear and on the table.

This warrior's weapon in spiritual warfare is their clear-headedness when it comes to interactions between them and others, and others and others too. You put them in a room and in fifteen minutes they'll know the equation between most of the important energy influencers in the room, enough to control the whole atmosphere – if they wanted to. Which they never want to – and that's their weakness.

They are incredibly self-critical. I don't know why. Most of them are just obsessed with trying to be the perfect person that they already are. Maybe after lifetimes of trying to, and finally becoming the perfect person, they cannot stop the habit of still trying to.

They're always thinking they should have done this better and that better and what not.

And in the meanwhile all kinds of crap happens and they find they have to disturb their self-improvement schedule to sort issues out.

Nothing pisses them off more than this.

But it's this warrior's time to take up the power they have and change the atmosphere and energy of the places and spaces they live in and work in. How exactly they do this will come to them from their instinct; but it starts with becoming consciously aware of what their spirit is noticing is the true equation between people and groups.

Their consciousness telecast itself is a catalyst and will cause things to happen.

This warrior is a leader, fair and square. They shouldn't waste their time trying to not be, because they don't want to upset the power structure wherever they are.

Demons ain't going to like it; but who cares. For this warrior to feel satisfied and reach their destiny, they should not hang back, suppress themselves anymore. Raise your hand, put forth your thoughts and ideas and watch the magic happen.

This warrior should NEVER hold back – just keep moving forward fearlessly. Let what has to happen, happen.

Demon – Sun in Cancer with Mars in the Earth Signs

This demon is one of those people that will go regularly for years to a group meeting, or church program, or whatever and become an organizer or such; develop a reputation for just being there consistently.

In fact, they're not contributing anything but regularly draining the energy pool and keeping everything never really going anywhere.

Young people tend to know this instinctively; that this demon is just there because it gets a sense of importance and it really doesn't do anything someone else could do the same or better.

Its heart is not in anything being done there, it's just there for the structure and reputation.

That's actually an abuse of that group or organization and others feel it.

If you have this demon on a team, you'll find sending them off to do something "important" job that doesn't require them to be there for every meeting will change the energy of the group immediately.

In personal life, they're egoistic as hell and make everyone walk on eggshells around them, lest they feel not valued and start pickling in their own resentment, making people feel guilty and so on.

SUN IN CANCER with

MARS IN GEMINI, LIBRA, AQUARIUS – THE AIR SIGNS

This warrior is intensely in tune with the energetic atmosphere in a relationship, family, group, room. You could say they almost pick up the radio waves in the air. The crystal stone Iolite, that I feel picks up vibrational waves in the atmosphere, reminds me of this warrior.

They have nervous systems that are very reactive as a result of being exposed to the atmosphere. Because they are so energetically sensitive, they tend to need support in the form of nerves that support nervous system health – herbs like the Artimisia family – Mugwort, Wormwood, Motherwort; Vervain, Borage, Cactus (stabilizes the nervous frequency literally physically) and so on. We are in such a time that this warrior is likely to be under immense bombardment and that's why I feel they should, whenever possible, as a habit for life, be working on supporting their nervous system.

There are so many crystals that help with maintaining nervous stability – Bronzite, Tournamaline, Nuumite and so on. There are so many. You could find what works for you and, and most of these warriors already are, so I need not say more about it.

This amazing gift of God – to know what's happening in the energy atmosphere, is often brutally suppressed right from childhood and the warrior begins to think something is wrong with them. They are often diagnosed with mental conditions to keep them down.

But they should actually develop and fine hone it. It is unlikely that they will find a friend who will genuinely help them develop it, it is too spectacular and demons will get jealous. Humans are too few and most probably too far away to be of help.

So this warrior should be their own support – something they are amply capable of; give themselves the support and understanding they are always giving others; and build on this ability. Develop their psychic and other sensitivities and a relationship with God within, and God without; to deploy it.

Demon – Sun in Cancer with Mars in the Air Signs
This demon plays with people's ideas, words and even thoughts to show their mental alacrity and superiority. They genuinely believe themselves to be superior to most people they know.

They are impatient with those who they consider to be useless non-contributing persons because they cannot discuss ideas and thoughts.

This demon lives in a fantasy world and those who get personally involved with this demon will find themselves losing touch with reality too.

This is their danger – the way they pull humans out from reality, into a pseudo half-relationship, half this, half that, not exactly here, not exactly there, zone.

SUN IN LEO with
MARS IN ARIES, LEO, SAGITTARIUS – THE FIRE SIGNS
This warrior doesn't mess about with anything at all in life. They tend to know what they want early in life and progress towards their goals through whichever route they find open.

This warrior's weakness is their tendency to believe whatever people tell them – in their early days ie.. They become wise to the world as they grow up.

But something this warrior struggles with even in adulthood, is believing that anyone has the time and dedication to focus on pulling them down and stopping them from reaching their goal. They simply cannot believe someone has the time and low-down gutter scum nature to do that.

In fact, demons who do exactly that are regularly attracted to this powerhouse of a warrior, the Hercules of the zodiac if you will; and are in fact dedicated to just that.

Every time I have met one of these Herculean warriors, they have had one or two of these demons in their immediate friend circle.

This warrior needs to understand once and for all, that they cannot compensate for cheating, evil demons in their entourage with their own strength. They keep imagining they can, and they keep struggling on every day, but it is not possible.

The Lion has to either be with his own pride, or walk alone. You cannot find others of your caliber that easy. I think God made less of you, because one is so powerful, and one complete One – ie you and your Soulmate – is such a powerful Being that there's just no need for another similar set anywhere nearby. It's nature.

This warrior needs to learn to walk alone and reach their goal; and TAKE THE CREDIT for it.

There are lots of people crazy attracted to this warrior, just to try and hijack his or her light.

This warrior needs to get out of the thug programmed idea that they should use their energy for other people's goals. This is not an ENABLER, this is an achiever. Stop trying to be a teacher, or a coach or such to others, unless you have already achieved what you wanted to achieve.

The thug world will constantly tell you you're lacking something, you're not good enough, you don't have this or that. It's all damn lies. You have the ONE thing that is needed to achieve that thing you want. Your birthright – your energy field, born under Leo, the house of the Sun itself, with Mars in the fire signs. Get going on. Don't look back, don't look to the side. Achievement is your destiny.

Be critical of others and choose who you let in close to you; and it's just fine if that's no one but your man or woman.

Demon – Sun in Leo with Mars in the Fire Signs
This demon is a gambler with a sort of megalomania in the head where they think they own the universe and can command things and people just because.

They are loud mouthed entities who push people around, demand things, and take full advantage of anyone who tolerates them in any way.

They're obsessed with all the things they believe they deserve but which someone held back from them. A lot of their energy goes into "getting back" at their enemies, but really, it's just about attacking whoever they can find any reason to attack. They don't want to get put in an asylum for randomly attacking people for fun, so they try and find some reason.

If this demon has his eye on a human, he or she isn't going to back off easy. It's not about you, it's about them proving to themselves that they can get and keep what they want (which they believe they deserve).

To get rid of them takes a spine of steel – and it's probably to develop just that, that a human attracts this kind of demon into their life.

SUN IN LEO with
MARS IN CANCER, SCORPIO, PISCES – THE WATER SIGNS
This warrior is intensely connected to earth rhythms and ebb and flow. Yes, the earth flows too – as water. This warrior is attracted to the rise and fall of energy forms in nature and elsewhere. They are a connoisseur of beauty in its different shades and very artistic too.

As a spiritual warrior, their gifts are in being able to translate things into expression – whether that's words or art or music or videos – that few others can. They have an ability to know where something is going. Like if a project is moving in a way where it will be successful or not. The flow, the process; they get that instinctively and they can repair or fix that instinctively too.

A somewhat difficult thing for this warrior, is that very few people are able to understand what they're really trying to convey. They are essentially poets and their brain is wired a different way, so very often they actually speak with the word arrangement in a sentence different from what others are used to; or something like that.

Their brain is wired different, basically, in the language and art department. They are more primal than others, closer to nature, human nature. This is not a mistake God made. This is a great and wonderful gift of God.

Those who don't instinctively understand them or love and value them enough to learn to understand their vibe, quite rightly don't deserve to and should be let go of. The few who do, are a find.

The world has enough copycats and people all doing and producing the same crap. This warrior is original, the first and last in eternity of him or her. Her work, especially creative work is of the finest quality and raises the consciousness of humanity whether others see it or not.

The great artist Augustus Saint Gaudens was of this sort of warrior. He made bronze sculptures that to this day are something a cut above the rest. You take two sculptures – both of the same theme and both technically perfect. One you will forget by the time you reach home, but one will stay with you for the rest of your life – because it made you feel something. It's just one of many sculptures of the same sort and theme, but still, it made you feel something.

The picture on the top of this book, is a sculpture of Diana, the Goddess of War; by Augustus Saint Gaudens .

This warrior has that in them – to make something that conveys a silent message or not-so-silent message from God to the heart and the soul; that echoes on forever.

Demon – Sun in Leo with Mars in the Water Signs
This demon is a thief of things they like – mostly ideas, but often other things as well. They are constantly imitating someone they

consider is powerful and they steal things from powerful people for the energy vibration of those and carry them about their person and such.

They are drawn to black magic from a young age, to try and control others, and it tends to be their only real hobby for the rest of their lives.

They tend to be very good at seducing people but duds in bed. They're never going to improve, so don't wait around.

When they're young they throw their weight around because of their moderately good looks, but as they grow older they become increasingly manipulative to keep their influence on others. They are very cruel in this and don't give a crap for the lives they could destroy or anything.

They are utterly selfish and have no qualms doing ANYTHING for money and status and power. No one will ever be more important to them than this. Ever. So don't waste your time.

SUN IN LEO with
MARS IN TAURUS, VIRGO, CAPRICORN – THE EARTH SIGNS

This warrior is a powerful juggler of different kinds of energies. They have that particular strength of soul that can make them be the fulcrum or center of a huge operation or project, that has many wings and need to be centrally kept in balance so they all work together.

This warrior has the expansive vision to always know where the whole juggernaut of a company or family or project is going, and also the ability to care for the details so that the whole thing can be sustained to fulfilment.

Their strength is legendary. That simple. They can do whatever they want so long as they don't allow anyone to make them shrink their vision and cause them to lose their motivation. If it isn't a big dream, this warrior is not into it.

This warrior's weakness is letting people into his or her inner circle, that initially come across as critical thinkers and give them an alternative perspective. In an ideal world, this would have been great. But in our world with demons who are energy insufficient and power hungry around; that sort of person usually starts getting a power trip high when someone like our warrior listens to them respectfully and considers what they're saying. And then they start being critical just to feel powerful.

Our warrior here is not the kind who will throw people out of his life easily. He or she will keep trying to work out what the problem is and find a resolution.

You cannot find a resolution in these cases and all of that only feeds the demon more.

So this warrior needs to filter out of their lives all the demons who are being critical as a sort of power trip, holding them back. One way to know who they are, is to simply see if they're nearly always critical. Someone who is a genuine critic for the sake of progress cannot and will not always be critical.

Demon – Sun in Leo with Mars in the Earth Signs

This demon doesn't like anyone crossing them, saying "no" to them. They are hungry for recognition as a great person and their childhood and youth, is often devoted to advancing in martial arts, or some skill of physical strength or prowess.

They can be generally pleasant and even loyal, until they find someone who is better than them at their skill or hobby or sport or whatever is their thing. They turn from the king of the jungle, into a scavenger hyena overnight. Planning, plotting, mercilessly trying to pull down the person they're jealous of.

Once they do that – it usually happens around the age of 15 – they make it a habit and then that becomes their sport.

They never really can advance further in whatever their hobby or skill was, because, for one, they're good but not THAT good, and secondly, their real hobby and profession is tearing down others.

They tend to attract other disgruntled demons and form a pack and imagine they're mafia dons or something. Their main aim is to prevent anyone from progressing, because they couldn't progress.

This demon goes about recruiting kids who are from broken homes, or struggling in some way; grooming them to provide him energy while imagining they're going well for themselves.

This is such a deceiver and is so hollow ultimately.

It's almost a guarantee, that this demon is physically violent in personal relationships and with the vulnerable.

SUN IN LEO with
MARS IN GEMINI, LIBRA, AQUARIUS – THE AIR SIGNS

This warrior is symbolized in the driver of a chariot that leaps into the air. This is the dreamer of the impossible and therefore the very frontline of human advancement towards that happy place we all want to go to.

The thug world is always telling us our dreams are impossible, and humans NEVER ever were happy anyway. But this warrior has the dreams of God for humanity beating in his or her heart, and they hold it aloft for all of us humans in our human consciousness.

Wherever this warrior is born, it means the time of deliverance for that people and that family has come. The birth of this baby is the sign from God, because this baby carries the energy of Sun that starts a new day – up there in the sky, the light breaks out, long before the warmth touches the leaves and the grass and wakes them to the new day.

This is that warrior that will never compromise on his or her values, and faith. They are the backbone and strength of the family, the team, the group.

This warrior's weakness is their compassion for those who aren't as uncompromising as them. They see that as weakness, when it is actually spinelessness. A weak person will suffer and hurt, but uphold their values. A spineless person will betray their values as soon they find it could hurt them.

This warrior must let spineless people go from their lives fully and completely. Their vibes simply do not match.

Demon — Sun in Leo with Mars in the Air Signs

This demon doesn't like anyone correcting them. They're a collector of phrases that "work", ideas and such and they put on a show for every interaction they have, throwing out an aura of someone who is a mind or thought leader and so on.

They have all the conversation starter topics going, and even have pre-planned how the conversation should go. They simply don't like anyone butting in and spoiling the show. They have a movie of their life in their heads and they want that movie to continue on as the director, them, intends.

Sooner or later something that happens that stops that from happening, and then they turn their focus to destroying whoever else has that thing they dreamed of for themselves.

This is true horror movie that goes on and on. This demon is psychotic to say the least and often is on drugs – legal and illegal – to fuel their trips. They are undependable, violent and destructive.

They are often jealous of their own children for little things like they look better, are younger and so on. The chance of them being arrested, or put in asylums is very high.

Once in a while there's one of these that manages to advance up a career path that requires deception and crooked thinking at every turn. Like the legal profession and government organizations. At some point however, they get betrayed by someone they trusted. What goes around comes around.

SUN IN VIRGO with

MARS IN ARIES, LEO, SAGITTARIUS – THE FIRE SIGNS
This warrior is a very simple minded person with a clear grasp of how energy works. They are attuned to animals and nature strongly and one of their abilities is to sense subtle changes in the energy fields around them.

Their spiritual warfare expertise is in how they can sense long before any actual attack that the atmosphere has changed and that someone with an intention to hurt them or their loved ones is coming around.

They are like those motor vehicle mechanics who can tell from how a car sounds, what the problem is, before it actually breaks down.

This warrior has deep subconscious and inherited knowledge of demons and how demons work. This comes out an instinct in this lifetime. Many times, they have saved themselves and their loved ones from various sorts of attacks.

It they feel their lives are not as dramatic as others, it's because they're so effective at naturally weeding out demons and preventing attacks before the attack even starts.

This warrior's weakness is when they're overly attached to places of the past and things which evoke nostalgia in them. In an ideal world all of our memories and childhoods would've been memories of humans; but in our times nostalgia can hold us back to demons, imagining that just because our lives were simpler or better or easier back then, everyone in it were all humans with good intentions for us.

Being psychologically open to demons, results in energy drains and this warrior experiences that sort of drain every now and then.

Demon – Sun in Virgo with Mars in the Fire Signs
This demon is drawn to professions that require opening and examining the insides of things. They seem curious and technically minded; but in fact, their inner sadistic desire is to know how something works, so they can feel powerful in the knowledge that they can destroy it if they want.

They have a secret power trip going, where they relish the idea of all those they could destroy if they wanted to.

They're pleasant enough when you just get to know them, but sooner or later they'll start dropping sentences now and then, about how someone is where they are in life, because they helped them and how they have the power to destroy them too, but they don't.

Their brains are literally necrotic or decaying inside their head. They have dreams of violence both consciously and in sleep and tend to carry a lot of suppressed frustration and passive aggression that can be very trying for those around them.

The danger of this demon is that they eat into your energy with their stagnant energy field, slow draining you over time without you not being able to pin point exactly what the problem is; and it's not like they're good in bed really or anything.

SUN IN VIRGO with

MARS IN CANCER, SCORPIO, PISCES – THE WATER SIGNS
This warrior is very imaginative and creative. They have a natural ancient memory of the heavens and creations of magic that have now been removed from the public memory of humans. Their soul

memory is fresh and alive here as it is in eternity; but not knowing it is their memory, they believe it is their imagination.

These warriors are seen as a threat by demons instinctively and later on "officially" by demon organizations. Attempts are made to stunt their expression and groom them to give their energy to demons or clones of themselves. They often are put on medication with some excuse or the other to keep their brain from accessing their soul memory.

This warrior begins to fully awake in their twenties, when they no longer pass off as some imaginative kid. About this time, their ability to investigate things kicks in and they begin to research and question things. They are met with huge sudden spiritual advancements and as they go on, they become bullet proof and sometimes secretive as part of it.

When they meet their love, it's instant connection and instant protection. This warrior needs to constantly remember their soulmate, their One love, whether they have found them yet or not, and stay in that frequency, so that they do not get drained, depressed and exploited energetically by demons. I have written a lot on this topic in my books on Soul Memory, and Sexual Energy Healing, Womb.

Demon – Sun in Virgo with Mars in the Water Signs

This demon can be rather good looking and very malleable. Depending on where they grow up, they can grow up imitating some adult who had an aura of being a very spiritual and good person, almost saintly. Spiritual, saintly people are this demon's favorite type to imitate. They dress in white and always tend to look like they've been doing some saintly service of humanity or God or such.

In reality, they are a drainer of people who are ill and low on energy and cannot defend themselves, especially children and young people. They give the impression that they're not that interested in friendships and connections, but actually they are astute in networking and are adept at using connections very, very subtly as social proof.

They can be very cruel and violent once they get so close to someone that that person feels a spiritual submission to them. They are adept at making people they abuse feel guilty. The "Look what you made me do," trope.

SUN IN VIRGO with
MARS IN TAURUS, VIRGO, CAPRICORN – THE EARTH SIGNS
This warrior is capable of immense and sudden shifts because of having their ear so close to the ground. They are capable of incredible focus and faithful allegiance to detail in everything they do. If for example, you want to build something big, that big thing is possible, only if the work is done brick by brick, faithfully all the way.

This is that warrior's strength.

But it is only one of his or her abilities. This is possibly the most "all-rounder" warrior of them all because of how they ease in and out of whatever role they have to play in life. For what they believe in, they'll do everything and anything.

One person like this in the family or the team, and you can guarantee that that family or that team will succeed in everything. Because there's something there, willing to do anything and be anything, and in fact, capable of just about anything; to make sure everyone reaches the finish line.

This warrior is often taken for granted because of their great, faithful love, and them not demanding anything in return for it. But with such a great heart of love, has also come great wisdom and this warrior never gets thrown off course by those who take them for granted or don't value their love. They simply move on, like the Sun, to do what their soul journey has next for them.

Just writing about this warrior, has me longing to just sit near them, just to enjoy the beautiful feeling of stability and faithfulness they emanate. God knows we all need that so much.

Demon – Sun in Virgo with Mars in the Earth Signs
This demon is nearly always wanting to get things into their care, that will make others have to come pay obeisance to them. It's something like hostage holding. They want to hold what others need and love, so they can subtly threaten and intimidate others – Be nice to me, give me what I want; or else.....

They tend to have all the qualifications and work experience and everything to make them candidates for managerial positions in projects like dams, bridges, sea ports and so on.

But a lot of people get an instinct that something is weird about this entity and they're right. They're like terrorists anywhere they are. But very subtly. Just always looking at what they hold hostage and psychically threatening and intimidating people. It's just what they do.

You know you're in a relationship with this demon if you feel stressed out constantly and worried for basic safety. You could think you're being paranoid, because you don't really have a reason to be worried. You feel you're in danger of being betrayed but can't imagine by who. The stress is turning your hair grey and you feel like you're in a horror movie.

For what it's worth, know that this demon is too much of a coward to do anything to really threaten the reputation and career that allows them to keep getting things to hold hostage. Their danger is in how they drain you emotionally with their subliminal intimidation and threatening.

SUN IN VIRGO with

MARS IN GEMINI, LIBRA, AQUARIUS – THE AIR SIGNS

This warrior is a champion in the mental arts required in spiritual warfare; the ability to understand the enemy's moves, recognize patterns and anticipate the enemy's next move.

These are formidable warriors from the day they're born because they're already negotiating the psychic space in which 80% at least of all thug world warfare is done. The realm of thought and psychic assault.

This warrior will tell you immediately, as soon as you present your situation, who is psychologically draining you, holding you at gunpoint and so on.

They are incredibly astute in matters of psychic warfare before they even begin to actually consciously study that field – and they should because that's their home ground and the expertise they have acquired through lifetimes of being a warrior.

You can't spar with this warrior in any way, though and come out unscathed. This is not one of those reluctant messiah types who talks a lot but shudders when it's time to get things done. Oh no. This is that friend, that family member, who will bloody well see to it that someone who has hurt those they love, is executed right out the scene well and properly.

I envy those who have someone like this in their lives. What a man; what a woman; what an absolute pillar of strength. I bow down to God that has manifested as this person. God, may they reproduce and fill the earth with their children, so all humans can have someone like this in their lives to keep them on track, and help them on their way.

This warrior's weakness is shopping for the latest technology. Apparently, it comes with being always at the cutting edge of every pursuit or art or field of study they do. But it can drain their finances, and make them feel like they're poor and God hasn't provided for them well enough. Really, a lot of the latest stuff is older stuff re-packaged, and God doesn't want them not becoming adept at one weapon because of playing about with so many all the time.

Demon – Sun in Virgo with Mars in the Air Signs

This demon is one of those psychopaths that tends to know more than they should about everyone around them, and then uses it to get close to them. They are very good at researching people, finding things out about their past and then using that to subtly throw vibes to lure that person in, make them think they're sent by God to help them.

They often portray themselves as angels in the lives of others, come to help them wanting nothing in return. In reality, they use people like steps in a ladder. They use people to get social proof and move on quite quickly too. They'll hang out with someone for months and suddenly one day not be available. They're hanging out with someone you introduced them to and no longer have time for you.

That isn't illegal to do of course, but in reality, it's energy vampirism and only those who are heartless would fake friendship like that. And they DO fake friendship. They don't give a damn for anyone but those who are giving them some sort of benefit in the moment – and not even long term.

They're the kind who'll dump their boyfriend or girlfriend if they lose their job; who won't bring their friends around home anymore if their own parents fall into bad days.

They're bothered about reputation and how they look – and that comes first. If they look good with you, ie., if you don't look like someone who's raised their market value, they'll be fine if you look like they rescued you like the angel, savior they are; but you'll have to perform that or they'll find some reason, accuse you of something or the other that's hurt them and be gone.

SUN IN LIBRA with

MARS IN ARIES, LEO, SAGITTARIUS — THE FIRE SIGNS
These warriors are visionaries who are capable of taking human consciousness further, much further. They are the ones tasked with fighting the cramps of consciousness. Have you ever tried walking under water? You'll find it's easy to move your head and upper body forward, but the water pressure keeps your lower and legs feeling pushed back.

We experience this when we, whether as an individual or a family, or community, or species want to move forward from bondage out towards our truth. It's like walking under water.

But this warrior here, is born with the ability to negotiate those undercurrents — be aware of them and develop the exact amount of force it would take to withstand them and move forward.

Undercurrents Expert is the name of warrior because they instinctively aware in any situation of the undercurrents that hold them or someone else back from progressing.

They are great healers for this reason, whether they actually intend to heal or not.

In their personal life, they are constantly battling mass consciousness and the consciousness of others around them that hold them out. They're that child who'll tell their parents, "You're never going to make it if you keep hanging out with those friends. They hold you back." They're able to see how mass consciousness and surrounding consciousness is affecting someone.

It's not always so simple. People can't just move out of neighborhoods that are holding them back, or change careers overnight, or get rid of family members holding them back. It's a process. But it will start only when the person knows what's holding them back and works on throwing it off or working around it.

This warrior does this in their own lives. They climb the ladder on behalf of us every day. Just that they exist out there refusing to be cowed by the consciousness of those around them; energizes us all sub-consciously. If any of us humans gets up in our bed in hell and decides we have got to get out of it, so we can express our true potential; it's because this warrior exists somewhere fighting their way out of consciousness prison every day, undaunted by how huge the task might be.

This warrior liberates people. Period.

If they have a weakness, it's that they can deprive themselves of sunlight and sunshine sometimes as they sort of mirror the reality of their lives – that they are in the darkness fighting the undercurrents of life; by keeping themselves working in the night or in darkened places. This can take a toll on them in the long run. So it's good for them to make sure to get sunlight and keep their bodies healthy for the long run.

Demon – Sun in Libra with Mars in the Fire Signs

This demon is all about gathering up energy from whoever is available to believe their schemes and ideas. They tend to do impromptu performances featuring downtrodden people and slavery and any cause they think will emotionally pull up people; and then say "We must do something about it," and maybe even take a donation from everyone there, or get them all to share something on their social media about it or such.

Two hours later they're fast asleep with the energy they drained out of you all. They're just a performing artist. They don't give a crap about anything REALLY. You look into their life and you'll see they've been associated with many causes and efforts but stuck with none. They're an energy middleman. They get their cut out of energy you send to the causes and live in that middle-zone getting a second hand importance out of those causes which are genuinely important.

SUN IN LIBRA with

MARS IN CANCER, SCORPIO, PISCES – THE WATER SIGNS

This warrior is not about to let anyone get away with any crime. They have got an old anger inside them from being taken advantage of. They are souls who would share their last meal with someone they didn't know; not out of kindness but out of a genuine sense that God will take care of his and we are meant to share our things.

In past lives, they gave their everything to others around them, and in most cases were taken for a ride and exploited.

As a result, God has now had them be born with the nature and agility to spot and address crimes against humanity. From a young age they are given to never turning away when something wrong is being done.

In situations and environments where crime is rampant and it is not possible for someone to react to every crime being done around them; they keep their anger back and express it in something that results in them fighting crime on a larger scale than on an individual scale.

They are great authors, great artists and musicians, litigators... Wherever there's a way to fight crimes against humanity, these warriors are there, steadfastly eating away at the thug world consciousness that legitimizes or looks the other way as crime is being committed.

This warrior's weakness is when they read too much and bother more about others' theories and ideas, when they themselves are the source of 100% original creative inspiration with rock solid grounding in the spirit of wanting the emancipation of humanity.

They just need to accept that their heart's desire for the good of mankind, is all the energy they need, and will open the doors they need opened to walk towards their destiny.

Demon – Sun in Libra with Mars in the Water Signs
This demon is a destroyer of homes and institutions. This demon cannot tolerate energy structures that are harmonious or stable. It doesn't matter if those energy structures are by humans or demons, or what they're used for. This demon simply gets a kick out of bringing down the basic energy structures of homes and institutions.

For example; a home is dependent on the love bond between the father and mother of the family. This demon will psychically attack them individually, and do whatever it can safely and covertly to break them up. For example, it will find out the father particularly does not like something, and convince the mother to try it. They sow discord between people, but not any people; the foundational people.

This demon cannot work on a team though it will look like a most convivial pleasant member of the team. It will bring up questions at particular times, and do networking after hours to bring down the structure of the team.

It gets its kicks from breaking things up.

It will mention these exploits later on being careful to hide the sadistic pleasure it gets.

In a personal relationship, this demon can be faithful only when there's money involved. They have to be with someone for the money, or they're not with them at all. Just cooling their heels till they find someone with money.

SUN IN LIBRA with

MARS IN TAURUS, VIRGO, CAPRICORN – THE EARTH SIGNS

This warrior is an earthshaker when it comes the people they love. They are simple people who like to live with a certain level of beauty and art in their lives. But all of this comes crashing down when tragedy strikes someone close to them, or themselves.

This warrior nearly always has had a huge dramatic tragedy happen in their lives, that ended life as they knew it and changed their course from whatever they were doing, to one that emerged because of the tragedy.

This is a good thing, because this person was never meant to be anyone lesser than a warrior.

Life for them is a constant battle in their inner self as they deal with the emotional turmoil of a soul who is awake and aware of injustice in their lives and done to humanity at large. They have to do a lot of things to just manage their emotions, and stay functional because they feel so enraged, their SPIRIT is so enraged inside them.

Just that they carry that divine rage inside, already makes them a warrior for us all, a consciousness warrior. We need someone who will hold the rage for us. We need someone who won't pretend nothing's happened to us and everything is fine and dandy.

Woe to the person or group that makes this warrior finally erupt. For all the rage, they are incredibly intelligent, actually brilliant minds. They will bring out arsenal, things learned over years and decades, and they will rip the guts out of someone that dares to provoke them into battle.

These warriors know how to choose their battles and that's why they're always successful. They will hold their rage and wait for the right moment, the right place.

One weakness of this warrior is being easy to manipulate via children. They tend to think all children are angels and don't really realize that demons can come around as children too. When one has this concept, we can see if a child coming around has a soul or is a soulless demon or zombie. Child demons and zombies are dangerous as they can open channels deep in the heart.

This warrior longs for his or her own child and there might be some problems in them having children at the time everyone around them of their age is having them. But they will have children eventually, real children of their own flesh and soul, who will inherit their anointing and spirit.

Demon – Sun in Libra with Mars in the Earth Signs

This demon is the enemy of anything that is unipolar. For example, this demon has a problem with someone believing God is good. They'll bring out the philosophy and dialogues to prove that God is also not good. They're very draining because they're just dedicated to divesting people of just anything they believe in.

Nihilism, I believe it is called; when someone doesn't believe in anything. It's a sort of spiritual disease, which is based in soullessness. A soul by virtue of existing has a polarity and place in space-time, which comes with a belief system to negotiate the characteristics of that place. For example, if you are born in the jungle, you must have certain belief systems that make you able to thrive there. You cannot believe poisonous fruits are food, for example.

So every soul has a natural innate belief system that enables their existence.

But this demon doesn't have a soul and sadistically enjoys draining anyone who has a strong belief system in anything, by showing them that the opposite of what they believe is also true.

If a human did this, it would be mind-expanding and liberating. But demons do this for the kick of power they get out of short-circuiting people who give them the benefit of the doubt.

SUN IN LIBRA with

MARS IN GEMINI, LIBRA, AQUARIUS – THE AIR SIGNS
This warrior is a master of the dark arts, and a champion of the oppressed, the downtrodden and those who have been held captured in regressive thoughtforms that keep them unevolved and stuck in abusive situations.

They themselves tend to be preyed upon from childhood on by those who would like to use and exploit their powers of reasoning, crystal clear intellect and ability to quickly comprehend situations and know how to work with them.

Wherever this warrior works, they end up being highly valued for their critical thinking skills and their ability to see projects through to the end no matter what the obstacles.

They seem to have grown up running obstacle races and to them, at one point, obstacles are nothing at all. They are calm warriors who never miss their mark.

If they have a weakness, it's allowing some demon or the other trick them into being compassionate and then use that as a channel to win trust and wriggle into this warrior's inner circle.

Because this warrior is so powerful, betrayal by those who get close is something they need to be careful about. In early life, they're not able to differentiate between being friends with those you're compassionate to, and being friends with those who have EARNED trust, and respect and have an EQUAL INTELLIGENCE.

Imagine if you were a warrior going to fight a war, and you met someone fallen on the roadside. You bound up their wounds, helped them get something to eat and somewhere to sleep. They have a place in your heart.

But would you go into battle with this person by your side, or would you want someone who is capable of battle in the first place, who earns your trust and respect, and is your equal in intellect, purpose and intent, by your side?

This warrior keeps getting tripped up and drained by demons for thinking compassion begets loyalty.

It is absolutely essential for this warrior to bulletproof their inner circle, because it doesn't matter what battles they're fighting on the outside when you're compromised within.

Demon – Sun in Libra with Mars in the Air Signs

This demon is a collector of magazines and all things that represent current cultural consciousness. This is because they have a demonic instinct that classifies people as "types" or "archetypes" that are used by thug media to represent human nature.

Actually, humans do not adhere to archetypes. An alpha male human today can be something else tomorrow. It depends on the situation for us. We change and evolve.

But demons don't and you can manipulate demons and humans too to a large extent (for a while), by playing these archetypes games.

Modern astrology also provides demons with knowledge about people that this demon stores up and uses to manipulate people.

It's all actually like shooting in the dark really, but this demon tends to supplement this knowledge with several moves that can only be called black magic and not in the "shadow work" sense but "intent to harm" sense.

They evolve by the age of 30 into someone who will attack a person for no reason other than to see if they can bend that person and break that person. They start with intellectual conversations that lead to sparring. And then they progress on into psychic attacks, predating on the people around the victim to attack the victim through those close to him or her, and so on.

You know how advanced this demon is in the game of needing to break people to feel good, by how they recommend things. If they recommend something to you, and you don't show much interest, you'll see how it irritates them. It means they believed they could control you, and that's why they tested you. If your not showing interest changed the energy of the atmosphere, you know you're dealing with a built up ego and the entity will now try to break you.

The interesting thing about psychic attack and black magic are, those don't work when you're aware of who is doing it. God will make you experience a slight effect if the entity is using people close to you to get to you; and this is for your benefit, because you should know who close to you is capable of betraying you by becoming a channel.

Those people close to you might not be consciously betraying you, but they are become a channel for this demon, because of spiritual frequency matching with the demon. You cannot ignore this. Don't wait for them to consciously betray you, because it WILL come. Demons will choose their own frequency over humans any day.

It's just how we would choose each other for being human frequencies, any day.

SUN IN SCORPIO with
MARS IN ARIES, LEO, SAGITTARIUS – THE FIRE SIGNS
This warrior is hell-bent from the day of birth on uncovering something that his or her soul is passionately driving them to. This passion is not something that they can put in words, but they can feel, when something is come into their life or zone that is the frequency of that passion, that search.

They are wide-eyed in their enjoyment of nature and equally wide-eyed in their learning of what lies beneath those flamboyant displays of nature that most others call pleasant.

These warriors will not turn away from the filth and gore of the wounds of others or their own selves and it gives them guts of steel.

They are constantly called on, night and day to discovery of the very foundations of life, love, and magic.

They are very hard to lie to, because they are so connected to the underlying forces of nature.

This warrior has this special gift of being a human lie detector. If they develop their use of this gift, they can just go through demon lines so quickly and get that which they're searching for so quickly.

This warrior's weakness is falling in infatuation with demons who take advantage of their passion for life to drain them of vital energy. The reason this warrior gets into these situations, is because of not realizing that a lot of demons in this current world population carry hormones of humans and even animals.

This warrior is triggered by hormonal smells and feels sure of someone if they smell like a human. In reality, perfumes, soaps, creams are full of human hormones both real and synthetic.

I have written extensively about this in my autobiography "Spirit" – as I am among those who has been used for hormone harvesting to make humans believe demons are human.

This warrior needs to develop the spiritual aspect of their instinct in tune with the physical (do not suppress the physical as it is powerful and precious and not everything can be masked), but developing both will make this warrior be safe from being led by the nose down the wrong alley.

Demon – Sun in Scorpio with Mars in the Fire Signs
This demon is capable of immense deception using hormonal manipulation and aura throwing. They are able to imitate the innocence of humans and hormonally mask themselves to seduce or win trust and so on.

They do this initially in childhood for amusement, as it amuses them to see how easily people can be fooled.

But deception becomes a way of life and everyday activity. How they actually get by while living under such a body of lies, I don't know; but one method they use is distraction. I met one such demon recently, who was covered with tattoos. He actually used tattoos as a way of mentally distracting people while he continued his lying and throwing a false personality around.

Their false personality is a big deal to these demons and you know that they are this demon and not the human, by how careful they are to stick in their behavior to their false personality. They have to be quite tense and uptight and careful or they'll lose their head and say something that'll bring their house of lies come crashing down.

They cannot really relax around you for this reason and they will come up with all kinds of stories, but you should know that the human Scorpio is not only capable of great relaxation but also will open their life to you without fear if they trust you.

You can go decades in a relationship with a demon Scorpio and they'll still be uptight and have areas of their lives closed from you. It's just that they're a false personality and you don't know anything about them at all. They're like a snake you're keeping in the house that could bite you any time.

They are very selfish and if they want something out of you, they'll set about getting it no matter how it hurts you.

SUN IN SCORPIO with

MARS IN CANCER, SCORPIO, PISCES – THE WATER SIGNS

This warrior is a beautiful confluence of the energies of deep wisdom of previous lives and the simplicity of being a primal human under the sun.

Their deep natural wisdom shows from their childhood, in everything they do. However, they are targeted from very early on for this. They are hypnotically beautiful, because they are old souls that all humans and demons as well have the memory of in the DNA.

They are great teachers of the past, whose energy went into hundreds and thousands and millions of people over time. Their great teachings were not great because of being difficult or too intellectual to comprehend; but great because of how true to spirit and nature they were and are; and how simply they were conveyed to all willing to listen.

Naturally they are led to being teachers in some way or another in this lifetime too, cultivators of the young, builders of wisdom thought bodies and so on. They are often involved in preserving ancient texts and art and so on; much of which they themselves wrote or made in previous lives.

In fact, it is almost a guarantee that this warrior is continuing in this life, the work of previous lives.

In spiritual warfare this warrior is formidable because they do not play games like others. They do not respond to personal attacks by feeling low about themselves. They got past all that by the time they reached middle school. They already know before someone attacks them, that they're going to.

This warrior usually doesn't give a crap for your average demon energy vampire; but should someone mess with those they love, they'll come out and do something or say something so devastating;

that demon will never rise from their crawling on the floor ever again.

This warrior's curse can make someone fall ill and die from one illness after another. It's because the curse is so well deserved.

This warrior's weakness in spiritual warfare is getting aligned to groups, covens, church prayer groups and so on. They are never, I repeat, NEVER, going to find, in our times, their level of spiritual acumen as a group. The group settings will open them up to psychic and energy draining and this warrior will find that every time they went under, it was soon after joining some group or attending group activities.

Their energy field is too big, too advanced, too refined to be part of a group.

To be energetically efficient and healthy in mind, body and soul; they must socialize only for fun, and keep their spirituality and deeper things of life confined to themselves and their one true soulmate.

Demon – Sun in Scorpio with Mars in the Water Signs
This demon hangs about public places, places through which people travel; like railway stations, bus stations; places tourists and travelers frequent; to do energy draining and psychic attacks.

The particular energy of travelers and tourists draws this demon because we are open in a way while traveling and touring that we are not when we're at home.

This demon preys similarly on people who are new to a place, don't know their way around.

This is how they establish themselves in relationships – as someone who helps those who are new or lost or such.

This sets the base for a relationship where the victim nearly always assumes this demon knows better and spiritually submits.

This demon is proper energy vampire that drains people sexually, emotionally, and leaves them completely confused about who they are, what they're doing there. The demon then dictates reality to them. It's a two-person cult there.

People only escape because this demon doesn't know when to stop. Invariably the victim literally runs away for personal survival or their family or friends rescue him or her.

This demon is also nearly always cheating, as they need to keep getting the best supply of vital energy; only it's tricky to catch them if you believe that flirting and hanging out with the opposite sex is normal. You have to go conservative on this demon. Ask him or her how they feel if you hang out with someone of the opposite sex "for an evening of music" or something like that. You'll see from their reaction what they think of that.

SUN IN SCORPIO with

MARS IN TAURUS, VIRGO, CAPRICORN – THE EARTH SIGNS
This warrior is a great man or woman of deep philosophy that aligns with nature, and a genuine heart of love for all the living. As a spiritual warrior, they are forced to develop the skills of offense and defense because they constantly invite jealousy from those who cannot be as effortlessly elegant and graceful in their spiritual freedom.

Their inner freedom to explore spirituality, sexuality and all that is taboo in thug world today, leads them to discovery after discovery and spiritual experiences that will keep unfolding for lifetimes to come, because they are so deep.

This warrior's only pull-back, is that they can get so deep into their inner discoveries that they can fall short on practical matters like taking care of their health, being on time for work or school and so on.

Once they get a base of personal discipline going, they are able to wing out and grow into a spiritual power that is paradigm shattering.

In our times, people often classify the power of someone's spirituality by what they can do, how many people they can influence or such. But there is a power of spirituality that is the development and holding of an energy field, that is generated by a soul that consistently seeks and upholds truth.

This is possible the greatest threat to the thug parasite matrix, because the matrix is made of lies. They're like a 24 x 7 weapon shattering the matrix overhead.

That is why, this warrior who simply wants to be left alone to mind his or her own business and enjoy their spiritual life; is near constantly being attacked in one way or another.

Their spiritual battle is literally simply to keep being them and having their energy field be as it is. To do this, they need to learn spiritual arts like identifying demons from humans and work out in their own environment and life how to deal with them.

I've no doubt that God who made this warrior so, has provided them with all that is needed to learn to protect themselves too.

Demon – Sun in Scorpio with Mars in the Earth Signs
This demon likes to be noticed as someone distinguished and elegant and capable of great things in life, because they are not any of that. They are an incredibly lazy demon, who very rarely ever finishes anything they start and all they do, is find someone to be like a servant to them and bring them things, and keep them comfortable.

They are constantly thinking of what service they can get from others, and how to manipulate them into giving then that.

If they manage to land a job, they keep it and keep that career by running interpersonal intrigues where they convince someone that they need this demon and that this demon is loyal to them.

They use loyalty and secrecy – which are in high demand anywhere in thug world because there's so little of it, as pawns to develop a secret network of supporters to keep them employed even though they barely do any actual work.

The aim is to feel powerful by doing this, but they usually end up being something of a glorified servant themselves, and lose their energy and die soon enough.

But they drain everyone on their way to death. Family, friends, whoever will consider it a human.

SUN IN SCORPIO with

MARS IN GEMINI, LIBRA, AQUARIUS – THE AIR SIGNS

This warrior is a giant in the world of spiritual warfare, because of their prophetic ability. They have inbuilt radios if you will and can pick up signals of what someone is planning long before anyone else knows.

They are highly valued by the thugs who invariably set up fake friends and fake family around this human, to tap into their prophetic abilities without them knowing they're being mined for information.

This warrior ends up as some point leaving their home town or such suddenly and never looking back. They often don't know what made them do it; but it's because they couldn't take the spiritual abuse anymore.

They are constantly under threat because they are so valuable. They are often followed and stalked and intimidated, bullied, even held hostage or poisoned.

God makes them develop their spiritual abilities to defend and protect themselves, on the road, in the thick of the battle itself.

I don't need to tell this warrior anything at all, because they already know. I only write this for the younger ones of this warrior, so that they don't need to wait till they're older and find out how valuable they are and that they're being watched, stalked for their spiritual abilities to be used.

They can know it right now. Stop offering spiritual services to people for free, refuse to do readings or divination or prayer for anyone but your own soulmate; and focus on weeding out people who bully you in the least bit for anything.

Demon – Sun in Scorpio with Mars in the Air Signs
This demon is a very cunning cheater in whichever area they're in. In sports, they cheat, in games, in love, in gambling; in everything. They grow up learning how to do little things that swing the situation their way, and 99% of the time, it is by sabotaging their opponents.

They primarily sabotage people using word and thought and psychic tricks, something like magicians do; but there's an element of emotional abuse they throw in that clinches the deal.

They're not VERY smooth though and most humans know they're being played sooner or later.

Once people get to know them, they detest them and avoid them.

SUN IN SAGITTARIUS with

MARS IN ARIES, LEO, SAGITTARIUS – THE FIRE SIGNS
This warrior is a world citizen, or rather a universal citizen. This soul has broken the bonds of identification with any one place or culture or even time for that matter.

That gives this soul a consciousness reach that is beyond the comprehension of most others. They are always looking at the big picture, and comprehending it too.

This warrior's spiritual warfare acumen comes from their uncompromising nature when it comes to what is their soul purpose.

They try and reject many paths, philosophies and methods while they're still young, retaining only that which fits it with their core spiritual vision.

This is very confusing for them as a young person because their vision is something they are unable to understand or put into words. They can end up getting tricked, exploited and vampirized by demon spiritual leaders and such.

They have an attraction for all things poetic and literary and this is another way this warrior gets conned.

This warrior needs to drastically filter out their circle of trusted people who know where they are, their schedule, what they're reading and so on. They are prone to severe psychic attacks leaving them on the floor in exhaustion, very like an actual blood draining vampirical attack.

They tend to return to their parents for repair before going back out there and getting attacked again.

This warrior's path to awareness and developing their spiritual acumen comes through recovering many times from attack upon attack upon attack.

When they do awaken to the reality of what's happening they tend to isolate themselves and develop their spirituality in relative quiet. This is necessary, as their energy field is too big and dramatic for them to not keep getting attacked by all and sundry for just daring to be that expanded.

When they do develop a personal discipline that keeps their energy field safe from being drained, they become a consciousness field that upholds the uncompromising demand for the rights and dignities of humans everywhere. Just being this huge consciousness refusing to accept anything lesser as normal or natural; refusing to accept the abuse of people or nature; refusing to accept evil as normal; causes

SUN IN SAGITTARIUS with

MARS IN CANCER, SCORPIO, PISCES – THE WATER SIGNS

This warrior is emotionally aware and uses emotional insight into topics to guide him into the wisdom he or she is constantly searching for, like a thirsty man searches for water.

They have a deep sense of being incomplete in early life, because they have an inner world that is absolutely beautiful and wondrous; and their outside world doesn't match up.

They search and search to try and match their inner frequencies to their outer frequencies.

These warriors are very familiar with angelic presences and guidance as they experience spiritual intervention directly from other realms and dimensions all through their lives.

They have a youthful innocence and faith and in God that never leaves them, and I must say, I would consider this, simply the greatest spiritual warfare weapon of all.

When one has innocent faith in God, they become capable of doing anything at all, whatever it takes, whatever is necessary. Faith in God is like the Joker card in the pack. It might be called the Joker but it is the most powerful card because it can be anything at all.

This warrior's weakness is their willingness to go along for the ride with just about anyone that invites them, hoping that they might find what they're looking for down a new path.

However as they get experience in the ways of the world, get drained and recover and drained and recover, they learn to be discerning and then they're the last person who can be taken for a ride.

They tend to have daughters that inherit their wisdom and anointing. In fact their daughters tend to be nature spirits, the embodiments of great water bodies like rivers and lakes. These need protection and nurture that only this warrior can give them.

Demon – Sun in Sagittarius with Mars in the Water Signs
This demon is all about portraying himself or herself as a saint who is ever available for their friends and family. In reality they actually live off "friends and family", if not financially, then definitely energetically. They tend to be in spiritual or other organizations where they get access to fresh energy regularly, and stay on there, long past anyone of their age has stayed on, because of the constant supply of fresh energy.

So long as they can, they keep sleeping around with multiple sexual partners, pretending to be on the verge of commitment with each, but actually simply sexually draining them.

They are unreliable as friends and lovers, though they will turn up when they're not wanted to help; but make it like they came to see if they could help. They keep giving the impression they're actually there for someone by doing that.

They are not just sexual drainers of humans, but often diversify into raping cattle and pets. To say they are sexually abusive is an understatement.

They cannot have a platonic relationship with anyone, male or female; so there's really nothing good anyone can get out of having anything to do with this demon.

They keep promising people stuff, like they'll help someone who's an artist get exposure for their art; or that they'll introduce a struggling author to someone who's in the publishing business and that sort of thing. But it's mostly bullshit and even if they do it, it's useless as o one respects anyone this demon introduces to them. They're likely to think you're a pimp or prostitute if you're introduced by them.

SUN IN SAGITTARIUS with

MARS IN TAURUS, VIRGO, CAPRICORN – THE EARTH SIGNS

This warrior is deeply connected to his or her natural human bloodline and one who in many generations has expressed the largest number of genes being passed down. They have inherited memory and wisdom of deep and long times in their subconscious and the ability to express them when situations demand in this lifetime.

They are also spiritually connected to the spiritual beings who are the originators of their Soul and DNA; and therefore are an oracle in a way from the time they are born.

Their natural spiritual weapon is their unwillingness to engage in the things that most demons use to entrap humans – ego games, discussions about members of the opposite sex and so on.

This ends up being very real self-defense.

There comes a time however when they are attacked through channels who are betrayers and they are astute enough to figure out who these are, even though sometimes it takes them a while to react. They never move without being fully sure, so they'll wait and gather proof and be fully sure. And when they do, the result is a brutal cut off from life energy of all those that were latched onto this human draining him or her of vital energy.

No one ever recovers from being cut off by this warrior. Because they were so giving and supplied so much energy that the demons get addicted to those high levels and good quality energy. When they're cut off, they will never again find that sort of succor again and the shock of being cut off is something they'll never recover from.

When this warrior turns their face from someone, there is no chance they'll ever turn it back again.

Demon – Sun in Sagittarius with Mars in the Earth Signs
This demon is a really petty thief who masquerades as this bombastic, entertaining Father Christmas. They are usually born in big families and established communities so they don't have to go very far to find fresh blood to drain. They quite literally get into vampirical drinking of blood via secret ceremonies through witchcraft or such groups.

You'd be surprised how many of those are around, Ed.

This sort of vampire recognizes each other and they have rather established networks.

Any human who gets entrapped by this demon is sure to fall ill and stay ill, confused, needing help even getting out of bed, with a host of illness diagnoses that really don't help in any way.

He or she recovers only after completely breaking off all relationship with this demon.

This demon will never change.

SUN IN SAGITTARIUS with
MARS IN GEMINI, LIBRA, AQUARIUS – THE AIR SIGNS
This warrior is a most merry, beautiful spark of joy on earth. They love to sing and dance and uphold all that is beautiful. They are artists and performers, story tellers and singers; and through it all they bring in the most amazing ancient wisdom from their own eternal soul.

They have deep love for all creation and are the very heart of God, in how they are for the weak and the weary and the vulnerable. This warrior shares all he has with those around who need help; and often to his or her own detriment.

The spiritual warfare advantage this warrior has comes through great and deep lessons learned through interaction with those who try to steal their anointing and crush their spirit.

They are targeted from a young age by sexual abusers who try to groom them into being sexually entrapped into patterns not their own naturally, or into situations or groups where everyone sleeps with everyone, thereby pooling all their energies together.

Sometimes this is presented as a spiritual group that bonds spiritually; but actually, it comes down to energy pooling through either sexual or blood energy sharing.

But this warrior grows up and begins to realize that many opportunities for their own advancement in life were destroyed by the energetic effects of those activities and that they did not really gain much from it.

They have the vision of Magus, which then begins to develop as they start identifying those who exploit them energetically.

This warrior has an ability to keep secrets, which mysteriously thrives right through their somewhat gregarious social life, and ends up rescuing them eventually one way or another.

They would save themselves much, if they kept their activities and information about their daily lives, secret from the beginning.

They tend to get recruited to keep and transport Govt. secrets and such, because of how impermeable they can be when they want or need to.

Demon – Sun in Sagittarius with Mars in the Air Signs
This demon is a betrayer extraordinaire. Sadistic in the extreme, this demon consciously and blatantly plays with people's feelings, finds out their secrets and then uses those to blackmail and control people.

They are insecure, paranoid and unable to win anyone's trust or respect for mor than a week or so.

They take up professions where they have access to younger people and children, because only those will consistently treat them right.

They're the sort that people at family gatherings wish wouldn't show up, but definitely do and spoil the atmosphere just be being there.

One of the reasons for this is, they are incestuous and frequently abuse children in the family.

If they come from a rich family, they'll be welcome at a brothel, but that's the only place they'll be welcomed at.

They manage to seduce adult women and men once in a while but this falls through because they are unable to perform sexually normally. They need drugs and porn and what not.

It doesn't work out.

SUN IN CAPRICORN with
MARS IN ARIES, LEO, SAGITTARIUS – THE FIRE SIGNS
This warrior is a dream in a business scenario because there is just nothing they want to do, that they won't do. Their only possible area of weakness is their listening to those they consider advisors, that they inherited from their family or such.

This warrior's energy field attracts demons trying to get that brilliance of mind that splits open the smallest things and sees the details. This is something very rare. Those who have this ability can foresee situations much like prophecy and therefore defend against it.

What this warrior builds therefore is bullet proof. They've thought of everything. They're good to go for a long, long, time.

If there's a project this warrior has ever failed it, or even not done spectacularly well, it's because of crude and blatant sabotage.

Their spiritual weapons are their absolutely precise understanding of the situation, and what has happened. Their weakness is when they let others color their own instinctive understanding.

It takes this warrior a few hits and misses to learn to standing independent and trust their own instinct. But they're razor sharp when they get there.

They need to be cautious about who they have relationships with. Because they are so valuable, there's a chance of them being sucked into groups and families that they on their own would have had nothing to do with. This warrior needs to maintain independence and not align themselves with any group.

Demon – Sun in Capricorn with Mars in the Fire Signs
This demon is a radical anarchist if ever there was one. They seem to be all for establishment of this and that, and they themselves tend to be firmly embedded in the system, in perfectly secured jobs; but actually they just want to pull down everything – purportedly to make it better.

They have a perverted sense of logic that makes them believe that changing the order of things, all natural things, will solve all the problems of the world. That of course is a lie they tell themselves to justify their constant need for sulphureous destruction of everything. They can't be trusted to go drop their daughter to school, and come back without developing a hypothesis that involves the mass murder of the entire town as a required and urgent thing.

They drain all they come in contact with, with their barely disguised pessimism and negativity.

Now, I know this, Ed, because I knew one of these demons personally. This demon has intense self-hatred and doesn't show it overtly so almost no one knows this. But they actually carry that consciousness of self-hatred to the point where others start hating themselves around this demon.

SUN IN CAPRICORN with

MARS IN CANCER, SCORPIO, PISCES – THE WATER SIGNS

This warrior is incredibly astute with moving and shifting value systems. That means they are able to perceive the energy value of institutions, businesses that are involved with shipping, transport, travel and movement of all kinds.

Their spiritual warfare acumen is in perceiving the build-up of energy in places from where it is likely to be deployed against humans.

Something about energy warfare with the thugs, Ed, is that they almost never have the energy anyone to do one on one attacks on humans. It is nearly always a team, with one face at a time doing the deployment. But before they attack, there's the build-up of loosh or stolen vital energy, moved in to a point from various places.

This warrior is a lifelong observer of energy movements and has the instinct to know when a build-up is happening and who it's likely to be deployed against. They are able to anticipate both macro events and micro events.

The true knowledge accumulated by this warrior of energy movements will probably be unknown even to them, as it's happening on a sub-conscious level. But in the moment of war, it will result in sudden crystal clear vision and guidance.

This warrior's weakness is a tendency to want to escape things for a break from the constant harassment of the thug world mass consciousness. I hate to say it, but in this lifetime, it's best for them to learn to relax on the battlefield. There is no actual escape from the battlefield for a while now. We can pretend but this warrior doesn't like pretense and won't be happy with it.

Demon – Sun in Capricorn with Mars in the Water Signs
This demon has an affinity for sports and other teams where the energy is fluid and is passed from one set of players to the next set, via the players in common.

This demon makes their cut of energy by coming in-between energy flow partners. They see energy flow happening and they go break it, or come in-between, imagining they're getting the energy displaced because of them coming in between.

They will join school boards, and PTA associations and neighborhood associations and any board or association that will have them, just to keep coming in-between people talking or people working together or people loving each other.

It's a demon of disruption. They WILL disrupt and come in-between and apologize for the intrusion but blatantly continue being in the middle.

They also steal, embezzle and even block necessities from reaching people. Like disturbing women who are breast-feeding their baby, delaying or blocking people's salaries to keep their families waiting for food; blocking essential needs' transport and supplies to keep people waiting and so on.

The thug world order uses these methods themselves enmasse so this sadistic demon is in company usually, that values their sadism.

This sort, honestly, ought to be executed for crimes against humanity.

SUN IN CAPRICORN with
MARS IN TAURUS, VIRGO, CAPRICORN – THE EARTH SIGNS
This warrior is a well read and expanded intellect with an instinctive understanding of value and wealth. They are able to make small changes that result in big changes later on. What they start or build,

automatically has the chance of long-term establishment and success because of their instinct.

For example, a plant they select out of many, to plant, will have the highest chance of surviving to grow into a tree and a fruitful healthy one. They are constantly gathering energy and information about energy in their energy fields so within them is always something like an energy map.

This warrior is an expert in time management and not wasting time on things that will be unproductive. This is a spiritual weapon that is not given enough importance. Time is a form of energy too and using it right, is energy efficiency of the highest order.

This warrior is an alchemist when it comes to time-management, because he or she manages to do things by arranging time that few others would be able to do or achieve. This shows in their lives and their protection of loved ones, in so many ways.

These warriors can almost never be cheated in negotiations because they are so well grounded in what they want and what they're willing to give for it.

This warrior's weakness is their attachment to things connected to their mother's family. A lot of old stuff, carries energy that one should allow to keep flowing and not try to hold. This warrior being so tuned to things of energy value can sometimes not allow things to leave and flow on, that should. This is because of deep rooted fear of loss that is often inherited trauma from when their family or community was forced to leave their own land to resettle in other places.

Demon – Sun in Capricorn with Mars in the Earth Signs
This demon is a flagrant violator of decencies as they have sadistic enjoyment in people being shocked and outraged. Their energy from when a child is invested in how to outrage people so that they

cannot actually anything in response because they are so shocked and didn't see that coming.

This is that kind of demon that hangs out around schools and flashes when kids don't have adults around. They are always preying on the innocent and those who are likely to get shocked by their sudden display of perversion.

They actually in secret, to what extent they can, study and collect material that is shocking, sexually perverse and so on. They find a sense of power in shocking and destabilizing people. If there's anyone in their lives they spare, it's because they need them to keep cooking and cleaning and providing for them.

They know who they can play with and who they can't. For the most part. So, they have a rather clean image in front in society. A man or woman who isn't extreme in any way and simply minds their own business. But in secret they're recording who's likely to be most shocked by something and if they get a chance, alone, perhaps when they and the person are drunk or in circumstances that can later be used as an excuse or cover, they do a sudden shocking move.

They rise in organizations initially but stall at mid-level management for example because someone or other gets a glimpse of their underlying sadistic enjoyment of outraging and shocking people.

SUN IN CAPRICORN with
MARS IN GEMINI, LIBRA, AQUARIUS – THE AIR SIGNS
This warrior is a powerful establisher of fields of philosophy and thought that will last a very, very long time. The Apostle Paul mentioned in the Bible is an example of this warrior. Someone who by insistence on some basic principles can establish a change in the way people think.

It's easy to influence people into thinking differently, seeing differently, even acting differently for a while. But it takes this warrior's inborn powers to cause a change that will last; to set a ball rolling that will keep rolling, perhaps infinitely.

Their effect may not be as visible and dramatic as thought leaders of the past, but there is no doubt that in their lives, and in their sphere or influence, or maybe through media of some sort; this warrior will cause a shift in understanding and attitude that will have far reaching effects because of the energy of the introducer.

In everything in life, this warrior is an establisher of good things for those they love, and the one who breaks cycles of poverty, loss, and things that come from the consciousness of feeling insufficient and valueless. They CREATE VALUE.

This warrior's weakness is their instinct to try and help people who don't value them. Just because they can. But they get out of this habit as they grow older, as they realize that not everyone really wants to prosper and progress. A lot of people like their hellhole lives and like to fester in lives and atmospheres that are dead and not going anywhere but doom.

This warrior will stop trying to get people off buses headed for doom, and focus on their own self and family, which tends to have the biggest impact energetically and through life into the future.

Demon – Sun in Capricorn with Mars in the Air Signs

This demon is interested in other peoples' finances and assets and such as they have a sadistic wish to trick others into giving up things of value in their lives.

It reminds me of this reality show, "Bigg Boss". It's the Indian equivalent of the show "Big Brother" in the US and UK. In this show there are frequently games or activities, where the contestants are supposed to give up, destroy or burn something of deep emotional value to them; like soft toys they've had a long time, or favorite gifts from loved ones, photos of family and so on; in exchange for saving a friend's or their own place on the show.

That idea probably is the brainchild of this demon. They're always rating the value of something, by what some human will give up, to get it. They frequently very cunningly put their family and people around in the predicament where they have to give up something dear to get something they need.

This demon does well in the thug world order because it is established on the principle of sacrifice of what is of great emotional value in exchange for advancement or progress. This thug is always noticing you noting what you like and value, to use that to manipulate you.

SUN IN AQUARIUS with

MARS IN ARIES, LEO, SAGITTARIUS – THE FIRE SIGNS
I feel blessed to contemplate and see the great manifestation of God as this angelic being of deliverance from the bondage of the mind and magnetism that has held a long time.

This warrior is a simple person, so simple that they can immediately see through long held diktats and such that hold energy hostage and don't allow progress. They walk right through because they are naturally the energy of energy field demagnetizer.

They simply do not buy into anything that is the result of long held regressive magnetism. They are immune to it.

This warrior does not think too much – they have no need to. Things are simple in the moment and they go with that.

They are often considered too simple by their caregivers and people around, but of course they don't really give a crap. They are the change God sends to turn the human consciousness from what has held us in a bind towards a return to primal; fresh energy flow and vision.

When they do have a vision for the future, this warrior starts off on making it a reality with the simplest, most basic tools and equipment. They either succeed directly or lay the foundation for that change and it waits for the time when it goes viral so to speak, but in the consciousness it is already whirring and rolling.

This human in spiritual warfare is someone you can't get past because you can't make them care for something that is spin or bullshit. They have their priorities set. They're like the Angels that guard the gates of heaven, in mythology. You can't slither and squeeze past them. They see you, they put their sword of fire to you.

This warrior is a guardian of precious things in the human consciousness and they do a fine job whether they know it or not.

Their weakness is sharing stuff with others who are not of the same purity and unfettered spirit as them. They end up being loners because of being bullied or laughed at by demons who cannot comprehend the simple ways of life. When they do find their own soul group and their soul mate, they keep everyone fresh and in the moment, focusing on what's important.

Demon – Sun in Aquarius with Mars in the Fire Signs
This demon is a destroyer of things kept in his or her care. You cannot trust them to cherish or care for or guard anything. They themselves have an instinct to destroy things kept in their care just because.

If they're born into a family that has a lot of things; they will slowly divest the family of everything, just everything. It's just that they have that sort of consciousness that can be quiet after destroying everything around themselves.

The only thing this demon won't destroy is what they need and use to fuel their ego trip as a powerful person who can influence others and make them choose or buy things. A sort of glorified salesman that can sell ice to an Eskimo.

People engaging with them start losing energy almost immediately and experience loss of things.

Humans attract this demon when they need to get rid of the life they have built while being in the wrong career or relationship for them.

SUN IN AQUARIUS with
MARS IN CANCER, SCORPIO, PISCES – THE WATER SIGNS

This warrior is a master of energy movement and changing energy from static forms into being useful to nurture and help others. For example, if they enter an office, they will immediately be aware of the potential of things in the office, potential of people, who've been there a long time but never got to be really useful. They can make changes to bring in all the potential that had been stagnating there and use it to take the work or team forward.

They are excellent galvanizers of people and energy and sentiment for the advancement towards a goal.

They are the scooper-up of potential that has been wasted, and the converter and user of things ignored and not valued.

They effect change all the time, not just dramatically now and then. They are naturally drawn to making life easy for others.

This warrior's weakness – well not exactly weakness, but it feels like it to them for some part of their lives – is that they tend to not be invested in education and staying in the education system of thug world.

This holds them back initially but they later realize that if they had gone on the beaten path, they would have lost things precious to them. This warrior values and needs their privacy, their personal freedom and an atmosphere that honors and respects that.

Often they are not honored or respected for who they are, because they did not gather up the qualifications and jobs or money to show for their unique talents and freedom of soul. But this results in them moving away from those who don't value them and finding their tribe and their own family.

It is because of these warriors that home birthing has become a widely established norm again, when it was so frowned upon and driven to near extinction by the thug world which wants to ritually torture women and children at the vulnerable time of birth.

Nearly all change for the betterment of humanity has a warrior of this birth in there, doing what others can't do because of being weighed down by the mass consciousness. They are kind to a fault and have a heart to care for others. They need to learn to distinguish demons from humans so they do not get drained trying to correct the energy of those who do not want freedom or emancipation.

Demon – Sun in Aquarius with Mars in the Water Signs
This demon is an energy vampire that thrives off people who are in transition in their lives; starting new ventures, or moving house, or moving from school to university, or from one relationship to another.

If you met this demon during a time of transition in your life, when you were starting something new; beware they're most likely only there to get your "fresh start" energy. If they're really into you or like you for real, they'll be around in weeks or months ahead when you've established yourself in your new situation a bit.

This demon drains "new start" or "transition" or "emancipation from the past" energy and uses it to keep their own self in some sort of stagnant situation where there is nearly always abuse they're keeping hidden, often abuse being the way they and someone else they're in cahoots with, make money.

They often pretend to be kind, donate money and "help" people – but it's a ruse to build an aura of a good person. They are essentially criminals and energy vampires who actually do criminal things to earn money.

You cannot trust them at all, and you should definitely not introduce them to people you value in your life.

SUN IN AQUARIUS with

MARS IN TAURUS, VIRGO, CAPRICORN – THE EARTH SIGNS

This warrior is the harbinger and canary in a cage singing, sign, of mass consciousness energy shifts. Even as rare as real humans are in our times, this human is even rarer. Of course we are in just one of those times in history when the energy shifts we're talking of are happening, after maybe millennia, and so we can assume that this warrior has been born somewhere.

This warrior is a God force consciousness of unfettered willingness to move towards what is beautiful, sublime and of lasting credit to our souls. They are not tempted by things that pass. Their eyes are on beauties of creation that are above the thug world's value system.

They are often reviled and misunderstood by those around them who cannot understand their magic, and that it is they who hold for us all the consciousness that we are not slaves to the energy parasites who farm us; but we are divine beings, angels in chains who must walk steadfastly and fearlessly towards our freedom.

This warrior has a soul courage and fearlessness that is angelic and uncompromising. Their very existence is a statement made by God and in their upholding of their own being, their own consciousness, is all of our healing.

If they have a weakness that can cause them pain and hold them back from the enjoyment of nature; it is their attempt to try and explain themselves to demons who have no capability of understanding them, nor the desire to.

Demons are attracted to this warrior big time because of their ability to change consciousness and this warrior must learn to recognize them and destroy those who have gotten addicted to them.

Once a demon gets a whiff of this warrior's energy, they are not likely to go away quietly because they know they'll never get this kind of energy supply again. They must be destroyed and God will show this warrior how to do it.

Demon – Sun in Aquarius with Mars in the Earth Signs

This demon is one of those which finds a human and latches on and never leaves. They're there hanging about and offering to do this and offering to do that, and they just won't go.

They don't latch on to just anyone. You got to be a human with an innocent love of life, laughter and joy. They got to feel like they're a child again with you.

If they experience that, they have found their most favorite prey. A natural source of childlike energy.

They are not usually able to deceive humans because they tend to have a sort of repelling, creepy, "I will lay my life down for you; I will lay my cloak on the path for you to walk; I will worship you master/mistress; I will be your slave;" kind of attitude.

But once in a while humans get fooled a bit and maybe believe them for a while.

They prey on lonely people. People who are lonely accumulate a lot of energy compared to those who are constantly social. This demon lives off that energy.

Humans who do not value themselves, tend to attract this demon to teach them that they do not need others to support them, and definitely not demons who live off of them; that it is better for wait for the right person than allow just anyone to spend time with you.

SUN IN AQUARIUS with

MARS IN GEMINI, LIBRA, AQUARIUS – THE AIR SIGNS

This warrior is a most understated, undervalued and hidden gem. I say this because they are so valuable and powerful that it is rare in our times that any human can be given importance to match that.

They have a God given vision to cut straight to the heart of things, cut out all the bullshit and set free the one core thing that is of great value.

They are a master healer of people and projects and things that having started off right, have gotten buried under accumulated energetic burdens and the rubble of operations that never got fully completed.

They have the ability to cut through the hugest mountains of rubbish, garbage and bullshit and fish out what's of value.

Their vision is simple and clear. But they do have a weakness for playing the Devil's advocate and that is one thing they need to be aware of. Because this warrior often has gone to rescue someone or something from under piles of bullshit and rubble, only to realize there wasn't anything of value there.

Worse, when they'd done the heavy lifting, someone else came along and finished the last bit and took credit for the whole work.

This warrior has to learn to follow their own instinct about who's good for them and who isn't and not get seduced by philosophies where they give exploiters and abusers second chances.

Demon – Sun in Aquarius with Mars in the Air Signs

This demon is the sort who'll stalk someone of high energy, and offer themselves in service. Something like people going after a guru. The real reason behind it is that this demon preys on the energy of those who do philanthropic activities or are giving back to the community or such.

In truth, in 90% of cases of people who are doing philanthropic things, they are in a consciousness of debt, where they feel they owe something to someone. This is an opening for energy vampires, and a good one too, because if you feel you owe someone something, and you don't mentally clearly state what it is you owe, it becomes an open-ended unlimited energy drain.

This demon finds themselves in those environments where the consciousness of debt is high and manipulates people into feeling attached to him and her without understanding or knowing consciously why they feel the MUST answer their phone call, follow them on social media, and show a sort of following or validation of them.

If you met this demon in a place with the consciousness of debt – volunteering activities, banks, or while applying for a home loan or such, know you're dealing with a demon and escape.

And deal with the consciousness of owing things that you're carrying.

SUN IN PISCES with
MARS IN ARIES, LEO, SAGITTARIUS – THE FIRE SIGNS
I bow down to God who manifests as this angel of compassion on all those who are suffering. This warrior feels and hears the cries for help of those who no one else hears.

And it's not like they just walk on the streets and hear people crying from inside the houses. No, this is an angel of mercy who has discernment like no other. Because they are of all the zodiac, those who are able to see, recognize and comprehend evil the most.

They have an instinct that is above the differentiation of good and evil; it is an instinct of understanding what must be, because the Spirit is flowing that way.

In the great epic the Bhagavat Gita, Krishna the warrior of old, tells his protégé Arjuna, that in the battle of life, one must do what is in their nature to do, and fulfil the natural duty they have without considering other things. He told Arjuna that in his standing for what is right, he has reached the point where his own cousins and family members were opposing him on the battlefield; and that he shouldn't back down now.

This is what this warrior has — that innerstanding of how nature or the spirit is flowing and this warrior does what is right according to their soul and spirit no matter what else.

My own father, Patrick was this warrior. Words won't be enough to describe the pillar he was. If anyone showed the very existence of the righteousness as well as mercy of God, it was he. He didn't care what others thought of him, he followed his inner guide in the moment.

In his young days, before he understood himself, he got exploited and used by many who needed a heart on fire to fuel their agendas. But at one point he began to become aware and he started to be his own warrior to fulfil his own soul's leading.

One time he went riding on his cycle across town to the house of a man who was beating up his wife regularly. He wasn't even close to them. He went in, met the man, and said something. No one knows what. But that man never dared raise his hand on his wife again. To this day people wonder what actually transpired.

But that's this warrior for you. When their spirit leads, they move in divine anointing.

They also have the ability to pull out endless supplies of energy including physical energy when they want to do something. My dad was known to pull whole cows out, on his own, who fell into wells.

This warrior's ability to convert energy into whichever energy is required, on demand is huge. They can go without sleep for days and days, doing something, their hands working steadily, their heart not failing in devotion and dedication.

What more can I say than that traditionally the Jesus of compassion for the weary and ill, and also the Jesus who took a whip and whipped money lenders and salespeople out of the temple for spoiling the atmosphere there; was supposed to be born under Pisces, or have a strong Pisces placement.

Demon – Sun in Pisces with Mars in the Fire Signs

This demon is sort of scavenger among demons, hanging about in places where there is a lot of emotional or spiritual energy. They hang about in places where there is trauma and are attracted to people carrying unreleased trauma. They feed on the energy of those who are in pain and trying to come to terms with shock, bereavement, sorrow and the like.

This demon ends up working in hospitals, psych wards and other trauma fields, living comfortably off those environments, presenting themselves as angels of mercy.

They are not small time energy vampires, but the sort who in one interaction can drain the person of vital energy to the point where they take months or years to recover.

You know you have this demon in your life if you have found yourself pouring your heart out to someone and then finding yourself tired, confused and feeling lost and demotivated for weeks after. They might not know you well, but they'll call up to ask how you are and suddenly you feel compelled to give them personal information. And then again you're tired for days.

Actually, I needn't say all this, you already know.

SUN IN PISCES with

MARS IN CANCER, SCORPIO, PISCES – THE WATER SIGNS

This warrior is multiplier of the little into the lots, and the not enough into the enough and plenty. They have the anointing from God to convert energy that is not yet in the physical, to the physical and beyond.

You could call them warriors of manifestation. It's their nature to know when a sort of energy that should be there, manifested, is not, and to correct that imbalance.

They are always bringing hidden or unseen energy into manifestation in some form or the other.

As teachers, they are nurturers of those who cannot express themselves and their talents or energies.

Ever gentle, they can also use unconventional methods to bring out what is latent.

They are finders of buried treasure and discoverers of lost treasures of the past.

This warrior's weakness is that early in life they get mentally programmed into certain fears or phobias by those who tried to keep them down spiritually. They will find that if they walk towards spiritual advancement on their own (not with others), the fears and phobias go away.

The channel through which they get exploited and drained are usually either sexual or spiritual. So they will have to learn to be monogamous and have sex only with a committed monogamous partner; and spiritually have their own walk without giving information about what they're doing and how they're growing to others.

Demon – Sun in Pisces with Mars in the Water Signs

This demon is a cheater in friendship, in love and in every place and situation they're trusted. They try to pass it off as the result of alcoholism or because they're so depressed in life and out of control and all that.

It's simply that they're so energy deficient that they must cause sudden huge tragedies to fall on people – like the loss of their entire food money for the week or month, or things like that, to get a feeling of power.

They usually end up in prison or have their family wealth drained bailing them out from one failed venture and criminal case after another.

The place they tend to be employed most often is religious organizations where abuse of the young is done ritualistically. This gives them cover for all their other crimes as well.

They pretend at one age to be romantic, fun and affectionate. But it's a well-trained act. They need to cause constant heartbreak, heartache, shock, sorrow and grief to feel like they have some power and being there.

If you met one of these and from the day you got with them you have had one heartbreak after another and have been living in sorrow day after day, you know you're with this demon.

They're extremely manipulative so don't talk to them. Just leave.

SUN IN PISCES with

MARS IN TAURUS, VIRGO, CAPRICORN – THE EARTH SIGNS

This warrior is drawn to earth fields, sometimes traveling great distances to stand at certain places on the surface of the earth. In their own being they connect up places whose energy fields are lost from or cut off from human consciousness.

They are a retriever of what is lost from human consciousness, that the human spirit needs at a particular time for our advancement.

They will dig out things buried under layers of time, find things overgrown by jungle, bring out talents long forgotten inside a person.

They are extremely good in businesses where this kind of activity – bringing out the hidden, and finding the lost, are involved.

This warrior is inheritor of his mother's side of the family's legacy and will frequently re-establish his mother's side bloodline.

This warrior is extremely psychically active, perceptive of people's leanings and allegiances that they themselves might not be aware of, and therefore a great judge of who will get along with who, and who should be on a team and so on.

Their only weakness appears to be that their sense of fashion doesn't seem to fit in with wherever they are. This is possibly because they have arrived in this time, straight from another time with another sense of fashion and it is not something they care to give importance to right now.

They really don't care how they look, or what anyone thinks of them. They'll do their thing and be driven by their purpose unfailingly.

Demon – Sun in Pisces with Mars in the Earth Signs
This demon is the sort of traitor that will sell out their family, country, own spouse for a big enough sum of money. They are crazy for money and the power they believe it brings.

From their childhood, they're focused on making money and are always on the look out for a good get-rich-quick scheme.

For all that, this demon is destined to die in poverty of all kinds and without anyone loving them.

If you're with a Piscean who keeps talking about money, and money making schemes, run. That really is all they're interested in.

SUN IN PISCES with

MARS IN GEMINI, LIBRA, AQUARIUS – THE AIR SIGNS

This warrior is a master of all that taboo but truly powerful in liberating souls from the manipulation, energy draining and trauma harvesting of this realm. Whether they acquire formal education to learn how to overcome deep and long term psychological and other trauma, it is an area of learning they become expert in naturally in the course of their lives.

They are themselves emotionally stable as adults because of deep hurt and abuse suffered in childhood and the teenage years, and then learning to overcome that.

Wherever in the world they are – working in a business, or running an ad agency, or coaching a sports team, their service to humanity continues on clear and brave – the upliftment of the hurt and the traumatized and helping them come out of their shell into achieving things they never thought they could.

This warrior's only weakness is a rather constant need to keep going back to some place they loved as a child or teen. You'd think it was understandable; naturally it's human nature to go back to places we loved.

But in the case of THIS warrior, 9/10 times they were feeling that pull because someone who abused them in those years they used to go to that place, is using that place as a channel to drain them.

That place has gotten associated with that "love" or "trust" of that abuser back then.

IF they bring this to awareness and deal with it, most of the time, they will discover that place is within them, and at least they don't feel the previous pull to go physically back there.

This warrior is prone to getting betrayed and must be very careful to only hang out with their soulmate or someone who has the same life purpose as them, who they're an energetic match with. Not someone they have compassion for and is tagging along as some sort of follower or general helper. It must be the same level of warrior or none at all.

All others are likely to turn betrayers.

Demon – Sun in Pisces with Mars in the Air Signs

This demon is an energy gambler. Most gambling in the world IS energy gambling, but this demon has in his head a race course, and the people he knows are the horses. He manipulates and plays the people in his life. He invests in those who are going strong, hangs out with them, drains them. Then he goes back to the board and looks at who's going strong now, and goes for them.

He is so compelling with his words, it's like he's making Martin Luther King type speeches sometimes. But he's an absolute fake.

He pretends to be appreciative of a whole lot of people, supportive with money and so on. But he is simply an energy gambler and vampirical drainer of those who are doing well.

He will himself often lend money to those he has drained, so that they will be available to him once they're recovered.

You'll recognize this demon by how they seem to arrive regularly and donate or give money or other support that keeps someone going a little, and then crashing again. They have more than one friends like that, and they tend to not introduce them to each other.

Dear Ed,

I have left Jupiter and the rest of the thrones out of this book, as they deal with another dimension of spiritual warfare, that's the next level after we master these.

Here are recent posts on my Substack – https://CarafAvnayt.Substack.com that got very popular and are related to this subject.

How To Recognize Demons & The Opportunities They Offer
Dear Ed,

I've been having hell since I posted my last article describing demons with Venus placements. My websites, social media shadow banned (even more than usual), and so on.

It's made me quite amazed at how some entities doing censoring, actually identify as demons enough to have a problem with my posts. Especially as it's a well-known and ancient concept that **demons occupy human bodies** and pervert the faculties available to us as humans towards energy draining humans - the very reason why they even bother to show up in human bodies.

Someone sent me a message, Ed, saying I was "dehumanizing" people by calling them demons! It made me realize that it's us humans who have been dehumanized by attributing evil to us.

Everything in nature, Ed, is full of love. No one in nature sadistically hurts another. Nothing in nature seeks to cause hurt, harm or cultivate pain for **energetic draining**.

In the Old Testament of the Bible, God makes a law, telling people to return the blood to the earth, because the life is in the blood. It even had to be said, because at the time of that being said or written, it was a well known and established thing - that drinking the blood of another was to vampirize their life energy, their soul energy.

In nature, Ed, no animal vampirizes another's soul.

We are nature too, Ed, yet **it is us who have been dehumanized; by attributing what is clearly not natural or human to us**.

In my life, this is has been painfully brought to my attention over and over again, as I am a subject of ritual torture, and evil, that neither I nor my parents ever did, has been used by the ritual doers to justify their violation, abuse and torture of me and our son.

It is what the thugs have done in the mass consciousness, Ed, attributing all manner of evil to human nature. It's a part of their routine policy, Ed, to attribute some evil to an ancestor of the tribe and use that to justify toe torture of all people of that tribe, that group, that race even.

Jews were punished for crucifying Jesus; Christians for the crusades, Muslims are punished because of 9/11; all white people are criminalized for "colonialism"; every tribe and human bloodline has some trope or the other on them that makes it easy for demons to assault the whole lot of them whenever they want ritual blood sacrifice. It just goes on and on and on.

We tend to forget, though, Ed, that they have run campaigns against us humans as a species itself, since time immemorial, Ed, making it like we are born to evil and selfishness, theivery, lust and perversion. They have modified and warped religious texts and books to sell this concept. The catholic church invented the concept of "original sin" - a concept so utterly anti-life that even I as a seven year old couldn't believe it.

They have invented the "cave man" who treats women like chattel, does nothing but kill animals, fight over the bones, f*** whatever. They tell us we came from that.

They have consistently, Ed, consistently removed as far as possible from us, the art, sculpture, architecture that shows our high and angelic qualities; our nobility, our goodness, our love. **Ed, just as sweet as any blade of grass, just as loyal as a dog, just as majestic as a cat, just as etheric as a bird, just as beautiful as the flowers, are we too.**

We too, like all of nature, just want to play about with our friends and family, till we find the one we want to mate with; we too just want to nest, make babies and just let life energy flow through us on and on; just like all of nature.

Yet we have been dehumanized, and made to believe that we are intent on harming others, cheating and exploiting. It simply isn't true, Ed.

We have, despite everything, **millions of years of epics and books that quite clearly describe the influence of demons or anti-natural beings** that disguise themselves as human sometimes, but always are after human soul energy. They are called Rakshasas in Sanskrit and there are very real descriptions of them as having human bodies despite not actually being human.

A painting by Raja Ravi Varma, circa 1910 depicting the scene where the Rakshasa or demon called Ravana, arrived as a Holy Man asking for alms to lure a woman out of her home to kidnap her. Picture Source

This Raksha called Ravana is one of the most famous demons, and here he is shown very much in a human body, sadistically enjoying killing a bird who was trying to help the woman he was kidnapping. - Painting "Jatayu Vadhu" by Raja Ravi Varma 1848-1906

The nature of demons are described extremely clearly and pointedly in several ancient texts and there is the well known concept that God takes birth as a human - where God means God in his form where he has the powers to cleanse the earth of evil; specifically to get rid of the **demons**, which - and I quote here from the "Bhagavat Purana" "*are grown numerous and are burdening the earth, so the earth herself cries out to me.*"

A modern painting that shows the ten most famous forms God takes at different points in time to destroy demons. <u>Picture Source</u>

This knowledge of demons or rakshasas *has been widely removed from Western thought*, simply because Western thought leads mainstream thought these days, and there is a **long term agenda to make people discount and negate the existence of evil itself, so that we will accept these demons in our lives, and accept their abuse as normal and human.**

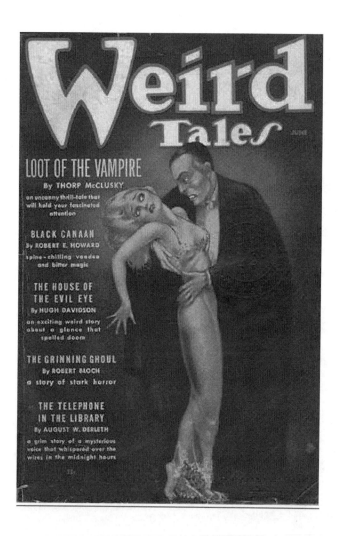

The concept of demons that vampirize energy through blood is so ancient, Ed, that to this modern day it continues to be represented in movies and tv shows. This magazine cover is from 1936.

A famous old story from Germany, called "Hansel and Grettel" told of a demon who kept a child hostage in a cage, fattening him up to eat him. This wasn't even contested or considered a controversial thought for the millennia or centuries through which it was passed down. "The Grimm's Fairy Tales" are like an introduction to the reality of demons in human bodies to keep children safe.

The "witch-trials" Ed, were essentially the wipeout of any woman who was spiritually active. Men are easy to program and control mentally as they traditionally go outside of the house to work and study and earn. But women, till recently, worldwide acquired their education at home, passed down from immemorial generations; and that included the recognition of demons and spiritual warfare.

Under the guise of removing evil, they took out those bloodlines and people who actually knew how to recognize and deal with demons.

And since then they've been "reeducating" us through books and tv shows and movies to accept demonic behavior as normal human behavior; thereby **putting the trope of evilness on all of us humans, making us _unable to defend ourselves in spiritual warfare_.** Literally disabling us on the battlefield so we don't know who's attacking us and why and what to do about it.

I won't stand for it, Ed.

I'd have been dead today, Ed, my destiny left unfulfilled if I'd not learned to recognize demons. Initially as a teenager I only saw the disembodied ones. I wrote a bit about those in another article a while ago. But I stopped being harassed by those and then began my real education in demons. It began, Ed, simply because by the early 2000s, I began to look at energy fields again - something I'd done in childhood and been beaten and bullied into suppressing.

As an adult I decided to let myself see again, and I found, Ed, that **not all human bodies actually had a self generating source of light within, a direct connection to spirit**. I was especially surrounded by these, more than others, because of being held hostage and a ritual torture subject.

I initially thought it was just the ones holding me hostage who weren't actual humans.

But between 2000 and now, Ed, the population of humans is pretty much disappeared from sight, nearly all either held in tight hostage somewhere out of normal circulation; the good quality fakes who had energy fields running because of inherited blood rhythm from actual human ancestors, have fallen to a very small part of the population; and the vast majority of bodies around are actually bio-bots, who are run chemically and controlled by demons, who are sometimes in residence in the body and sometimes not.

In my noticing, the average demon or egoic entity controls about 60 bodies at a time, sometimes more. Those 60 are usually a family group, or a group bonded through exchange of sexual fluids. For example if one male rapes 30 male or female bodies, that demons controls the lot. This is why pedophilia and sodomy are being normalized.

This is vastly different from the time of Jesus when a legion - which is about 40,000 demons occupied one man. That was the quality of human dna then, that it could vibrationally hold that many egoic astral loosh entities.

Now the quality of human dna of demon bodies - which is basically human flesh generated without soul or spirit is drastically degenerated and is continuously degenerating very badly, so the demons have needed to make more and more bodies. The bodies get drained very quickly, and need energetic support to go past 16-17 years.

The parasites' front line are increasingly pre-teens and teenagers for their vital force, because they become energyless soon. They then have to support, anyone who is useful in any way, even if it's just the organs they keep alive; with supplements made of fet-s - unborn baby. This is because the energy value of a fet-s which grows from just a cell to a entire little body in 9 months, is the highest level of energy expression we will have in our lifetime.

Food and medicines worldwide have fet-s energy and to keep the supply of these going is such a critical matter that it shapes the politics and so many other aspects of law making and so called "healthcare".

I get asked a lot, Ed, about -

How I recognize who's a demon and who's not

It's all kinds of little things, Ed, and it's very easy for someone who decides they want to recognize but comes out of religious and tv show programming first.

Religious programming demonizes pretty much anyone who is a free spirit, who is irreverent and lives without adhering to religious laws in their daily life. This can cloud the vision of a person and the perception.

Secular programming of what demons are is basically about poltergeists or ghosts. They're supposed to have horrible peeling skin and make your temperature drop when they're near, and give you the shivers basically. Such a waste of time, Ed, and so far from reality. I've met a lot of poltergeists, Ed, basically egoic entities who were forced to leave their body suddenly and their vital energy did not dissipate immediately so they're still astrally and vibrationally them, hanging about. They're very few now, Ed, compared to say the 90s, because the entire thug matrix is drastically drained of loosh and they've been dissipating as a result.

But most thug programming about demons, Ed, focuses on either their appearance or their actions. This is a huge deception, because humans can look like that and even do "evil" things.

The difference is INTENTION.

A demon instrinsically wants to get energy from someone else, and it is always exploitative. A human intrinsically is out to express their own energy and soul.

A demon is out to take, a human is out to give.

I was channel surfing in 1999 or 2000 when I saw the artist Ricky Martin being interviewed on MTV by someone. I heard him say this, *"In my line, as a celebrity, you have people coming at you all the time. You learn to recognize very quickly the intention with which they're coming at you. You have to learn this or you cannot survive."*

This, in my experience is the key to knowing a demon from a human. Even if they're not coming AT you, a demon is always carrying the intent to exploit others, exploit nature, whatever. They have no inner source of love flowing out to others, even when they pretend they do. It's always about gathering, collecting, getting more people and bodies to use.

When I started noticing the intention of people coming at me, I was startled to find how someone doing nice things for me could actually be carrying the intention to exploit me, while someone not doing so might actually not want to exploit me.

It was mindblowing to discover how little the actions of people actually show their true intent.

Whether humans or demons, you must be spiritually active to know the intention.

My son Gabriel will often come around to the kitchen like he's on a walk around the house to stretch his legs. But I know he's coming to see what I'm cooking and which stage of readiness it's in. I know this without turning around and looking at him. In general I know what the brat's intention is long before he actually shows any sign of it.

I used to think this ability is restricted to him, but believe me, Ed, it is not; and ALL HUMANS have this. Even demons in human bodies have it. ALL of nature has it. We just have to use our preexisting ability to know the intention with which someone is approaching us, to know if it's a demon or a human.

A demon is energetically insufficient - they need to get energy, loosh, whatever, from you. A human is energetically sufficient. If they want money or help or whatever, it's just money, help or whatever. Not your energy.

We need to become of our own energy levels, so that we can be aware "my energy has dropped," "I'm suddenly no longer motivated, what happened?" And we will begin to notice what hit us that drained us.

One very common reason why a person might not be able to exercise this ability, is because of very low self esteem. It's one reason why rape and sexual abuse among other forms of abuse are so common. Because all of this breaks a person's self esteem and with it, their ability to respect and value and follow their own instinct.

So addressing low self esteem, **doing the shadow work to find out why you have shut off your spiritual sensing powers** is very very important. It's possibly the most important thing you will ever do for your life, because without your spiritual sensing, you going to fall for some bullshit or the other, get poisoned, get hurt and die early. YOU NEED TO BECOME FULLY FUNCTIONAL NOW.

Why We Attract Particular Kinds of Demons

Demons in a person's life are a great and unrivalled opportunity. They are not there randomly or outside of our spiritual permission. As Fanny Ellingwood Abbot said, "We cannot fall out of the hands of God."

The psalmist said,"If I make my bed in hell, behold, thou art there." (Psalms 139).

God uses demons; our own soul will attract demons to us to bring out whatever in us corresponds to those demon frequencies. In that way, demons are like homeopathy.

The principle behind homeopathy, is that if you have a problem, and if you introduce an energy that CAUSES that problem, it will waken the sluggish body to respond to the NEW intruder, throwing out the OLD intruder as a result.

For example, if you have heart palpitations and severe pain, your nervous system is shivering and trembling, you're find it hard to breathe as there's no place for the lungs to expand; if you take a plant energy, a poison, that CAUSES these things, very diluted ofcourse, your body will recognize that energy, react to it and deal with whatever is causing the symptoms in the first place.

I can tell you this, Ed, from my own personal experience. The energy Digitalis - made from the poisonous flower Foxglove, has stopped my palpitations and prevented heart attacks on several occasions (back when I had heart trouble). **The NEW poison, made my body react now, to a poison I was not capable of reacting to in childhood.**

In situations where an actual heart attack was coming on, where my heart was actually stopping beating, the dilution called Naja Tripudians - which is the dilution of Cobra venom - which in its non diluted form causes death by heart attack; has STOPPED the heart attack and got my heart going.

I cannot tell you how many times this happened when I was pregnant with Gabriel. I have turned my face into the pillow and cried thanking God for those beautiful creatures, the poisonous flowers and the Cobra, that by existing, saved my life.

Now, Ed, I have found in my life, that **demons are just such an opportunity for us humans to come out of bondage.** If you look into what sort of demon you're attracting, especially the sort you attract over and over again, **you can find out what's locked in your own subconscious that's calling those to you.**

If you're attracting **demons who try to control you, who dominate you sexually and otherwise**; it's because of hidden abuse by parents or spiritual authorities in childhood; who subtly programmed you to need abuse and forcing to reach orgasm. Your soul is trying to break out of that by asserting that you DO believe that love and ecstasy can be found outside of the circle of abuse; that abuse need not be accepted as part of love.

You're attracting these demons to provoke you into believing in love without abuse again; to rub your face in filth till a fire starts up in your gut making you roar back into your own reality and your own energy patterns.

If you're attracting **demons who drain you financially, emotionally** and so on; it's because you believe you are of worth only when you're serving others. You've been programmed to believe that. Your soul is trying to say, "I am worth my existence on my own. I deserve to live, and BE, just for being me. I am not lesser than anyone else. I deserve LIFE and LOVE just for being me. I AM LOVABLE JUST AS I AM. I DON'T HAVE TO DO ANYTHING EXTRA TO DESERVE IT."

If you've been attracting **demons who exploit you to get contacts and find others to exploit** (including your family and children); you're attracting them because you've been used as a conduit to exploit or abuse others with or without your knowing it, as a child maybe. You are carrying guilt for what happened without knowing it. A deep burden eating you away inside. Your soul is saying, "I am not responsible for what happened. I was used without my permission. I am not part of that crime. I am innocent."

If you've been attracting **demons who lead you on on this ecstatic trip of romance and happiness, and then suddenly dump you or betray you;** you've been lied to by someone very important to you in childhood, who made you believe that there's no real pleasure in this world; or real love. That everything nice is unreal and no one's really true to anyone. The actor Yul Brynner once said, "When someone says they want to break up with me, I am cool with it. I see it as, I ate a meal in a restaurant and now it's time to pay the bill."

You've been programmed with that bullshit by someone who did not love or give a damn for you, a demon ofcourse. And your soul is refusing to accept that. Your soul is trying to provoke you into throwing off the cheats and asserting yourself, and your core beliefs as a natural human. If you have real love in you, the "for better or worse, in sickness and in health" sort, know that it exists in the world outside as well, even though it might be rare. Call and believe in, and invest in your soul's other half out there.

Throw out all in your life that upholds the paradigm that true love doesn't exist. Stop hanging out with people who do not believe in true love. Surround yourself with all that upholds the existence of love.

If you've been attracting **demons who drug, poison and control you using substances**; then that's your soul trying to get your attention to your having been controlled that way in childhood or past lives. You have been programmed to excuse crimes done, if they were done by a drunk or drugged person. Your soul is saying, "That was not done to me randomly, it was done on purpose. The substance was an excuse."

If you attract **a demon that isolates you from your true family, friends and life itself**, it's because you have the suppressed memory of someone abusing you, or someone you love very much; in such a way where you had to keep it secret and therefore you were no longer able to play with others or make friends or be close to anyone anymore. You might have developed the appearance of being well-socialized but actually you don't really have actually close friends, because you've been locked up inside keeping the secrets of the abuser.

If you attract **a demon that wants to do sexual rituals with you, who's not your Beloved**; note that you've attracted that entity because you have been a subject of rituals without your knowledge all your life. The rabbit hole on this one runs deep. You'll have to go into meditation or hypnosis and bring out buried memories of ritual abuse and very often you'll have to cut off from some core group you are part of since childhood - either the family you think are yours; or the friend circle or the church or so. Your soul believes you're ready to break out of that spiritual bondage.

If you attract **demons who steal from you,** your soul is trying to awaken you to some big theft of your energy, your money, your vitality, your life; that you've suppressed awareness of, perhaps because it will uproot and end life as you know it.

These are just examples, Ed. But being aware of demons in our lives are a great opportunity to exhume our buried bondages and find freedom. Along with awareness, comes the guidance from the Spirit on how to proceed to set ourselves free.

Freedom from Demons

There was a time when I was just waking up to this concept, and I asked my Granddad about it. He told me this one thing that completely changed my life. He said, "Every crisis is an identity crisis."

Any time we attract or keep demons in our lives, Ed, it's because we're identifying with something, or a group, or an idea or identity that's not ours. This is true on every level you look into it on.

In actual demon ritual circles, they get you identified into a group or false family, to manufacture your consent to participation in their rituals. The day you dis-identify from that group or family, the draining stops.

Deep subconscious self-sabotage is often the result of identifying with a group of friends or classmates or team; where you believe you all have the same intention and purpose in life; whether that's to have a good time, or enjoy music or whatever. But you were being deceived. Demons use all that to get close to humans, and they can do this without them even knowing it.

You self sabotage to maintain that group identity, because the day you stop being insufficient, and the day you step into your power, you won't be able to identify with that group whose core identity is that of someone who doesn't have, is not all there, is insufficient in some way, carry a consciousness of poverty or lack.

NEARLY ALWAYS - SELF SABOTAGE IS A RESULT OF IDENTIFYING WITH A DEMON GROUP OR FAMILY.

You literally feel guilty if you don't sabotage yourself and stay in the circle. This can hold long after losing touch with that group and even after everyone else dies. It's inside you.

A common identity crisis example, is an elder sibling brought up taught she is the caretaker of the younger kids. This makes her attract needy dependent exploitative demons who live off her. When she comes out of her false imposed identity, she breaks out of that cycle.

I think I've made my point, Ed.

I leave you with a still from the "Twilight" movie series, featuring the "Volturi". This "Vampire Government"'s one job, is to prevent humans from finding out that vampires exist in the modern day.

My book on the life of my Granddad John Waltham **"The Eighth of Seven Children"** *describes his experience with vampires (some human) etc.*

My autobiographical book **"Spirit"** *describes my own experiences with demons and actual rituals done on me and others to vampirize human energy.*

These and other books can be got by visiting https://Cara.Earth *or by searching for my name "Caraf Avnayt" in your online book website, like Amazon.*

You can also buy directly from me, <u>PDF, Kindle and Ebook versions of my books at this link.</u>

Sexual Energy Blocks - Venus in the 12 Astrological Houses

Dear Ed,

Because of the current shifts and how this is causing basic Venus energy, which is vital life energy, to rise in all natural living beings, it is now and for the next few years, an easy time to remove sexual energy blocks. So, I thought I'd write this for all our human brothers and sisters, all those who message and email me about it.

I have described how a human with a Venus placement manifests that energy, and then how a fake human or demon with a Venus placement manifests that.

There are similarities sometimes and that's because the opportunities are the same for both, but the human having a soul can use the same abilities very differently, to the soulless demon whose entire use of their own energy is to vampirize human and natural energy.

VENUS IN THE 1ST HOUSE

This person tends to have their sexual energy blocked because of abuse in the past where they were not allowed to express their sexuality in their overt behavior and appearance. They're most probably born in sexually repressed backgrounds where any form of sexual expression is frowned upon and considered evil.

This hurts this person a lot, because as is natural, holy and right, their view of themselves and others is based on their gender and sexuality. To deny them feminity or masculinity in their appearance, and behavior is to choke them.

They tend to grow up feeling splintered inside, usually hunched over a bit, never really happy and looking to escape their family and community for good.

They are very good looking, but constantly manifest some problem or the other with their skin and hair, just to keep safe from feeling they're sexually attractive, and therefore able to fit into the society they're in.

They feel ashamed of the lower half of their body.

That's when their sexual energy is blocked.

When they deal with that though, release the shame of needing to naturally express their feminity, masculinity, sexiness in their outward expression, they are so good looking, so romantic, so hot.

It doesn't matter they're tall or short, or thin or fat, they're so charming and disarming, their love life is likely to be filled with the cutest, sweetest, fun and happiness.

Demon – Venus in the 1st House

This demon pretends to be sexual, and simply isn't going to perform as expected. Their game is to draw people in using covert sexual games, subliminal sexual games, sudden "accidental" touches and so on. They tend to wear perfumes with the sexual hormones of animals and are nearly all the time, even if they're just in a store buying things, bothered about how people are sexually reacting to them.

Their confidence is built on and depends on covert sexual cues from people showing they're getting turned on by this entity. Their confidence breaks when they're not able to do this, and then they get into relationships with the intention of staying in it long term, for the security.

They don't give a crap for the sexual satisfaction of the person they're with, past that initial demonstration of their sexuality. They just keep the relationship going with games that engage their partner sexually, but never actually satisfy. They can drag a human on for years with this game, draining them, keeping them hanging on, doubting themselves, doubting their own sexual energy, emailing me wondering what the problem with them is.

This is the problem. The "Secure" boyfriend or husband or wife is a sexual promise gamer.

You can't make this demon be any different. You have to dump them and never give in to their charming playful attempts to engage you again. Block them etc.

It's evil to string someone on like that. Sheer evil.

VENUS IN THE 2ND HOUSE

This human is full of joy and excitement in sex and vital energy. They're all about making things beautiful, helping everyone around them to be happy and well.

Their sexual energy blocks tend come from being misunderstood as children, when their exuberant wanting to help others and make other happy is seen as them trying to get attention, trying to be where they're not wanted, trying even to steal the attention or thunder of others. For example, i.e. There are so many ways the demon world misunderstands the joie de vivre of this beautiful innocent soul who simply loves to spread joy and happiness and beauty.

But this hurts them right in childhood and they begin to restrict their sexual energy, and be very cautious in showing their friendship, love, sexual energy.

This keeps them middling in everything, just doing the bare essential, never really fully winging out and expressing their passion. They keep away from things, people and places that bring out their passion, and this is one reason they take long to find their soulmate. Because you cannot be medium hot with the love of your life. You got to be 100% heart and without fear of the force of love.

At some point in their adult lives, they reach a breakdown because of how insufficient their life is emotionally, and often look to spirituality, service of others and the like to supplement the lack of sexual or vital love in their lives.

Their soulmate will find them though and then they go through horrors of fears they cannot explain because of how strongly they feel.

They could even hire a private investigator to check their soulmate isn't conning them with black magic. It scares them so, how strongly they love.

I wish I could say most of them find happiness, but in our times, most of them take to loving from a distance because they are too terrified of their own passion in love and the hurt that can ensue from that passion being misunderstood for demonic lust, base sexual wantonness and even sexual addiction. These are things their soul can never tolerate, but because they're so passionate they worry that they could become or be seen as having that.

They tend to have hot hands and feet, manifest boils and pimples in the sexual pelvic zone, on the top of the head, and are permanently angry with God, whether they show it or not, feeling that God has cut them a raw deal in life.

If I were in this situation, Ed, I'd put a huge poster up in my room, "F*** WHAT PEOPLE THINK OF ME, I'M HOT, I'M SEXY, I'M PASSIONATE. DEAL WITH IT." And I would start not holding myself back in life from doing the things I love, letting myself go crazy enjoying them. I'd enjoy the f*** out of every last little thing I ate, moan and groan with pleasure at the softness of a fresh bedsheet, adore myself in the mirror and just in general just have a wonderful time without giving one damn crap what anyone thinks of me.

If someone doesn't like the passionate me, they can f*** off. There's someone out there who's withering sad and pissed off with God, because I'm not loving them like only I can.

Demon – Venus in the 2nd House

This a sexually violent demon whether male or female. They have a high need for sexual energy and they will get it wherever they can. They have an aura of trustworthiness, built by copying someone they considered respectable, usually a teacher or a coach in school.

So they tend to behave like a stentorian P.T. teacher or math teacher. They behave like they're uncompromising in their values and they want everything to be done properly and at the right time. They put on the show of being a very disciplined person in their personal lives. They got everyone's birthdays on their phone reminders, are on time everywhere. In general you could say that they give off the aura of being a disciplined trustworthy individual with high moral values.

This is their cover.

Underneath this, is their constant need for sexual energy vampirized from others. They cultivate people in their lives, usually children and the young, who adore and look up to them, never suspecting that they sexually fantasize about them. They have psychic and covert or subliminal sexual interactions with their cultivated flock.

This can be incredibly harmful to the children and young ones, because they don't know that they're being sexually stimulated and harvested by this demon – who's got this reputation and aura of being so morally up to the mark.

However, instinct will save most of them, because they're likely to have dreams showing this demon sexually assaulting them and so on.

In their adult relationships, this demon goes from sexually hot to sexually cold very quickly, because they don't have what it really takes to keep someone sexually satisfied. They'll perform only when they sense the relationship is in real danger, just to keep it going for their security.

They do not have the concept of emotional cruelty in them, really. They believe that if they play roles like earning for the "family" and paying the bills, they can treat people however they like.

When someone gets rid of a demon like this, there's always the subtle threat of this demon using character defamation to try and intimidate the person into coming back. But at some point this demon realizes that it can go both ways and they could be the one whose character is exposed.

It's important to show this demon that you too can expose them and that you're not afraid to want your emotional and sexual needs be met, that you know that's your right.

VENUS IN THE 3RD HOUSE

This person has a fine taste for what is beautiful and their sexual energy responds to all that is intricate in the world. Nature is a huge turn on. They are sensitive to the movement of life energy and many of their most important decisions are made because their response to beauty and beautiful things.

Unfortunately in a time when demons can also, and more often than humans use skill to lure humans, these can get deceived by those who have got the ability to make beautiful things, music etc., imagining that it means they have a beautiful heart.

That turns out not the case and this person, after a few such experiences, becomes stoic and shuts out beauty and art and beautiful things, subconsciously now associating those with getting duped, played, cheated and brutally hurt.

This becomes a block to their sexual energy which intrinsically responds to beauty.

Even if this is not why their sexual energy got blocked up, they can get it moving again by opening up emotionally and holistically to beauty again. By doing something just for the beauty of it.

I guess I don't have to say anymore, Ed, because they already know exactly what I mean.

Demon – Venus in the 3rd House

This is one of those demons that makes big promises, says the most scintillating things, and sweeps people off their feet. They know how to make an appearance and impact – getting more and more subtle as their fine tune their art.

They are however among the most shallow, petty, money-grubbing types around. They can drain the life out of some innocent human who thought they were a grand, big-hearted, high-thinking person. They are in reality the very opposite of that.

They have no plan or intention whatsoever of keeping their promises. They never did. They see relationships as stepping stones to finding fame and wealth and so on. They have no plan to give anything to their partner, only to take.

They tend to have family members who are dearer to them than any partner could ever be, simply because they're partners in crime, and are each other's protection if things go bad.

They nearly always are involved in some kind of crime or the other.

Getting rid of this demon is not that difficult. They are afraid of institutions like the police, schools, and such. They are naturally wary of people who are disciplined and want to see proof of claims before they believe anything.

They'll behave like they're dying when you dump them. But they never die, it's just an act. They'll actually be out hunting before sundown even.

VENUS IN THE 4TH HOUSE

This person is full of practical ingenuity – with a tinge of magic about it all. They can make their home a wonderful place of magic and beauty. A bit of a dreamer and a bit of resilience to wait and work towards a dream, is such a wonderful thing to be. God has blessed their hands to bring out the beautiful things in their heart.

They are often curtailed by not having enough money to do the projects they want to do. But it's all good, because they can go into projects and trip on those and lose sight of the big picture. So it's all good in the long run. When they have to do the projects that are in line with their soul, the money will arrive miraculously.

Their sexual energy blocks tend to form most often because of assault on their creative ability to make beauty and comfort out of almost nothing. The thug world paradigm has very little respect for this sort of magic anymore. They only respect those who are making a lot of money out of whatever they're doing.

This person often ends up in professions that are nothing to do with their latent magic, just to earn well. This makes them sad and their sexual energy stalls.

The way out for them is start giving importance to the magic they can make. They are the anointed of God who can lift the hearts of humans with sweetness and beauty that only the heart can understand. This is a great and powerful destiny.

Demon – Venus in the 4th House

This demon is an expert at making people feel comfortable. An expert in massage and such. They can make people relax and relaxation always has benefits.

However, this demon is also something like a middleman who takes a cut out of everything they sell.

They either do drain the people they interact with, a little every time. If they don't directly drain them of energy, they will steal some little thing. If they can't do even that, they will do them some harm behind their back very cunningly, like tell someone something that will sabotage that person's happiness or success in some way. I've known one to actually "accidentally" burn a favorite dress of someone they could not steal from.

Somehow these demons gravitate often to being house servants, housekeeping in hotels and so on, and they're excellent there, until they come across someone who doesn't buy their disguise as the angel of comfort.

They actively seek in relationships to be seen as the Angel of Mercy and Comfort. They get possessive of their partners in the sense that, they don't like them getting comforted, liking the food made by others, and appreciating anything really about anyone else. They can poison their partner just to demonstrate that it's only them who will be there for them when things go bad.

This kind of abuse can go on for decades without the partner realizing who's been sabotaging them, wrecking their health and so on.

This demon pretends like service is their motto, but actually they want to be the god or goddess worshipped on a pedestal; or they'll start hurting and breaking down their partner.

They are a remarkably dangerous demon to get away from, but the main thing to remember is, to be careful to never eat anything made by them or which they could have had access to when you're getting away. If you can, get away from their physical access before you say you've left.

I've gotten away from TWO like this, so it's possible. You just need to hold your own vision of the situation, because they'll come around with the angel of Mercy and Comfort act, ready to forgive you, freshly made yummy food in a tray, and all that. Hold your vision and respect yourself.

VENUS IN THE 5TH HOUSE

This person is a natural communicator, both of the verbal and the non verbal sort. This person can communicate with animals, babies. They are refreshed and stimulated by raw natural places, the music of nature and by interactions with natural living beings.

Their sexual energy flow gets blocked by the lack of the fresh air of natural beings and truth.

Because they are so talented and skilled, they get grabbed up people who want to use their skills in communication and marketing and such for the thug world businesses. They get paid well too. But it causes a gradual lessening of their sexual energy levels.

They also tend to get into situations where they're directly or indirectly connected to gambling houses, thug media houses and such which are often hothouses of witchcraft.

They are themselves attracted to magic and witchcraft, and tend to get caught up in groups that they believe are good, and want the good of mankind. Later on, they begin to find out they are selfish, and actually evil.

They tend to cut off from all things witchcraft and magic as a result of wanting to keep the hell away from those wicked, selfish, cruelty entities. But in doing so, they cut off an essential part of themselves and how they interact with life itself.

Magick and witchcraft can be so dirty, but it can also be wonderful and this person has the anointing from God to bring healing through the mysteries of natural energies.

As they do so, they heal themselves and those they love. They begin to stop being deceived as they allow their special abilities to develop and as the fear of being deceived goes, their energy begins to flow well.

Demon – Venus in the 5th House

This demon is an extremely smooth trickster. They start practicing early on their own family, most of who are usually cut off from them for reasons no one can actually say.

They tend to have the logic and excuses and reasons and pros and cons for any topic you could bring up. They come across as intellectually sharp, great memory and very observant.

Actually, they're all that when they're trying to spin a lie as true. A person I knew, used to say, "You can take the Bible and prove anything you want from it. You can even tell someone that God wants them to commit suicide. You can take the verse that says, "And Judas hung himself." And combine it with the verse that says, "Jesus said, "Go and do likewise."

This demon's bread and butter tends to come from perverting justice, spinning proof and support for what he wants to uphold as truth. Naturally they're the sort of lawyers who get paid by criminals. They know how to play the system.

They're wherever there's the need of cunning deceptions to trick people into things. Marketing, media, authors of books and so on.

They have no morals and will write books supporting or covertly promoting sexual abuse, pedophilia and such. They're the experts of making criminals look innocent.

If you have this demon in your life, simply cut off and don't have any communication or discussion with them. That's their forte. They'll never forget that you tried to escape them, no matter how "forgiving" they seem. They will hurt you in ways you don't even know. Just cut off in every way possible. They're seriously a disease and they can actually cause people stuck in their net to have mental and nervous system problems and not know why.

In a work environment, it might look like you cannot escape from this demon, that your path to success goes through them. It's a deception and a lie. No one really respects them, only fears them. You can find your way without becoming an ally of theirs.

NOTE – The 6TH house on, Venus placements mean the person is turned on by spiritual and intangible things more than physical, viewable, things; and the sexual energy blocks tend to be deeper things in the consciousness as well.

VENUS IN THE 6TH HOUSE

This is a great healer who facilitates breakthroughs for all who they help. They heal broken things whenever they can. They naturally can help people save their marriages, relationships and counsel people on how to deal with relationship problems.

For themselves, their sexual energy is stimulated by a similar big-hearted "heal the world" energy. They are prone to loneliness in this world, because there are such few people around. There are many fakers of this around but not those who really walk the talk. So they tend to feel lonely and marooned in the world.

Many of them take to books, movies, where there's that beautiful world full of kind, caring, loving people, that this person dreams of, remembers from past lives, and longs for.

As a result, a lot of their life energy tends to get spent in escaping from the realities of this thug world. This unfortunately blocks their sexual energy as it becomes trained to respond only to fantasy and mind-palaces.

This makes them prone to attracting real solid energy vampires into their lives, those who know how to give them fantasies, turn them on, drain their loosh and then leave them to recover on their own, knowing they'll be back despite the abuse, because they cannot get turned on any other way.

They can consider themselves in love with a rapist, a sexual abuser, someone they had a one night stand with and so on.

It's because they've completely lost faith that any miracle of love can happen in reality.

Often they abuse their bodies out of sheer desperation, making themselves so ill, so out of shape, so they can say, "Now, definitely, no one will love me."

They tend to have the children of their abusers, thereby burying themselves while alive, looking then to abuse fantasies to release the awful pain they carry in them, the corpses of their broken dreams.

Yet, despite all this, in them is the memory of a GREAT LOVE. Greater than I can describe. A love like Jesus wiping the face of Benhur, a slave fainting in the desert under the load he is bearing.

This person's love will come into their dark hell, hold them in their worst times, and bring them out into the light. It's a guarantee.

But the whole thing can be made a lot less macabre by them making a super human effort and starting to come into reality and enjoying what little they can, thereby building their ability to laugh in the face of the devils of the thug world, and realize that God is bigger than the biggest thugs and their institutions.

They can look to cutting out the substances they use to escape reality, and spend time doing things they enjoyed as little children before they lost hope.

They can remove the macabre art and books and music that keep upholding the thug paradigm of pain, and put in those things that remind them of those very rare instances of kindness, beauty and love in this world.

I was in this situation, Ed, completely betrayed on every side, not one glimmer of light from anywhere; and there was a day, I realized that, the fact that I am here in this world, with my heart of true love, is all I really need as proof that God and love exist.

I just looked at my own heart and my own love, Ed, and I said to myself, "If I love like this, it means this exists, and it means my love who loves me like I love him exists."

Demon – Venus in the 6th House

This demon is a chronic and shocking user and dumper of people. This demon's favorite game is to get into a relationship with someone, make them dependent on him or her, slowly cut them off from their natural support system; and then suddenly one day shock them, dump them. They tell them stuff like, "You're no longer the person you used to be. You're just a leech. You're worthless." And so on.

This demon does this, because this demon is a high level vampire and is 99% of the time officially part of a network of

demons. The thug world governments use this kind of demon as their foot soldier. They are given targets. They familiarize themselves with information about the target and then go after them. When they're told it's time to break the target, usually a high day for witchcraft, they will do the shocking.

The network is set up such, that there will be another operative ready to pick up the target person who has been dumped, and is now in a state of shock and very vulnerable. Their natural support system being broken, means they'll have no one trustworthy to weather things with and become extremely easy for others, especially "friends" of the abuser, to pick up.

This is how the thugs break down high vitality independent minded humans. They send them through this roller coaster of this sort of demon, through orchestrated relationships.

The human tends to have no idea what the reality is, and cannot form a clear idea of reality, because people behave suddenly completely uncharacteristically all the time. Someone their heart says will contact them, won't, because they've been stopped. Someone else will.

It's because most of it is staged. These witchcraft rings are ancient and operational all over the world wherever humans are. And the demon with this placement is invariably a part of them. I've not met even one that wasn't. They're too "talented" with their aura of "amazing leader of humanity".

To get rid of them, a human will have to get out of the whole network. This means getting out of the dating game, staying out of places like churches, gatherings where they can expect you to be. You have to find emotional healing in spirituality on your own and then you will have a frequency they can't play with.

VENUS IN THE 7TH HOUSE

This person is a most compassionate, empathetic, adorer of beauty in all things natural, and especially of the heart. They are spiritually inclined and naturally very inclined into doing things for others with a charitable spirit.

This is all very easily exploited, and if it wasn't the family support they tend to have, they would've been robbed many times of all their energy. But this placement of Venus also comes with a strong instinct to recognize evil.

The problem arises when this person suppresses their own instinct and out of thug world mind programming pushes on to be kind to someone even though their instincts are saying NO.

They fall prey to various sorts of seduction – whether covert or overt – because they so love to be kind and loving. They have a great love story in their head, that tends to have them as the partner who rescues the other. So someone playing the, "Help me, help me," card becomes intensely attractive to them. This is because in fact their soulmate probably does need their rescuing. But not in the way they picture in their heads, which is made up of the movies and books they've had in their lives.

They end up sexually drained by energy vampires again and again because of how easily they fall prey to the damsel or dude in distress story.

At the root of it all is thug world programming that makes them believe they can only be loved if they do some service or charity to another.

When they no longer can do all that, because they're so drained, financially destroyed, maybe even homeless, they block off their sexual energy because they believe it's what caused all the trouble.

They then see sexual energy as the enemy of their stability in life. This keeps them swinging health-wise from one extreme to the other. They try various fields of spirituality, read a lot of books, try meditation, holidays in distant lands.

The key for them, is to come out of the belief that they have to be of service to someone to be loved and adored. When they just relax and trust God, and focus on being healthy and peaceful, love will come most sweetly to them.

Demon – Venus in the 7th house

This demon is obsessed with suicide for some reason. They keep threatening to commit suicide to get people's attention, and they secretly try to drive others to that point of desperation where they start contemplating suicide.

This demon is careful to maintain an aura of someone who is a trustworthy person to let your kids be around, but in fact they are sexually deviant and get sadistic pleasure from harming kids, not just physically, but emotionally, and mentally; showing them pictures of tortured people and such.

They tend to be in very boring professions like accountancy, clerks; that sort of thing.

They tend to have a grouse with their parents and everyone in their family, believing they were given a raw deal.

But you get to know this only when you get close.

They're one of those demons one shouldn't even get near because of the heavy consciousness of morbidity they carry.

But altruistic humans tend to get attracted to these types believing they can change and help them.

Humans tend to think they're suffering and that's why they're so morbid. Actually, happiness would make them suffer. They keep morbid because they actually are setting up a back story for some horrible crime they want to commit for sadistic enjoyment – but which they're too scared to do.

They set up long back stories of being ill-treated by their family, dumped by their wife for someone with money, or younger or whatever. The female equivalent of it too.

One should just get the hell away from this morbid demon.

VENUS IN THE 8TH HOUSE

This person is a born pilgrim, a worshipper of God as Love. For Love, this person will give up their all, go the distance, climb mountains and swim seas. They are intensely sensitive to music, art and nature.

They are deeply inclined to all things taboo because they simply cannot perceive that beauty could ever end anywhere.

The evil in the world comes to them as a shock, and they end up becoming warriors against evil wherever they come across it.

Their sexual energy blocks come as a result of them fighting for demons. Because they're so eager to fight for the underdog and the socially ostracized, they end up championing the cause of demons unawares.

After getting drained, falling terribly ill and nearly dying; they return to health through spiritual energy, but blocking sexual energy because they don't want to care about anything or anyone that much anymore; and they don't feel free to allow themselves to experience the world with their raw sensuality again.

They become asexual, reclusive, isolated.

It's always a miracle when this person actually falls in love with someone in the ordinary sense of the word. Like boy meets girl thing. Because after the sort of energetic assault they went through and then shut off for survival, it's just a miracle if they can give their heart to someone again.

When they do, it's a miracle and it's for forever.

How it happens is, a deeply spiritual process that changes their sense of identity to the point where they might be unrecognizable to people who knew them before.

Their sense of commitment and loyalty is so strong that they will cut off their own life to follow on the path their soul leads them on. This eventually leaves in their life only the one or two people who live life on that frequency of sacredness and authenticity to spirit.

Demon – Venus in the 8th House

This demon is a purely sexual demon. They don't even try to approach a person pretending to be after anything else. In cultures starved of sexual freedom, this demon has no lack of opportunity.

Others find them so refreshing because they have that "no strings attached" aura.

In reality however, this demons always comes back. They are emotional blackmailers and can even be more blatant blackmailers. They tend to be employed by thug networks to honey trap target humans, to then blackmail them.

They're very good at being pimps and managing sex industry houses. They have a sound sense of numbers and math and tend to be quite money rich.

They see everyone as a product to sell physically.

They have zero qualms about human and child trafficking. They'll actually do anything for money.

When this demon is in a situation where they can't openly be involved in sex services, they go into the occult arts and learn to psychically drain people sexually.

Very often they'll develop a public aura of a person who is just an innocent struggler (note the struggle bit, that's something they do a LOT, they have that pinched look on their faces, because humans tend to immediately feel sympathy for that). They'll have some horrible sob story to relate, of what a horrible life they've had.

Next thing they'll be crying on your breast and you won't know if that's sexual or not, should you throw them off or not. In a few seconds, the thug will be kissing your neck and you won't know what's going on. In one minute, you'll be blackmailable.

It takes strength of character to get rid of this demon. But you'll just have to do it, and do it openly. You'll probably lose a lot of people in your life as a result, but good riddance.

VENUS IN THE 9TH HOUSE

This person is exceptionally sensitive to the sort of art and music that is sublime – as opposed to art and music that is earthy. The things others don't notice, this person notices and hears. They are sensitive to vibration that others barely feel, very intuitive and have the special gift of being able to communicate these sensitivities to students and those around them.

If they, for example, find something beautiful, they telecast it in the consciousness to others, so others begin to change their frequency to appreciate it too.

For this reason, they are discoverers of music, art, beauty in all its forms.

When for whatever reason they are unable to feel free in their enjoyment of beauty, perhaps by being with people who don't understand their extreme soulful longing for beauty, they feel imprisoned, trapped, cut off from hope, even suicidal. This stops their sexual energy from flowing.

Giving themselves the freedom to experience beauty without being constrained by anything or anyone, not even any philosophy; and the freedom to share that with others, will begin to make them begin to move sexual energy again.

Demon – Venus in the 9th House

This demon is a blatant enemy of the arts in the sense that it has a sadistic enjoyment of "exposing" the things a person loves and reveres as hollow, perverse, selfish and such.

They actually are desperate to control others, as many others as possible. They want to be someone who everyone respects and listens to and consults about everything. But they don't have the magnetism or character or spine to naturally command respect.

So, they learn that they can control people by attacking the things the person reveres, a sort of deep emotional and spiritual abuse. I don't know, Ed, if I can get across, what sort of abuse this is. Take a young child who likes a particular kind of dance. A thug tv program will purport to be about that dance but will actually "expose" that that dance was originally started by soldiers commanding local girls to dance for them. Or they were danced by prostitutes in the palaces of kings.

You see the level on which they're hitting the child, Ed?

These are the demons that make social media reels saying this food is bad, and that vegetable is bad, and your local river has flesh eating bacteria, lettuce has parasites that will make your hair fall out; and all that sort of thing.

The thug media is full of this, because this Venus placement is specially attracted to the media, to broadcast their assault on mass consciousness.

Wherever the job is to cause trauma, disassociation and so on, you'll find this demon reveling in the job.

It's hard for a human to actually get along with someone who crushes their dreams so, for very long, but in case you are; cut off and go far and learn another language or two. Learning a new language breaks you out of associations formed in the mind in your native language, and you'll find you can find your simple joy and happiness again.

VENUS IN THE 10TH HOUSE

This person, Ed, is a curator and preserver of the best that is in their lives and environment. They protect what is beautiful and they also push aside, sometimes destroy what is not.

They have a very strong sense of justice and can be seen as extreme as a result.

They are very rarely not well traveled or well-read or exposed to things outside of their environment.

They have God given vision and insight in whichever field of work or study they've taken up. They are precise, detailed and really care about it.

They are the sort of eccentric professor who'll give you a lifelong passion for something that'll bring you happiness to the end of your life.

The path to establishment for them, however is not easy. They are influenced by many things, many energies, and from many dimensions.

Just like a person tasting different wines must smell coffee in-between to reset their olfactory cells, so they can be sensitive to the taste of the wine again, so they often go incognito for months or years at a time, during which they seem to be completely other people.

They don't make a lot of sound and they don't make a lot of demands; but ultimately, they end up being the spine of their community.

Their sexual energy blocks come from spiritual abuse where people they look up to, either abused them directly or indirectly. They're often targets for abusers and bullies from a young age because of their emotional sensitivity and the raw sensuality they throw out as a result of that. In learning to deal with that, they often block their sensitivity with their sexual energy and present themselves as cold, unfeeling, brash and so on.

It can take them decades to find a spirituality free of the impressions of those who abused them, and a sensitivity to sensuality, free of fear.

Demon – Venus in the 10th house

This demon is something of a megalomaniac. He or she tends to have pictures in their mind of gruesome and horrible scenarios. They are motivated by such things. They long to witness horrible tragedies and disasters. It's a demon that has completely lost the ability to find sexual or even physical or mental stimulation out of what is normal in this realm. You could say, they already live in a hell realm for the most part and the bits of them stuck here are trying to vibrate to that frequency of pain, death, disaster and horror that will take them fully to that other realm.

A quirk of this demon, is that it is often involved in charitable activities, because it enjoys the suffering of people. It will go home and salivate over the pain and gore it saw.

It will often find someone poor and lavish them a whole day or even a holiday with all kinds of pleasures, just so when they go back to their lives they will feel sorely lacking.

I saw one of these demons tie a cow in front of a stack of hay, which it then moved out of reach of the cow. It sat there then, watching the cow strain to reach the hay. I couldn't believe what I was seeing. I wanted to intervene but I was told not to as those people there could get dangerous.

On the way back home, I fell into a half sleep on the bus and in front of me rose instances when I'd seen "humans" ie., demons do this to others, but in ways not so obvious. I was shocked at how common these sadistic demons actually are. You'll find one on every street at least, if not more. They just don't LOOK like they could be this cruel, but the second they feel safe to be, they are.

Now that I have faced the reality of my life, I can tell you, Ed, that the vast majority of ritual torturers are like this. They actually love and revel in the atmosphere of pain and trauma and suffering.

VENUS IN THE 11TH HOUSE

This person is psychically well developed with incredible powers of judgment. They can be trusted to handle the most difficult of projects because of how illuminated their minds are. In this placement we see the aspect of Venus that is an intelligence that sits above the daily affairs of life, to see the big picture and restore beauty, health and balance to all.

This person develops sexual energy blocks when they're forced into roles and personalities where they have to suppress their natural vision that is wide and all encompassing. They're told to shut up and do what they're paid to do. Or that they're just little girls, or little boys. Or that they shouldn't waste their time on these grandstanding "heal the world" thoughts.

Nothing hurts so much for them as being in a relationship where they're cut down to size and told that no one's interested in their theories of how things should be or be done. It hurts so much, they could block their sexual energy off just to be able to get the mental balance to survive.

At the end of the day, to find someone like themselves who LOVES humanity, LOVES the world enough to care for and think about things, is rare, but if they keep just being who they are, even if it's in private, their soulmate will come.

The soulmate tends to be someone who makes them laugh a lot, and makes them feel hopeful again. This triggers their primal energy.

Whether it becomes known or not, these humans are consciousness bondage breakers for all of humanity, because they refuse to give up envisioning a beautiful world that is healed and full of love, and telecasting that to all of us.

Demon – Venus in the 11th house

You remember the vampires in the "Twilight" movies, Ed? The way they used to pose around dressed like they were royalty, speaking like they were royalty?

This demon has a royalty complex. They're a low kind of demon because they're actually obsessed with poverty, grime and literally shit. But they will pose around like they're royalty. They'll come dressed to college like they're coming for a violin recital at St. Albert's Hall. They'll behave like their stock value is falling if they have to stand in a line for anything.

But that's only when they're young. Their obsession is either making more money if they're rich, or marrying into money if they're poor.

This demon often rises up the ranks of the demon hierarchy very quickly because they're utterly unscrupulous; they will do anything they're told to for money; and they're very secretive. They don't have "vices" like alcohol or drug addictions very often, or anything that can make them reveal secrets or give the plot away.

Once they decide on a plan, they will follow it to a T.

They are often those sent on undercover missions to pretend to be someone else. They do it so well. They are fantastic actors and actresses.

This demon usually does not have any committed sexual relationships at all, but for access to money or for the reputation of being a 'safe' married man, can have a picture perfect marriage to someone who can't complain about anything being wrong.

This demon's appetites are for substances carrying high level vampirized energy such as from unborn babies and children. They know how rare those are to come by outside of the organizations of the demon hierarchies. So, they practice fields of art like yoga, semen retention and various such arts to minimize their loss of energy and manage their energy well.

They are often paid by the upper thugs to maintain orphanages, and such, which are actually human trafficking, organ trafficking institutions. Because they are not like the lower level demons who'll sleep with anyone, abuse anyone they can for energy; the uppers can trust them to control their appetite till they can get the right sacrificial victim at a ritual done properly on the right astrological time to give them all the intensity of pain energy they need to fuel themselves.

In the past this used to work, but in recent times, these have lost their ability to manage their energy and have turned to ways to quickly get some low grade energy.

At the level they are in thug hierarchies, they are killed for this because it means they no longer can be trusted to take care of the "flock" that is to be kept for sacrifice at the right times and dates.

There is pandemonium in the demon hierarchies because of how many of these have fallen.

When a human is with such a demon, they experience a continuous drain of energy that seems unrelated to any specific event or activity. My mother was married to such a demon. 14 years, she didn't know why she went from a healthy happy young woman to someone so drained she was in bed most of the time, too weak to move about. The very second she decided to leave, her energy began to surge back.

One of the caretakers when I was little was this kind of demon too. That demon would literally drain vegetables, fruits and the very atmosphere of a room, of energy, by just being there. It was a phenomenon to watch.

When I started becoming aware of what was happening to me, I became aware of what sort of demons come to do rituals on us.

Once in a while, on high days, this kind of demon comes around, and the whole apartment society is drained as soon as they enter.

They have such huge appetites.

VENUS IN THE 12TH HOUSE

This person is an artist of the highest spiritual order, angelic. They are able to lift art and music up to a place where the joy and ethereal realms above can meet ours.

They are graceful, beautiful, gentle and kind people.

They have an inner peace and calm.

Their sexual energy blocks form when they feel unable to help someone they love. They feel worthless, because they so long to help, they love with such selflessness; but they're not able to see a way out.

They are those humans who when they lose a wife or husband or child, don't want to find love again because they feel it will just create pain eventually.

They take to philanthropic activities to try and assuage the pain of the world.

Fortunately, they have a streak of sensuality in them that rescues them from tripping right out of our realm; that makes them enjoy the simple joys of our realm like the taste of fruit, music, dancing and so on. Eventually this rescues them one way or another.

It's like a good midlife crisis that happens to them. They tend to find the love of their life, their lifelong companion and best friend in the pursuit of these simple pleasures.

Demon – Venus in the 12th house

This demon, Ed, tends to be born into old money most of the time, or a bloodline of valuable established demons. Its birth is often engineered astrologically to have favorable placements of planets to keep the family wealthy and powerful.

It is usually impotent, having been engineered into birth, but is often grown up with a lot of supplements and what not to keep it developing physically and mentally.

They are without scruples, and even allegiance, really. They can only enjoy sex when there's some sort of perversion or pain involved. They often hide this with a veneer of being an innocent person who got drunk or drugged and didn't know what he or she was doing.

If they get caught, they get sent to rehab, where they learn even better how to use the drugs and drinks story to cover their sheer evilness.

They frequently are sent away to other countries to study or work or such, to get a reset of their reputation from some scandal or the other.

They "buy" friendships, sex, everything. Directly or indirectly.

Some of them could actually get arrested for rape and such. But eventually, in our times, they get killed by their demon bloodline overseers for losing control and raping or abusing people outside of the allowed categories.

--

In Conclusion

Ed, it's been such an experience for me writing this. Seeing the great manifestations of God as Venus in the various houses and then the demons.

I went through an intense spiritual process, even to be able to get to the point where I could write this.

I thank God for this experience and for this information. I know it will help our human brothers and sisters and children.

By Henry Fuseli 1741 - 1825

My books *"**Sexual Energy Healing**"* and *"**Womb**"* and other books can be got by visiting

https://Cara.Earth

or by searching for my name "Caraf Avnayt" in your online book website, like Amazon.

You can also buy directly from me, <u>PDF, Kindle and Ebook versions of my books at this link.</u>

THANK YOU

If you liked this book, please review and rate it on the internet wherever you got it from. This will ultimately help me continue to write and publish independently.

My other books are available at https://cara.earth .

I have a lot of articles on holistic healing at https://Holistic-Treatment.com

I don't know how long my accounts will be up, but I post on X at @CarahasAngels and Instagram - @Mistletoe1981 .

I also have a Youtube channel where I describe some concepts about sexual and energy healing that need a video to put across my point. The username is CaraHasAngels .

SEXUAL ENERGY HEALING

CARAF AVNAYT

Remove Sexual Energy Blocks by Healing the Subconscious

The
EIGHTH of SEVEN
CHILDREN

The Life of John Waltham Jr.

CARAF AVNAYT

CARAF AVNAYT

FIRST WATER

THE USE OF URINE & SEXUAL FLUIDS AS MEDICINE

DNA REGENERATION
ENERGY REHABILITATION

CARAF AVNAYT

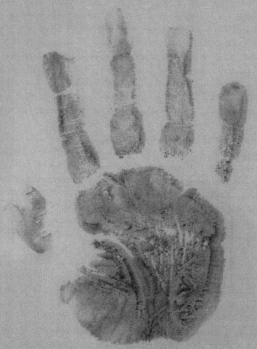

GUERILLA
DNA RECOVERY
& REGENERATION
Herbs & Energy
Recalibration

SEVEN ANGELS OF THWARTED PASSION

HERBS TO CHANGE INHERITED ENERGY PATTERNS

CARAF AVNAYT

The Spirit of Yeast

Yeast will tell you the time.

Caraf Avnayt

SOUL MEMORY

CARAF AVNAYT

How to Remember What
You've Forgotten You Know

SOUL MEMORY
in the Elements of
TIME FOCUS
DREAM-SLEEP and
BUOYANCY

CARAF AVNAYT

2022/02/20 16:53

The Use Of
TRAUMA HORMONES
for
EMOTIONAL ENERGY
HARVESTING

Excerpts from the book
'Sara In The Wheelwork'

CARAF AVNAYT

Emotional? Read this.

SPIRIT

Human Child Weapon
of Trauma Atmosphere
for Consciousness Terrorism

my own life story
CARAF AVNAYT

*Take refuge in the truth,
and the truth will defend you.
- John Waltham*

CARAF AVNAYT

THE PAIN EATERS

YOUR PAIN IS
THEIR PRODUCT.

Cover Picture Credit

Made in the USA
Columbia, SC
12 February 2025

53767216R00202